WHAT EVERY AFRICAN SHOULD KNOW ABOUT AFRICA

Rediscovering Our Past, Understanding Our Present, and Building Our Future

Dr. Chala Abdi

WHAT EVERY AFRICAN SHOULD KNOW ABOUT AFRICA

First edition, 2026. Independently published.

The historical, demographic, economic, and institutional information in this book is based on the sources cited. Statistics and institutional conditions reflect the dates and definitions used by the underlying sources and may change after publication.

ISBN: 979-8-9978340-0-5

Acknowledgments

No meaningful journey is completed alone. This book may carry my name on its cover, but behind these pages are people whose love, encouragement, patience, and belief helped me through every stage of the journey.

First, I want to express my deepest gratitude to my wife, **Sara Hussen.** Thank you for your love, patience, understanding, and constant support. Writing a book requires more than the effort of the person sitting at the desk. It also requires the patience and sacrifice of those who share that person's life. I am deeply grateful.

To my children, you are among the greatest sources of purpose in my life. You remind me that what we build today can reach far beyond ourselves. My hope is that you will always value knowledge, ask difficult questions, remain proud of who you are without being afraid to learn from others, and understand that a better future is something people must actively build.

To my entire family and to my friends, thank you. Some of you encouraged me with words. Some listened to my ideas. Some challenged my thinking. Your support, whether visible or quiet, helped carry me forward.

I want to offer a very special expression of gratitude to my uncle, **Dr. Nuru Said.** There are moments in life when the confidence of one person can change the way we see ourselves. Sometimes we do not fully understand the impact of someone's encouragement until many years later. A few words spoken at the right moment can remain with a person for a lifetime. His belief in me was one of those gifts, and I will always carry it with gratitude.

I am also deeply thankful to my colleagues, a good friend and mentor, **Efrem Tewelde,** you may never know that a conversation we shared about our continent eventually found its way into my thinking and, in some form, into the pages of this book. I am deeply grateful.

And to every reader who chooses to spend time with this book, my hope is not that every reader will agree with every conclusion in these pages. In fact, thoughtful disagreement is part of serious learning. My hope is that this book encourages curiosity, honest conversation, deeper knowledge of Africa, and a greater willingness to ask not only what the continent possesses, but what we can build with it. I am grateful for the opportunity to contribute one small voice to that continuing conversation.

A Note on Evidence and Statistics. This book distinguishes documented facts from estimates, projections, model results, and policy recommendations. It also treats Africa, sub-Saharan Africa, African Union membership, the WHO African Region, and other statistical geographies as distinct categories rather than interchangeable labels. Dates and geographic scope are stated where they materially affect interpretation. The purpose is not to make Africa's case through exaggeration, but to understand the continent through evidence strong enough to withstand scrutiny.

Contents

CHAPTER 1

Africa: The Cradle of Humanity

When many people hear the word Africa, a familiar set of images may come to mind: wildlife, deserts, safaris, poverty, conflict, famine, or colonialism. These images are not entirely false. They are simply incomplete.

Africa is much larger, older, more diverse, and more historically significant than any narrow collection of headlines or stereotypes can convey. Before colonial borders divided the continent, Africa was already alive with communities. From the marketplaces of Mogadishu and the trading ports of the East African coast to the commercial communities of West Africa, the cities of North Africa, and the settlements of Southern Africa, people were building lives, exchanging goods, developing skills, raising families, and connecting with neighboring societies and the wider world.

Life was not perfect. African societies faced conflict, inequality, rivalry, and hardship, just as societies elsewhere did. But those realities do not change a simple and important truth: ***Africa did not begin with colonialism. The continent already had a story. Colonialism profoundly changed Africa, but it did not create Africa.***

The Human Story Begins in Africa

To understand Africa's place in history, we must begin much earlier than kingdoms, borders, or written records. We must begin with the human story itself.

Scientific evidence places Africa at the center of human evolution. The Smithsonian Institution's Human Origins Program explains that humans first evolved in Africa and that the fossils of early humans who lived between six million and two million years ago have been found entirely on the continent. The same evidence shows that human evolution was not a straight march from one species to another. It was a branching history in which several early human species sometimes existed during overlapping periods (Smithsonian Institution, 2024a).

Our own species, *Homo sapiens*, also emerged in Africa. Fossils from Jebel Irhoud in Morocco, dated to roughly 300,000 years ago, extended the known history of our species and strengthened the case for an early *Homo sapiens* presence across a wide part of the continent (Hublin et al., 2017). In Ethiopia, research on volcanic deposits at Omo-Kibish established that the Omo I remains are older than about 230,000 years, making them among the earliest securely dated *Homo sapiens* fossils in eastern Africa (Vidal et al., 2022).

These discoveries should not be turned into a competition among modern countries. Morocco, Ethiopia, Kenya, Tanzania, South Africa, Zambia, and other parts of the continent have all contributed important evidence to the study of human origins. Modern borders did not exist when early human populations lived, moved, separated, and met again. The scientific record belongs to no present-day nation alone.

Research also cautions against imagining that *Homo sapiens* appeared suddenly in one isolated place. Genetic modeling published in *Nature* supports a more complex picture in which ancestral populations within Africa remained connected over long periods and contributed to the emergence of our species (Ragsdale et al., 2023). The details will continue to be debated as new fossils, dating methods, and genetic evidence become available. The broader conclusion, however, is well established: the evolutionary history of the human lineage runs deeply through Africa.

The larger point is therefore clear:

Africa is not a side note in the story of humanity.

It is central to it.

The history of humankind cannot be told seriously without Africa.

What Does "Cradle of Humanity" Really Mean?

The phrase *cradle of humanity* is powerful, but it must be used carefully. It does not mean that one modern African country can claim to be the exclusive birthplace of all humanity. Nor does it mean that science has answered every question about where and how our species emerged.

Human evolution unfolded over immense stretches of time. Populations moved as climates and landscapes changed. Some groups became separated; others came into contact. Different branches of the human family appeared, adapted, and disappeared. Scientific interpretations change when stronger evidence becomes available. That uncertainty is not a weakness. It is how serious research works.

When this book describes Africa as the cradle of humanity, it makes a broader and more defensible claim: the deepest evolutionary history of the human lineage, including the emergence of *Homo sapiens*, is rooted in Africa. ***Africa is therefore not merely where African history begins.*** It is where a fundamental part of human history begins.

Long Before Countries and Borders

Now imagine the continent tens of thousands of years ago. There was no Nigeria, Kenya, Ghana, South Africa, Senegal, Somalia, or Democratic Republic of the Congo. Ethiopia existed much later as a historical state, but not in its present territorial form. There were no modern passports, colonial boundaries, or national capitals. The political map familiar to us today belongs to a far more recent period.

People organized their lives according to the conditions around them. Kinship, language, environment, subsistence, migration, trade, security, and political authority shaped communities in different ways. Populations living near rivers developed possibilities that differed from those available in deserts, forests, highlands, savannas, or coastal environments. Over time, communities developed distinct economic practices, cultural traditions, languages, and forms of political organization.

This is important because the continent we now call Africa was never one culture. Its diversity is ancient. The name *Africa* describes a vast geographic whole, but it does not erase the many peoples and histories within it.

Africa Is Not One Story

Africa is not a country. It is not one people, one language, one religion, or one culture. It has never followed one historical path.

North African societies developed deep connections with the Mediterranean world. The Nile Valley supported some of the world's earliest complex states. Communities in the Horn of Africa formed relationships across the Red Sea and the Indian Ocean. West Africa became home to powerful states and long-distance commercial networks. Central African histories were shaped by forests, river systems, agriculture, migration, and trade. Eastern Africa included pastoral communities, farming societies, inland states, and Indian Ocean trading cities. Southern Africa developed its own settlements, kingdoms, political systems, and commercial networks.

These regional histories were never completely separate. People migrated. Merchants traded. Languages changed. Religions spread. States competed. Knowledge traveled. Sometimes interaction was peaceful and mutually beneficial. At other times it involved conquest, enslavement, or war.

The point is not to replace one simplified story with another. It is to recognize that Africa's history is too large and varied to be compressed into a single account of suffering or greatness. UNESCO's *General History of Africa*, created through decades of collaboration among more than 550 historians and specialists, approaches the continent as a whole while still recognizing its internal diversity and its relationships with the wider world (UNESCO, n.d.). That balance matters. Africa is connected, but it is not uniform.

Movement, Geography, and Connection

Human populations have always moved. Some movements took place within Africa; others eventually carried early humans beyond the continent. Fossil evidence indicates that early human populations reached parts of Eurasia roughly 1.8 million years ago, long before *Homo sapiens* appeared. Much later, populations of our own species dispersed beyond Africa and eventually reached every inhabited continent (Smithsonian Institution, 2024a).

Those journeys took place over enormous spans of time. Communities adapted to different climates and landscapes. Languages and cultures changed. Populations became increasingly distinct. Yet all living human beings belong to the same species, *Homo sapiens*, and share a deep ancestry rooted in Africa.

Geography influenced these movements, but geography did not dictate history. The Sahara could be a formidable barrier, yet routes across it also supported long-distance exchange. The Nile sustained agriculture and dense settlement. The Ethiopian Highlands created distinctive ecological and political settings. The Congo Basin supported societies adapted to one of the world's largest tropical forest regions. Savannas supported farming, livestock production, settlement, and commerce. Africa's Mediterranean, Atlantic, Red Sea, and Indian Ocean coastlines connected communities to wider worlds.

Mountains do not create governments. Rivers do not create civilizations by themselves. Deserts do not determine political outcomes. People respond to geography through knowledge, technology, institutions, cooperation, and conflict. Geography creates possibilities and constraints; human beings make history within them.

That history also challenges the old idea that Africa remained isolated until Europeans connected it to the world. **Africa Was Never Isolated.**

Another misconception is that Africa remained isolated until Europeans connected it to the wider world. Different regions participated in long-distance networks at different times. North Africa interacted with Mediterranean societies. The Horn maintained connections across the Red Sea. Eastern African coastal communities took part in Indian Ocean trade. West African merchants and states participated in trans-Saharan commerce. These networks moved more than gold, salt, ivory, textiles, metals, livestock, and ceramics. They also carried people, ideas, languages, technologies, religious traditions, and artistic influences.

Africa Was Already There: The First Hijra to Abyssinia

One of the most striking reminders that Africa was deeply connected to the wider world long before European colonialism comes from the earliest history of Islam. Around 615 CE, during a period of persecution in Mecca, a group of the Prophet Muhammad's early followers crossed the Red Sea and sought refuge in the Christian Kingdom of Aksum, in the region then known to Arab sources as al-Habasha (Abyssinia). The refugees did not travel to an unknown or politically empty land. They went to an established African kingdom with a ruler, institutions, international connections, and a reputation in the Islamic tradition for providing protection from injustice.

The importance of this story extends beyond religious history. It reminds us that Africa was already part of the political, commercial, and cultural world surrounding the Red Sea centuries before European colonial rule. Early Muslims looked toward an African kingdom as a place of refuge and security at a critical moment in the formation of their community.

The story therefore challenges any picture of Africa as a continent waiting to be discovered, organized, or connected by outsiders. Africa was already there—governed by its own societies, engaged with neighboring regions, and participating in events that would become part of world history. Not every African community was connected to distant markets, and those that were connected did not participate in the same way. The scale and meaning of exchange varied greatly by region and period. The responsible conclusion is simply that Africa was never waiting outside history for someone else to connect it. Many African societies were already connected to one another and to wider regional worlds.

Knowledge Existed in Many Forms

When people hear the word *knowledge*, they may first think of books, universities, laboratories, and written archives. Those forms of knowledge are important, but human knowledge has never existed only in writing.

African societies transmitted knowledge through oral tradition, apprenticeship, observation, artistic practice, religious institutions, practical experience, and written scholarship. Farmers studied local soils, rainfall, crops, and seasons. Pastoral communities learned about animals, water, grazing, and mobility. Builders developed methods suited to local materials and climates. Merchants learned routes, languages, markets, and negotiation. Political communities created different systems of authority, diplomacy, taxation, law, and conflict resolution. Oral specialists preserved genealogies, collective memory, and accounts of the past.

Written traditions also developed in several parts of the continent. Ancient Egypt produced one of the world's best-known early systems of writing. The Horn of Africa developed a long Ge'ez literary tradition. North Africa produced scholarship in several languages across different periods, while Islamic learning flourished in centers across parts of North, West, East, and the Horn of Africa.

No single kind of evidence can reconstruct all of this history. Written documents are valuable, but they are incomplete. Archaeology can recover material traces that written sources ignored. Oral traditions can preserve information and social memory, but they must be evaluated carefully, just as written records must be examined for bias, purpose, and context. Linguistics, anthropology, art history, genetics, and environmental studies can add further evidence. UNESCO's historical project deliberately brought several of these methods together rather than treating one source as sufficient (UNESCO, n.d.).

The responsible claim is not that every African society possessed the same knowledge or institutions. They did not. It is that knowledge existed in many forms and must be understood in its historical setting.

Diversity Is Not a Defect

Modern discussions sometimes describe African diversity mainly as a political problem. History tells a more complicated story. Diversity is one of the continent's oldest realities.

African languages belong to several broad language families and reflect long histories of movement, interaction, separation, and cultural development. Language carries more than vocabulary. It can carry memory, humor, poetry, values, religious ideas, and ways of understanding kinship, community, and the natural world. The same is true of food, music, architecture, clothing, agriculture, political organization, and religious practice.

This diversity should not be romanticized. African societies, like societies everywhere, experienced both cooperation and conflict. Kingdoms expanded. States competed. Communities fought. People conquered and were conquered. Diversity did not guarantee peace, but neither is it evidence of weakness. It is evidence of a long and complex human history.

The challenge for modern Africa is not to erase difference. It is to build institutions capable of managing difference fairly, peacefully, and productively. That question belongs to later chapters, but its historical roots begin here.

Pride Without Myth

When people discover that their history has been ignored, distorted, or undervalued, they may be tempted to correct the injury through exaggeration. That response is understandable, but it is not useful.

Not every ancient invention originated in Africa. Not every African kingdom was wealthy or peaceful. Not every ruler governed wisely. Not every failure can be blamed entirely on outsiders. Uncomfortable evidence does not weaken African history; refusing to face it does.

Africa's documented history is significant enough without mythology. The continent's role in human origins, its civilizations, commercial systems, intellectual traditions, political experiments, and cultural influence can stand on evidence. Where the evidence is incomplete, we should say so. Where scholars disagree, we should explain why. Where popular claims cannot be verified, we should not repeat them simply because they sound inspiring.

A mature relationship with history should allow two things at once: pride in genuine achievement and honesty about genuine failure. One does not cancel the other. This book will follow that principle, neither minimize Africa's achievements nor exaggerate them.

Why This Beginning Matters

Starting points shape understanding. If Africa enters the reader's imagination only through slavery, colonialism, poverty, famine, or modern conflict, the story begins too late. Those subjects matter, and this book will confront them directly. But none of them marks the beginning of African history.

Africa existed before European colonialism. Political communities existed before modern borders. Commercial networks existed before today's global economy. Systems of knowledge existed before colonial education. And the continent's place in the human story reaches much further back than any of these developments.

History should not become an excuse for avoiding present responsibilities. An ancient university cannot educate today's children. A historic empire cannot provide electricity, create jobs, or repair a failing institution. Past greatness is not a substitute for present achievement. But history still matters. It corrects misconceptions, deepens perspective, and shows that current conditions are neither timeless nor inevitable.

This understanding also changes the meaning of development. Africa does not need to choose between learning from the wider world and respecting its own history. Every successful society learns, adapts, borrows, and creates. Confidence is not the refusal to learn from others. It is the ability to learn without assuming that progress belongs to someone else.

The Journey Ahead

This chapter began as far back as the evidence allows us to go: human origins, migration, geography, diversity, connection, and knowledge. The chapters ahead will move through civilizations and states, trade and enslavement, colonial conquest, independence, economic change, regional integration, human development, institutions, and the choices facing the continent today.

Some of those discussions will be uncomfortable. They should be. A book called *What Every African Should Know About Africa* should not exist simply to make Africans feel proud. Its purpose is to help readers understand. Understanding requires evidence, context, humility, and the willingness to question both inherited stereotypes and comforting myths.

Stand anywhere in Africa and consider the depth of human time beneath the modern landscape. Countless generations lived before today's countries existed. Most of their names were never recorded. They were children and parents, hunters and gatherers, farmers and herders, traders and builders, healers and travelers, leaders and storytellers. Across immense stretches of time, human beings learned to survive, adapt, cooperate, compete, create, and move.

Eventually, descendants of African populations spread far beyond the continent. Today, *Homo sapiens* lives on every inhabited continent, in different nations, speaking different languages, practicing different religions, and creating different cultures. Yet all belong to one human species whose evolutionary history leads deeply into Africa.

That should inspire pride. More importantly, it should inspire perspective.

Africa does not need to be inserted into human history. Africa was there at the beginning.

The question for today's generation is what Africans will contribute to the chapters still waiting to be written.

Evidence Note

The science of human origins continues to develop. New fossils, improved dating methods, archaeology, and genetic research can change interpretations of particular populations and evolutionary relationships. For that reason, this chapter does not claim that one modern country or one archaeological site was the exclusive birthplace of humanity. The strongest evidence supports the broader conclusion that the human lineage has deep evolutionary origins in Africa and that *Homo sapiens* emerged on the continent roughly 300,000 years ago, while the precise relationships among the populations involved remain subjects of active research.

CHAPTER 2

The Africa They Were Not Taught About

Chapter 1 began before kingdoms, borders, or written records. It placed Africa at the beginning of the human story and showed that the continent's diversity is not a recent development.

Now the story moves forward.

Long before European colonial rule, different parts of Africa had cities, kingdoms, empires, trading communities, religious institutions, artistic traditions, centers of scholarship, and systems of government. These societies did not exist at the same time, and they did not form one civilization. They spoke different languages, followed different religions, and organized power in different ways. Some flourished for centuries. Others rose quickly and disappeared. They traded, fought, created, conquered, adapted, and sometimes failed.

The purpose of this chapter is not to replace an old insult with a new myth. Precolonial Africa was not a peaceful paradise, and every African ruler was not wise or just. The more important truth is also the more defensible one: Africa had complex histories of its own before European colonial domination.

There Was Never One Ancient Africa

The phrase *ancient Africa* can be useful, but it can also mislead. The Nile Valley developed differently from the western Sahel. The highlands of the Horn of Africa followed paths different from those of Central

Africa's forests and river systems. Swahili towns faced the Indian Ocean, while inland communities in Southern Africa built political and commercial centers around different environments and resources.

There was no single African political model. Some societies created centralized monarchies and territorial states. Others governed through councils, lineage systems, age grades, religious authorities, or combinations of institutions. Some left inscriptions and monumental stone buildings. Others preserved law, memory, and identity primarily through oral traditions and social practice.

That variety is not a complication to be removed from African history. It is the history.

Egypt and Kush: Power Along the Nile

Any serious account of early African civilization must include ancient Egypt. Egypt developed along the Nile in northeastern Africa and became one of the ancient world's longest-lasting state civilizations. Its surviving temples, tombs, inscriptions, and monumental architecture reveal organized government, religious institutions, specialized labor, and remarkable technical skill. At Thebes, the temples of Karnak and Luxor and the necropolises of the Valleys of the Kings and Queens still testify to the power reached during the Middle and New Kingdoms (UNESCO World Heritage Centre, n.d.-b).

The pyramids are often admired as engineering wonders, but their importance is larger than stone. Projects of such scale required agricultural production, transportation, planning, skilled labor, administration, and political authority. Monumental construction does not prove that life was equal or easy for everyone. It does show what coordinated institutions could accomplish.

Egypt was African by geography and deeply connected to surrounding worlds. Its relationships extended south into Nubia and north and northeast toward the Mediterranean and western Asia. There is no need to choose between these facts. A society can be rooted in Africa and connected beyond it. That pattern appears throughout the continent's history.

South of Egypt, in the Middle Nile region of present-day Sudan, the Kingdom of Kush became a major power. Kush was not merely an extension of Egypt. It developed political, religious, artistic, and architectural traditions of its own, even as the two societies influenced one another. From the eighth century BCE to the fourth century CE, the Kushite heartland included the royal city at Meroe and the religious centers of Naqa and Musawwarat es-Sufra. The surviving landscape contains pyramids, temples, palaces, homes, industrial areas, and water-management works (UNESCO World Heritage Centre, n.d.-d).

At one stage, power moved north. Kushite rulers conquered Egypt and governed it for close to a century, forming Egypt's Twenty-Fifth Dynasty. That episode corrects a common assumption that influences always flowed from Egypt toward the African interior. Relations along the Nile moved in more than one direction.

Kush also changed over time. Napata was an earlier center, while Meroe later became the principal royal residence and burial place. The shift reminds us that even a civilization discussed under one name was never frozen. Capitals moved, institutions changed, and political power had to be rebuilt from one generation to the next.

Aksum and the Red Sea World

In the northern highlands of present-day Ethiopia and Eritrea, Aksum grew into a major state during the first millennium CE. Its position connected the African interior to the Red Sea and to commercial routes reaching Arabia, the Mediterranean, and the Indian Ocean. UNESCO describes Aksum as standing at the crossroads of Africa, Arabia, and the

Greco-Roman world. Its surviving stelae, royal tombs, inscriptions, and palace remain reflect the wealth and power of the kingdom (UNESCO World Heritage Centre, n.d.-a).

Aksumite rulers issued coinage, and some inscriptions appeared in Greek, Sabaean, and Ge'ez. These were not decorative details. Coins made exchange and royal authority visible, while multilingual inscriptions spoke to different audiences. Together they offer material evidence of a state engaged in commerce, diplomacy, religion, and war beyond its immediate region.

In the fourth century, King Ezana adopted Christianity. Changes in Aksumite coinage, including the replacement of earlier religious symbols with the cross, help document that transition. Aksum became one of the early Christian states of late antiquity, while its political and commercial importance remained tied to the Red Sea world (Metropolitan Museum of Art, 2000a).

Aksum's history challenges another familiar image: that the Horn of Africa stood apart from the great exchanges of the ancient world. It did not. Aksum was neither a passive recipient of outside influence nor an isolated kingdom. It was an African power acting within a wider international system.

Gada: Power Beyond the Palace

Kings and empires are often the easiest institutions to see in historical records, but African political thought was not limited to monarchies. Among the Oromo people, the Gada system organized public life through generational classes, graded responsibilities, assemblies, rules of conduct, and periodic transfers of authority.

UNESCO describes Gada as an indigenous democratic socio-political system that regulates political, economic, social, and religious affairs.

At the heart of the system are important values such as Nagaa (peace), Waliigaltee (agreement), Safuu (moral responsibility and respect), Gorsa (wisdom and counsel), Araara (reconciliation), and Walif Yaaduu (collective responsibility). *Leadership rotates among these parties in an established cycle, helping reduce direct rivalry for power and encouraging orderly succession. Power is transferred at eight-year intervals, and the institution depends on members learning the laws, history, rituals, and responsibilities attached to each stage (UNESCO Intangible Cultural Heritage, 2016).*

This is significant because governance is more than deciding who sits at the top. It also concerns how authority is limited, how responsibility is transferred, how disputes are resolved, and how a community teaches the rules that hold an institution together. Gada approached those questions through a political tradition different from the royal systems of Egypt, Kush, or Aksum.

The Kgotla System of Botswana

In Botswana, the Kgotla developed as an important community institution where people gathered to discuss public matters, resolve disputes, and participate in decisions affecting the community. Traditionally led by a Kgosi, or chief, the Kgotla provided a space where community members could express their views before major decisions were made.

The Kgotla also played an important role in customary justice and social order. Its continued importance in Botswana shows that traditions of consultation and community participation were deeply rooted in African societies long before the establishment of modern colonial governments.

Both the Gadaa system and the Kgotla, along with other longstanding African traditions of governance, should be understood within their own historical and cultural contexts. The Gadaa system, for example, was shaped by rules concerning age, generation, gender, and membership. It was therefore not identical to a modern constitutional democracy based on universal adult suffrage. Likewise, the available historical evidence does not justify the popular claim that Gadaa was "the oldest democracy in the world." Such a ranking depends on uncertain comparisons and on how democracy itself is defined. No such claim is necessary to recognize the significance of these institutions. The documented achievement of Gadaa is substantial: Oromo society developed an enduring system of shared political responsibility, generational organization, public deliberation, conflict resolution, and scheduled transfers of leadership. The Kgotla similarly reflects a long tradition of consultation, public discussion, customary authority, and community participation in Botswana. These histories deserve recognition on their own terms, without exaggeration and without forcing them into modern political categories.

The Western Sahel: Ghana, Mali, and Songhai

Across the western Sahel, political power grew in close relationship with long-distance trade. Caravans crossed the Sahara carrying salt, textiles, metals, and other goods, while gold and commodities from regions farther south moved toward North Africa and the Mediterranean. These routes were not simply lines on a map. They depended on knowledge of water, terrain, animals, markets, security, credit, and political negotiation.

Ghana, Mali, and Songhai were among the major states associated with this history. They did not replace one another in a perfectly orderly sequence, and their borders shifted over time. Even so, their rise shows how states could use geography, taxation, military power, and access to trade to build regional influence (Metropolitan Museum of Art, 2000b).

The Ghana Empire should not be confused with the modern Republic of Ghana. Its heartland lay farther northwest, in areas now associated mainly with Mauritania and Mali. Modern Ghana adopted the historic name many centuries later. Ancient Ghana's importance came partly from its position between gold-producing regions to the south and the trans-Saharan markets to the north. Resources mattered, but location, organization, and control of exchange mattered too.

By the thirteenth century, Mali had become a major power. Its most famous ruler, Mansa Musa, drew international attention during his pilgrimage to Mecca in 1324-1325. Accounts of the journey and later representations of the ruler made Mali's access to gold known well beyond West Africa (Metropolitan Museum of Art, 2000b).

Mansa Musa is often called the richest person who ever lived. That description is memorable, but it cannot be measured responsibly. The territory, taxation, tribute, gold production, and political authority controlled by a fourteenth-century monarch cannot be converted into a reliable modern personal net worth. The historical record supports a strong conclusion without a speculative dollar figure: Mansa Musa ruled an exceptionally wealthy empire, and his pilgrimage made that wealth internationally famous.

Mali's importance was not limited to gold. Timbuktu became an important center of trade, religion, teaching, and manuscript culture. During the fifteenth and sixteenth centuries, its mosques and scholarly communities made it a major intellectual and spiritual center of West Africa (UNESCO World Heritage Centre, n.d.-f). Sankore is often called a medieval university. The comparison can help a modern reader, but it should not hide the institution's own form. Timbuktu's education grew through mosques, Qur'anic schools, scholars, students, and manuscript libraries rather than through a university organized exactly like one today.

As Mali's dominance weakened, Songhai became a major regional power, with Gao as an important political center. The Tomb of Askia, built in Gao in 1495, survives as evidence of the wealth of an empire closely tied to the trans-Saharan trade in gold and salt (UNESCO World Heritage Centre, n.d.-g). Songhai's power did not last forever. A Moroccan invasion in 1591 shattered its imperial control over many important centers.

There is nothing uniquely African about that rise and decline. States everywhere expand, compete, adapt, and sometimes collapse. The western Sahel belongs within that familiar human history.

Great Zimbabwe: Evidence in Stone

In Southern Africa, Great Zimbabwe offers some of the continent's most important archaeological evidence of precolonial political and commercial life. Built principally between about 1100 and 1450 CE, the site includes the Hill Ruins, the Great Enclosure, and the Valley Ruins. Its walls were constructed from carefully fitted stone without mortar, and the settlement became the principal city of a powerful state (UNESCO World Heritage Centre, n.d.-c).

Great Zimbabwe was not cut off from the wider world. Archaeologists have found objects that point to connections with the East African coast and Indian Ocean commerce, including glass beads, imported ceramics, and coins from Kilwa. Gold and other products moved outward from the interior while goods and ideas moved inland through regional networks.

The site's interpretation also reveals how prejudice can shape scholarship. During the colonial period, some European writers resisted the conclusion that Africans had built it and searched for foreign creators instead. Archaeological research established its origin among an African Iron Age population associated with the Shona.

The lesson is not that all earlier scholarship was worthless or that evidence never changes. It is that assumptions about what Africans were supposedly capable of doing affected how evidence was interpreted. The remedy is not a more flattering myth. It is better research and the willingness to follow the evidence even when it challenges inherited beliefs.

Benin: Art, Memory, and Conquest

In what is now southern Nigeria, the Kingdom of Benin developed a powerful royal court centered on Benin City. Court artists worked in organized guilds and produced cast-brass plaques and commemorative heads, carved ivory tusks, figures, and ceremonial objects. These works recorded rulers, officials, rituals, warfare, status, and relationships with foreign visitors. The familiar name *Benin Bronzes* describes a much wider body of art: many objects are brass, while others were made from bronze, ivory, wood, coral, or terracotta (Ezra, 1992).

This historical kingdom should not be confused with the modern Republic of Benin. Benin City lies in present-day Nigeria, and the kingdom's history is closely associated with the Edo people and the Oba's court.

In 1897, British forces attacked and occupied Benin City. Large numbers of royal and ceremonial objects were removed from the palace and other sites and dispersed through museums and private collections. The fact that so many are now seen in Europe or North America can hide the order of events: the artistic tradition came first; conquest and removal came later.

Museums have increasingly confronted that history. In 2022, American institutions transferred ownership of thirty Benin works to Nigeria, including twenty-nine from the Smithsonian Institution (U.S. Embassy and Consulate in Nigeria, 2022). The continuing debate over restitution involves law, ethics, preservation, access, and ownership. But the central historical fact is clear. European museums did not create this art. Benin artists did.

The Swahili Coast: African and Cosmopolitan

Along the East African coast, Swahili towns participated in Indian Ocean commerce for centuries. Kilwa, Mombasa, Lamu, Malindi, and Zanzibar rose to prominence at different times. Their histories cannot be reduced to a single city or period, but together they reveal a coast shaped by African settlement, maritime trade, Islam, and sustained contact across the ocean.

Kilwa Kisiwani, off the coast of present-day Tanzania, reached the height of its prosperity in the thirteenth and fourteenth centuries. Gold and ivory from the African interior passed through coastal markets, while textiles, ceramics, silver, and other goods arrived from Arabia, India, China, and elsewhere. Kilwa even minted its own currency. Its coral-and-lime buildings, mosques, palace remains, homes, and public spaces provide material evidence of an urban commercial society (UNESCO World Heritage Centre, n.d.-e).

Swahili culture was both African and cosmopolitan. Centuries of contact brought outside influences, but connection did not make the culture foreign. Swahili language and society developed on the East African coast through the lives of African communities engaged with a wider world.

This distinction matters. Egypt's Mediterranean connections did not remove it from Africa. Aksum's Red Sea trade did not make it less African. Islam and trans-Saharan exchange did not erase the African character of Mali or Timbuktu. Indian Ocean commerce did not make the Swahili coast an imported civilization. Cultural exchange changes societies; it does not automatically cancel their roots.

Africa Was Connected Before Colonialism

Seen together, these histories overturn the image of an isolated continent waiting to be connected by Europe. The Nile linked northeastern African societies. Caravan routes crossed the Sahara. The Red Sea joined the Horn of Africa to Arabia and the Mediterranean. The Indian Ocean connected the East African coast to ports thousands of miles away. Inland routes tied Great Zimbabwe and other southern African centers to coastal markets.

Europeans did not introduce Africa to trade, diplomacy, religion, urban life, or political organization. All existed in varied forms long before the colonial conquest of the continent. What later changed were the scale, direction, technology, and political control of many relationships, as well as the coercion through which some of them were imposed.

Connection, however, should not be confused with equality. Trade could enrich rulers and merchants while exploiting laborers, captives, or subject communities. States protected exchange, but they also taxed, raided, fought, and conquered. Slavery and other forms of servitude existed in different African societies before the Atlantic slave trade, though their forms and scale varied across place and time.

Precolonial Africa was not a utopia destroyed by the first outsider who arrived. It contained achievement and suffering, order and conflict, learning and inequality. These were human societies, not symbols created to prove either African greatness or African failure.

Pride Without Myth

Chapter 1 argued for pride without myth. The histories in this chapter show what that principle requires.

We do not need to call Gada the world's first democracy. Its documented political structure is significant enough. We do not need to calculate Mansa Musa's fortune in modern dollars. Mali's command of gold and the international impact of his pilgrimage are impressive enough. We do not need to turn Sankore into an exact copy of a modern university. Timbuktu's scholarly traditions stand on their own. We do not need to invent foreign builders for Great Zimbabwe or imagine a perfect precolonial peace.

Africa does not need an invented past. Its documented past is powerful enough.

That past also does not solve the present. Aksum's ancient trade cannot create a modern job. Mali's gold cannot repair today's institutions. Great Zimbabwe's walls cannot supply electricity. The Benin works cannot build a transport network. Historical achievement demonstrates human capability, but it does not excuse present failure.

The useful question is not simply, "Were our ancestors great?" It is: What did people build? How did their institutions work? Who benefited? Why did some systems endure while others weakened? What can be learned without pretending that the past can be copied unchanged?

Those questions turn history from decoration into knowledge.

A Continent Already in Motion

This chapter has moved across centuries and regions that should never be collapsed into one scene. The builders of the pyramids did not live beside the rulers of Songhai. Aksum, Great Zimbabwe, Benin, and Kilwa followed different timelines. Gada developed through a political tradition unlike the monarchies described elsewhere. Their peoples did not share one language, religion, identity, or system of government.

What connects them is simpler: they left evidence of African societies organizing power, producing knowledge, creating art, building cities and monuments, trading across distance, and responding to change. They also left evidence of rivalry, hierarchy, conquest, and decline.

That is why this history must come before colonialism. If Africa's political story begins with European conquest, it can appear that imperial powers arrived on an empty continent. They did not. They encountered states, communities, authorities, markets, beliefs, rivalries, and histories already in motion. Some African leaders resisted. Some negotiated. Some formed alliances. Some were defeated. None of them was living outside history.

Chapter 3 will examine how enslavement, imperial competition, and colonial conquest altered those histories. To understand the scale of that disruption, we must first understand what was already there.

Africa was not waiting to begin.

Evidence Note

The societies discussed here span more than four thousand years. Dates are sometimes approximate, names changed, and historical borders rarely matched modern national boundaries. Archaeological interpretation also develops as new evidence appears. This chapter therefore uses selected examples rather than treating them as a complete survey of precolonial Africa. It distinguishes ancient Ghana from modern Ghana, the Kingdom of Benin from the Republic of Benin, and historical institutions from modern political categories. It also avoids speculative rankings of Gada or Mansa Musa and does not portray precolonial societies as uniformly peaceful, wealthy, or equal.

CHAPTER 3

The Scramble for Africa

How a Continent Was Divided

Chapter 2 ended with a continent already in motion. Across Africa, people had built states, cities, trading networks, religious institutions, systems of law, and political traditions of many kinds. By the late nineteenth century, none of those societies was standing still. Rulers were reforming armies, merchants were extending trade, communities were competing over land and authority, and new religious and political movements were emerging.

Then the balance of power changed with extraordinary speed.

Within a few decades, European governments claimed and conquered most of the continent. They did not arrive in an empty land, and Africans did not simply watch as their sovereignty disappeared.

Some rulers negotiated. Some resisted. Some tried to play one foreign power against another. Some African groups allied with Europeans against local rivals. Others moved, rebelled, or fought long after a colonial flag had been raised.

The Scramble for Africa was therefore not one event and not one story. It was a period of competing imperial ambitions, military conquest, African resistance, unequal treaties, collaboration, and political calculation. Its results varied from place to place, but together they transformed Africa's map and the institutions later inherited by independent states.

A Continent Under Growing Pressure

European involvement in Africa did not begin in the 1880s. Coastal trade, missionary activity, the Atlantic slave trade, settler expansion in southern Africa, and the French conquest of Algeria had already created deep and often violent relationships. Even so, around 1880 much of Africa's interior remained under African political authority. The speed with which that changed is one reason the period is remembered as a scramble (Boahen, 1985).

No single cause explains the expansion. European industries wanted access to raw materials and markets, but economic calculation alone cannot explain every colony; some territories cost imperial governments more than they immediately returned. Strategic concerns also mattered. Governments wanted control of river routes, ports, and passages connecting existing possessions. The opening of the Suez Canal in 1869 increased the importance of northeastern Africa to European and Asian trade. National prestige and rivalry encouraged officials to claim territory partly because they feared another power would take it first.

Private ambitions helped push governments forward. Companies sought concessions. Missionaries and explorers supplied information, maps, and arguments for intervention. King Leopold II of Belgium pursued control in the Congo through organizations presented as humanitarian and scientific. In practice, his project became one of the most coercive systems of extraction in colonial Africa.

Technology altered what European armies and administrators could attempt. Steam transport, telegraphy, repeating firearms, and medical use of quinine reduced some of the obstacles that had limited European movement. But technology did not make conquest automatic. European powers still depended on African knowledge, labor, soldiers, interpreters, and allies. They also faced organized resistance. The outcome came from an unequal combination of military power, finance, diplomacy, local divisions, and repeated campaigns—not from a single invention or a simple story of European superiority.

Berlin: What the Conference Did—and Did Not Do

The Berlin West Africa Conference met from 15 November 1884 to 26 February 1885. Diplomats representing fourteen governments gathered in Berlin at the invitation of German Chancellor Otto von Bismarck. No African state or political community was represented in the negotiations.

The conference dealt especially with commerce and navigation in the Congo and Niger regions. Its General Act also established procedures concerning new European possessions on the African coast. A government making a new claim was expected to notify the other signatories, and occupation had to be supported by enough authority to protect existing rights and freedom of trade. These provisions are commonly associated with the principle of "effective occupation" (Federal Foreign Office, 1885).

Berlin mattered because it gave imperial competition a shared diplomatic framework and encouraged European governments to turn paper claims into administrative and military control. It also reflected a deeper assumption: European powers believed they could establish rules for African territory without the consent of the people who lived there.

But the familiar image of officials sitting around one table and drawing every modern African border is inaccurate. The conference did not settle the whole map. Many boundaries were negotiated later in bilateral agreements between European powers, imposed through military conquest, adjusted by colonial administrators, or inherited from earlier claims. Some changed more than once.

This distinction does not make the partition less serious. It makes the history more precise. Berlin helped create the rules and political momentum for a wider process. The actual division of the continent continued through treaties, protectorates, wars, occupations, and boundary commissions over the following decades (Boahen, 1985).

The resulting borders often joined communities with different political histories and separated people who shared language, trade, kinship, or religious ties. Yet it would also be misleading to imagine that every precolonial society had lived inside a fixed ethnic homeland. African states and identities had changed over time, and many communities were multilingual or connected across political frontiers. Colonial boundaries did not cut across a simple, perfectly ordered map. They imposed new territorial states upon a continent whose political geography was already complex.

Conquest Was Not One Story

European maps often colored vast territories as possessions before those areas were fully occupied. A treaty signed by one ruler could be interpreted far beyond what the African signatory understood or intended. A coastal foothold could become the basis for an inland claim. Military campaigns might continue for years after annexation was announced.

African responses were equally varied. Resistance was widespread, but it was not always united. Some leaders accepted treaties in the hope of preserving authority. Some sought weapons or alliances from one European power against another. Some communities cooperated because they faced older rivalries nearby, hoped to gain advantage, or believed accommodation would reduce destruction. Others rejected foreign demands and fought.

These choices were made under unequal conditions, but they were still choices. Describing every African as either a heroic resister or a willing collaborator hides the pressure, uncertainty, and local politics people faced. It also erases the fact that the same ruler or community might negotiate at one moment and resist at another.

The military record shows both African capability and the limits of individual victories. In January 1879, before the Berlin Conference but during the longer period of imperial expansion, Zulu forces defeated a British army at Isandlwana. The victory exposed British failures in planning and their underestimation of Zulu military power. Britain later returned with greater force and conquered the Zulu kingdom, but the first result cannot be dismissed simply because the war ended differently (National Army Museum, n.d.).

In West Africa, Samori Touré built a powerful state and resisted French expansion for many years. He reorganized forces, acquired firearms, moved his political base, and combined war with negotiation. His struggle was not the defense of a modern nation-state with fixed borders; Samori was also building and expanding his own authority. That complexity does not diminish the scale of his resistance. French forces captured him in 1898 after a prolonged contest (Boahen, 1985).

In Asante, Yaa Asantewaa, the Queen Mother of Ejisu, became the leading figure in the 1900 uprising often called the War of the Golden Stool. The conflict followed earlier British campaigns and a demand by the British governor involving the Golden Stool, a sacred symbol of Asante political identity. Her leadership challenges the habit of telling resistance only through male rulers and generals. The uprising was defeated, but Yaa Asantewaa remained a lasting symbol of political courage and defense of sovereignty (British Museum, n.d.).

In German East Africa, the Maji Maji uprising of 1905–1907 brought together communities with different grievances against colonial rule, forced labor, taxation, and compulsory cotton production. The movement drew spiritual and political strength from the belief that sacred water, *maji*, offered protection. German forces suppressed the uprising through military violence and the destruction of crops and food supplies, contributing to famine and enormous loss of life. The movement was broad, but it was not one centrally commanded national army. Its alliances and experiences differed across the region (Boahen, 1985).

These cases do not form a complete list. Resistance occurred across North, West, Central, East, and Southern Africa. Nor should defeat be treated as proof that resistance did not matter. People fought because land, authority, security, belief, and the right to determine their own future mattered to them. A movement's historical importance cannot be measured only by whether it won.

When Conquest Became Catastrophe

Some colonial campaigns went beyond military defeat and became systems of mass violence.

In German South West Africa, in present-day Namibia, the Ovaherero rose against German colonial rule in 1904, followed by Nama resistance. German forces responded with warfare, expulsion, confinement, forced labor, and lethal conditions that destroyed a large share of the affected populations. The German government now officially describes the atrocities committed between 1904 and 1908 as genocide (Federal Foreign Office, 2021).

In the Congo, Leopold II became the sovereign ruler of the Congo Free State from 1885 to 1908. ***The name suggested liberty; the system delivered coercion.*** Colonial officials and concessionary companies used forced labor and punitive violence to extract ivory and rubber. Communities experienced hostage-taking, punishment, displacement, disrupted agriculture, disease, and large-scale mortality. International criticism eventually contributed to Belgium's annexation of the territory in 1908.

The exact population loss cannot be calculated with confidence because reliable demographic records are incomplete. Estimates differ widely. There is no need to present a disputed number as settled fact. The documented conclusion is already devastating: Leopold's system made coercive extraction central to rule and caused catastrophic harm to Congolese communities (Royal Museum for Central Africa, n.d.).

Namibia and the Congo were not identical, and their histories should not be collapsed into one general account of colonial brutality. They do, however, show what could happen when distant authorities treated African lives, land, and labor as instruments of imperial power.

Ethiopia, Italy, and Adwa

Ethiopia's experience during the Scramble was exceptional, but it was not separate from African history. Italy established Eritrea as a colony on Ethiopia's northern frontier and sought to extend its power inland. Tension deepened after Emperor Menelik II and Italy signed the Treaty of Wuchale in 1889.

The Amharic and Italian versions of a crucial article did not say the same thing. The Italian text treated Ethiopia's foreign relations as subject to Italian control, while the Amharic text allowed Menelik to use Italy's diplomatic assistance without making it compulsory. Italy claimed a protectorate. Menelik rejected that interpretation, and the dispute helped lead to war.

On 1 March 1896, Ethiopian forces defeated the invading Italian army near Adwa. The victory came from a broad mobilization involving regional leaders and forces drawn from different parts of the empire. Menelik's leadership was central, but he was not alone. Empress Taytu Betul supported the war effort, advised on strategy, helped mobilize resources, and was present with her own forces. The victory belonged to a political and military coalition, not to one man (Boahen, 1985; Ofoego, 2015).

Adwa mattered first because of its immediate result. Italy failed to impose the protectorate it had sought, and the peace settlement recognized Ethiopia's sovereignty. At a time when European empires were conquering most of the continent, an African army had defeated a European colonial force in a major conventional battle.

The victory also carried meaning beyond Ethiopia. It challenged racist assumptions about inevitable European conquest and later became important in African and Black political memory. For people confronting colonial rule and racial domination elsewhere, Adwa offered evidence that imperial expansion could be resisted.

Adwa still should not be turned into a perfect national legend. Menelik's government was itself expanding, and different communities experienced that expansion in different ways. Ethiopia contained political rivalries, inequality, and conflict. A victory over foreign invasion did not make the state democratic or just in every other respect.

It is also inaccurate to say, without qualification, that Ethiopia was "never occupied." Adwa preserved Ethiopian sovereignty during the principal nineteenth-century partition, but Fascist Italy invaded again in 1935. Italian forces occupied Addis Ababa in May 1936 and organized Ethiopia with Eritrea and Italian Somaliland as Italian East Africa. Ethiopian resistance continued, and the occupation ended in 1941 (Library of Congress, n.d.-a).

The careful conclusion is stronger than the slogan: Ethiopia defeated Italy in 1896 and maintained internationally recognized sovereignty during the main Scramble, then endured and resisted Fascist Italian occupation from 1936 to 1941.

Liberia: A Different Exception

Liberia also remained outside formal European colonial rule during the Scramble, but its path was very different. The American Colonization Society established a settlement on the West African coast in 1822 for free and formerly enslaved Black people from the United States. The settlement became the independent Republic of Liberia in 1847 (Library of Congress, n.d.-b).

Liberia was therefore neither a European colony nor an untouched precolonial state. Indigenous African societies already lived in the territory, while Americo-Liberian settlers and their descendants dominated the new republic's political institutions for generations. The country also faced sustained pressure from European powers and depended heavily on its relationship with the United States.

Ethiopia and Liberia both remained formally independent during the partition of most of Africa, but they did so through different histories. Treating them as identical exceptions would hide more than it explains.

What Colonial Rule Changed

By the early twentieth century, European empires controlled most of Africa. British possessions stretched across parts of West, East, Central, and Southern Africa. France ruled large territories in North, West, and Central Africa. Portugal retained Angola, Mozambique, and other colonies. Belgium controlled the Congo after Leopold's personal rule ended. Germany held colonies until its defeat in the First World War. Italy and Spain controlled territories in the north, east, west, and the Horn.

These governments did not all rule in the same way. British administrations often governed partly through selected or recognized African authorities, a practice associated with indirect rule. French systems are often described as more centralized, though practice varied. Belgian, German, Italian, Portuguese, and Spanish administrations developed their own arrangements, and every empire changed over time. Settler colonies also differed sharply from territories where relatively few Europeans lived.

Still, colonial systems shared a defining feature: ultimate sovereignty rested outside the colonized population. Major decisions could be made by officials who were not accountable to the African people living under their authority.

Colonial rule changed more than flags. Some rulers were removed; others were incorporated into new administrations. Governments created districts, courts, taxes, labor regulations, police forces, schools, and territorial capitals. In some places, colonial officials strengthened particular chiefs. Elsewhere they reduced older authorities or recognized people who had not previously held the powers assigned to them. Local institutions did not simply disappear, but they operated within a new hierarchy backed by foreign force.

Economic structures changed as well. Colonial governments and companies promoted mines, plantations, and cash crops tied to overseas markets. ***Roads and railways were often designed to move minerals or agricultural products from the interior to ports. Such infrastructure could later serve wider purposes, and Africans used it in ways colonial planners did not foresee. But much of its original logic was outward-facing: extract, transport, and export.***

This pattern helps explain why neighboring African economies were often poorly connected to one another even when each possessed a route to the sea. It will reappear in Chapters 9 and 13, where the book examines trade, value addition, and continental infrastructure.

Colonial economies were not uniform. Some territories depended on settler agriculture; others on African smallholders, mining, concessionary companies, or labor migration. Some regions received more roads, schools, and administrative investment than others. These differences mattered after independence. There was no single colonial inheritance, but there were recurring structures of external control and unequal development.

The new territories also became the foundations of later African states. At independence, leaders faced a dangerous choice: redraw boundaries that had been established under colonial rule, or preserve them to reduce the risk of conflict. In 1964, the Organization of African Unity pledged respect for the borders that existed when member states achieved independence (Organization of African Unity, 1964).

That decision did not declare the borders historically fair. It recognized that attempting to redesign an entire continent's map could produce even greater instability. The boundaries endured, and Africans then had to build national institutions across territories that colonial governments had not created as democratic nation-states.

African Agency Did Not Disappear

Colonial rule imposed powerful constraints, but it did not bring African political life to an end. People continued to negotiate, resist, adapt, worship, trade, migrate, and organize. They formed churches, mosques, newspapers, mutual-aid associations, professional groups, trade unions, and political movements. They used colonial schools and courts while also challenging the purposes those institutions served.

Africans also served as soldiers and carriers in imperial wars. During the First World War, fighting spread across several African colonies, and large numbers of Africans were recruited or compelled into military and transport service. Germany's defeat led to the transfer of its colonies under the League of Nations mandate system, principally to Britain, France, Belgium, and South Africa. One imperial administration replaced another; self-government did not follow.

Yet colonial rule was never as permanent as it appeared. Veterans returned with wider experience. Cities expanded. Workers organized. Educated professionals challenged discrimination. Farmers protested prices and controls. Religious leaders, women, students, journalists, and traditional authorities all entered political struggles in different ways.

Pan-African networks connected arguments inside Africa with Black political thought across the Atlantic and beyond.

In 1960, seventeen new states were admitted to the United Nations, sixteen of them African. That December, the UN General Assembly adopted Resolution 1514, declaring the right of colonial peoples to self-determination and calling for colonial rule to end (United Nations, n.d.; United Nations General Assembly, 1960). Independence did not arrive everywhere at once, and in some territories, it required years of armed struggle. But the empires that had divided Africa were being dismantled.

Colonial History Is Context, Not Destiny

The Scramble altered Africa profoundly. It changed borders, political authority, land systems, trade, education, law, language, and infrastructure. It created institutions that later governments inherited and economic relationships they could not easily redesign.

Colonialism therefore matters to any serious explanation of modern Africa. But it cannot responsibly explain every event that followed. Independent governments have made choices. Leaders have built, neglected, or damaged institutions. Countries with related colonial histories have produced different results, while countries with different colonial experiences sometimes face similar problems. Global markets, the Cold War, domestic politics, geography, social movements, and individual decisions have all shaped the continent since independence.

To say that history matters is not to say that history decides everything. Inheritance sets conditions; it does not remove responsibility.

The same balance applies to resistance. Africans were not passive, but not every response was united or successful. Adwa deserves recognition, but Ethiopia's wider history should not be romanticized. Liberia remained independent, but its institutions contained deep inequalities. Colonial violence was real, but it did not erase African agency. The record is powerful enough without turning it into myth.

Chapter 2 showed what existed before conquest. This chapter has shown how foreign rule changed the map and redirected political power. The next chapter turns to the people who challenged that order and asks what independence was meant to achieve.

The colonial state was imposed from outside. The struggle for African self-determination would be fought from within.

Evidence Note

The Scramble was a continent-wide process, but its timing and effects varied greatly. This chapter uses selected cases rather than presenting them as a complete record of conquest or resistance. The Berlin Conference established rules and momentum for partition; it did not draw every modern border. African responses included resistance, negotiation, accommodation, and alliance, sometimes within the same society. Population losses in the Congo Free State cannot be stated precisely from the surviving evidence. Ethiopia preserved its sovereignty after Adwa in 1896 but experienced Fascist Italian occupation from 1936 to 1941. Liberia's independence emerged from a settler-colonization project and should not be treated as the same historical experience as Ethiopia's.

CHAPTER 4

Independence and the Search for African Self-Determination

From Colonial Rule to Sovereign States

Chapter 3 ended with a continent transformed by conquest. European empires had redrawn boundaries, redirected economies, and placed most African societies under foreign rule. Yet colonial authority was never uncontested, and it did not last forever.

Across the twentieth century, Africans organized in political parties, trade unions, churches, newspapers, student groups, professional associations, women's movements, and liberation armies. Some challenged colonial rule through elections, strikes, petitions, and constitutional negotiations. Others concluded that armed struggle was unavoidable. In many territories, these methods overlapped.

The result was not one African independence story. It was many stories, unfolding at different times and at very different human costs.

In 1960 alone, sixteen of the seventeen states admitted to the United Nations were African. That remarkable change in membership captured the speed of decolonization, but it can also create a misleading impression that the colonial era ended in a single wave (United Nations, n.d.-a). It did not. Ghana became independent in 1957 and Guinea in 1958. Algeria reached independence in 1962 after a brutal war. Angola and Mozambique remained under Portuguese rule until 1975. Namibia became independent in 1990. In South Africa, formal sovereignty had long coexisted with white-minority rule; universal adult suffrage in a national election did not arrive until 1994.

Independence was therefore an extraordinary achievement, but not a finish line. It answered one essential question—who had the right to govern—but immediately raised another: what would Africans build with that right?

Freedom Did Not Arrive Everywhere at Once

The uneven timing of independence reflected the diversity of colonial systems and African political struggles. In Morocco and Tunisia, negotiations contributed to the end of French protectorate rule in 1956. In the British Gold Coast, mass politics and constitutional change led to independence as Ghana in 1957. Guinea made a sharper break from France after rejecting the proposed French Community in the 1958 referendum. Across much of the continent, 1960 became the symbolic year of independence, but even that dramatic wave left large parts of southern Africa under colonial or minority rule.

This varied chronology matters because the word *independence* can hide very different experiences. A negotiated transfer of authority did not leave the same wounds as a long war. A territory with an established African civil service did not begin with the same administrative capacity as one in which colonial officials had severely restricted African advancement. A country surrounded by other independent states faced a different regional environment from one bordering settler regimes or active wars.

There was no single day when Africa became free. Decolonization was a generation-long transformation, and some struggles continued long after the first flags were raised.

More Than a New Flag

Political independence transferred formal sovereignty from a colonial power to an African state. That change was profound. African governments could make laws, conduct foreign policy, control national budgets, establish diplomatic relations, and represent their people in international institutions. Millions of people ceased to be colonial subjects and became citizens of sovereign countries.

But a flag could change in one night; a state could not.

New governments usually inherited the territorial framework discussed in Chapter 3. The borders remained, as did many ministries, courts, administrative languages, security institutions, and colonial legal traditions. Economies were often heavily dependent on a small number of exports. Railways and ports had frequently been designed to connect mines or cash-crop regions to overseas markets rather than to integrate national economies. Educational opportunity and trained personnel were distributed unevenly, both within and among territories (Cooper, 2002; Young, 1994).

These inheritances did not make failure inevitable. They did, however, shape the choices available to the first governments. Independence movements had promised dignity and freedom, while citizens also expected schools, hospitals, jobs, roads, land reform, and wider opportunity. The demand for rapid change was understandable. The capacity to deliver it was often limited.

This is the central distinction of the independence era: winning sovereignty and using sovereignty were connected achievements, but they were not the same achievement.

Ghana and Guinea: Two Early Signals

On 6 March 1957, the Gold Coast became independent as Ghana. Kwame Nkrumah and the Convention People's Party had become leading forces in the nationalist movement, but independence was not the work of one man. It emerged from years of organizing, elections, labor activism, public pressure, and negotiation. Ghana's achievement nevertheless acquired continental importance because Nkrumah tied national freedom to the liberation of the rest of Africa and to a larger Pan-African future (U.S. Department of State, Office of the Historian, n.d.-a).

Ghana also exposed a question that would follow every new state. The country had gained the authority to make its own decisions, but its economy remained highly dependent on cocoa exports. Nkrumah's government pursued ambitious infrastructure, education, and industrial projects in an effort to turn political independence into economic capacity. Some investments had lasting value; others placed heavy pressure on public finances. His government became increasingly restrictive toward opposition before he was removed in a military coup in 1966 (Cooper, 2002).

None of this erases Nkrumah's contribution to liberation or Pan-Africanism. It simply places him back inside history. A leader can help achieve national freedom and still make serious governing mistakes. Mature historical judgment does not require a person to be either a flawless hero or a complete failure.

Guinea followed a different path. In September 1958, its voters rejected continued membership in the French Community under the terms offered by Charles de Gaulle's government. Independence followed on 2 October, with Sékou Touré as the country's first president. France withdrew personnel and support with unusual speed, leaving the new government to manage an abrupt institutional break (Birmingham, 1995; U.S. Department of State, Office of the Historian, n.d.-b).

Guinea's choice represented a determined assertion of sovereignty, but the later authoritarian record of Touré's government must be judged separately from the legitimacy of the struggle against colonial rule.

Liberation gives a government authority; it does not place that government beyond criticism.

1960—and the Warning from the Congo

The pace of decolonization accelerated dramatically in 1960. That December, the UN General Assembly adopted Resolution 1514, declaring that colonial peoples had a right to self-determination and calling for colonial rule to end. The declaration did not liberate Africa by itself. Africans had already spent decades organizing, resisting, negotiating, and fighting. It did, however, confirm that permanent colonial rule was losing international legitimacy (United Nations General Assembly, 1960).

The Congo showed how fragile a transfer of sovereignty could be. The Belgian Congo became independent on 30 June 1960, with Joseph Kasa-Vubu as president and Patrice Lumumba as prime minister. Within days, the Force Publique mutinied against its Belgian officers. Belgian troops intervened without the approval of the Congolese government. Katanga, the mineral-rich southern province, declared secession, followed by South Kasai. The Congolese government appealed to the United Nations, which established the United Nations Operation in the Congo, known as ONUC (U.S. Department of State, Office of the Historian, n.d.-c).

Domestic rivalries, provincial secession, Belgian interests, and Cold War competition quickly became entangled. The United States feared Soviet influence; Lumumba sought outside assistance after Western governments failed to meet his requests; the Soviet Union became involved; and Congolese factions competed for control of a state whose national institutions had barely begun to function.

Lumumba was dismissed during the political crisis, arrested, transferred to Katanga, and killed on 17 January 1961. Declassified U.S. records show that American officials had sought his removal and developed assassination plans, although the plan described in those records was not the immediate method by which he died. Belgian and Congolese actors were directly involved in the transfer and killing. The full history remains a subject of continuing research, but foreign intervention is not speculation and should not be written out of the story (U.S. Department of State, 2013; U.S. Department of State, Office of the Historian, n.d.-c).

The Congo crisis cannot honestly be reduced to a story of Africans receiving independence and then failing to govern. Nor can every responsibility be placed outside the country. Congolese political conflict was real, but it unfolded inside a hurried transition and an international struggle over strategic influence and mineral wealth.

The lesson is sobering: international recognition can establish legal sovereignty, but it cannot instantly create a cohesive army, trusted institutions, a settled political order, or protection from foreign pressure.

Different Roads to the Same Demand

Algeria reached independence through one of the longest and most violent struggles of the period. The war that began in 1954 involved the National Liberation Front, French armed forces, European settlers, rival Algerian movements, and extensive violence against civilians. After the Évian agreements, Algerians voted overwhelmingly for independence in a referendum on 1 July 1962, and France recognized the independent state two days later (U.S. Department of State, Office of the Historian, n.d.-d).

Kenya's path combined insurgency, repression, mass politics, and negotiation. The British government declared a state of emergency in 1952 during the conflict commonly associated with Mau Mau. Disputes over land, labor, racial inequality, and political exclusion formed part of the wider setting. The colonial response included detention, executions, forced resettlement, and systematic abuse. In 2013, the British government expressed regret for torture and ill-treatment during the Emergency and announced a settlement covering 5,228 Kenyan claimants, while continuing to deny legal liability (Foreign and Commonwealth Office, 2013).

Mau Mau was important, but it was not the entire independence movement. Trade unions, nationalist parties, constitutional conferences, shifting British policy, and international pressure also mattered. Kenya became independent on 12 December 1963.

Tanganyika, by contrast, achieved independence from Britain on 9 December 1961 through a comparatively negotiated transition led politically by the Tanganyika African National Union under Julius Nyerere. The territory had been administered by Britain as a United Nations Trust Territory. In 1964, Tanganyika united with Zanzibar—whose own revolution and political history followed a different course—to form the United Republic of Tanzania (U.S. Department of State, Office of the Historian, n.d.-e).

These cases resist a simple formula. Armed struggle was decisive in some places and one influence among several in others. Negotiation could reduce violence, but it could also preserve old inequalities. The route to independence depended on local organization, settler power, colonial policy, regional conditions, and the willingness of an imperial government to surrender control.

Pan-Africanism Became an Institution

National independence also created the possibility of cooperation among sovereign African states. Pan-African thought had developed across Africa and the diaspora long before the 1960s. Independence gave it a new diplomatic form.

Leaders disagreed about how far unity should go. Nkrumah advocated rapid political integration. Others preferred gradual cooperation among states that retained their own sovereignty. The disagreement was not between people who cared about Africa and people who did not. It concerned what kind of unity was practical, how much authority national governments should surrender, and whether a continental union could be built before the new states had consolidated themselves.

On 25 May 1963, leaders of thirty-two independent African states signed the Charter of the Organization of African Unity in Addis Ababa. The OAU committed its members to cooperation, sovereignty, and the completion of African liberation (African Union, n.d.). It also embodied a compromise: Africa would organize collectively, but the member states would remain the principal political units.

The organization supported liberation movements and gave African governments a forum in which to coordinate diplomacy. At the same time, its commitment to non-interference limited its response when member governments abused their own citizens. That tension grew from a real historical concern. States that had only recently escaped foreign control were deeply protective of sovereignty. Yet the protection of governments could come at the expense of the people in whose name sovereignty had been won.

The OAU also accepted the practical reality of inherited borders. In 1964, its members pledged to respect the boundaries that existed at independence. They were not declaring those borders fair or culturally natural. They were judging that a continent-wide attempt to redraw them could produce even greater conflict (Organization of African Unity, 1964).

Liberation Continued in Portuguese Africa

While new states gathered in Addis Ababa, Portugal still ruled Angola, Mozambique, Guinea-Bissau, Cape Verde, and São Tomé and Príncipe. Armed liberation movements fought prolonged wars in Angola, Mozambique, and Guinea-Bissau. The anticolonial struggle weakened

Portuguese rule, while the wars also placed a heavy burden on Portugal itself.

In April 1974, the Carnation Revolution overthrew Portugal's dictatorship. The new government moved rapidly toward decolonization. Mozambique became independent on 25 June 1975, and Angola on 11 November (U.S. Department of State, Office of the Historian, n.d.-f, n.d.-g). Cape Verde and São Tomé and Príncipe also became independent that year; Portugal recognized Guinea-Bissau in 1974 after its liberation movement had declared independence the year before.

The timing should not be misunderstood. A change of government in Lisbon opened the final political door, but African movements had spent years fighting colonial rule. Independence resulted from the interaction of African resistance, military stalemate, international pressure, and political change inside Portugal.

In Angola, sovereignty arrived amid a struggle among the MPLA, FNLA, and UNITA. Foreign governments backed different forces, and Cuban troops intervened in support of the MPLA while the United States, South Africa, the Soviet Union, and other states became involved in various ways. A long civil war followed (U.S. Department of State, Office of the Historian, n.d.-h). Mozambique also entered a destructive post-independence conflict between the FRELIMO government and RENAMO, shaped by domestic choices as well as intervention from Rhodesia and apartheid South Africa (United Nations, n.d.-b).

These wars are often described as Cold War conflicts, which is true but incomplete. External powers supplied weapons, money, training, and political support. They intensified violence and altered the balance among local actors. Yet Angolan and Mozambican movements also had their own histories, constituencies, rivalries, and objectives. Africans were not merely pieces on an American-Soviet chessboard.

The Long Struggle in Southern Africa

Independence changed the regional balance even where colonial and minority rule continued. Zambia, independent on 24 October 1964, and Tanzania became important bases and supporters for liberation movements operating farther south (U.S. Department of State, Office of the Historian, n.d.-i). Their involvement carried real costs, including economic pressure and cross-border attacks.

Namibia's struggle continued for decades under South African administration. The United Nations challenged South Africa's claim to the territory, and the South West Africa People's Organization, or SWAPO, became the leading liberation movement. After years of war and negotiation, the United Nations Transition Assistance Group supervised the transition, including elections in 1989. Namibia became independent on 21 March 1990 (United Nations, n.d.-c).

South Africa presents a different problem of language. The Union of South Africa had become a self-governing dominion and later a republic, but most of its people were denied equal citizenship under white-minority rule and apartheid. Formal statehood was not freedom for the majority.

The end of apartheid was not the achievement of one leader. Nelson Mandela's imprisonment, release, and role in negotiation were historically important, but so were decades of action by the African National Congress, the Pan Africanist Congress, trade unions, civic organizations, students, churches, journalists, lawyers, underground networks, armed movements, and ordinary communities. International sanctions and solidarity campaigns added pressure, while F. W. de Klerk's government released political prisoners, unbanned major organizations, and entered negotiations.

On 27 April 1994, South Africans voted in the country's first national election based on universal adult suffrage. Mandela was inaugurated as president on 10 May (United Nations, n.d.-d). Political rights changed decisively. Economic inequality, segregated settlement patterns, and unequal access to land and education did not disappear with the ballot.

Here again, liberation was both an event and a process.

Independence Was Made by More Than Presidents

Public memory often reduces independence to a line of famous men: Nkrumah, Lumumba, Nyerere, Kenyatta, Touré, Kaunda, Ben Bella, Machel, Neto, Mandela. Leadership mattered, but this way of telling the story can make entire populations vanish.

Workers organized strikes and withheld labor. Farmers challenged prices, taxes, and land seizures. Journalists and teachers gave political language to public grievances. Students built networks across borders. Lawyers defended detainees. Religious communities created spaces for organization. Soldiers deserted, rebelled, or joined liberation forces. People carried messages, hid activists, raised money, supplied food, and endured reprisals.

Women participated at every level—as organizers, intellectuals, protesters, combatants, couriers, nurses, fundraisers, and community leaders—yet national histories have often treated them as supporters rather than political actors in their own right. The pattern differed from one country to another, but the larger point is clear: independence was a mass historical process, not a gift exchanged between an imperial governor and a future president.

Recognizing collective action does not make individual leadership unimportant. It makes the story more accurate. It also reminds citizens that sovereignty belongs to a people, not to the person temporarily occupying the highest office.

Leaders Must Be Judged as Human Beings

The generation that led Africa into independence worked under extraordinary pressure. Its members had to negotiate with colonial governments, unite broad coalitions, manage ethnic and regional tensions, create public institutions, and pursue development in a world divided by the Cold War. Many had endured imprisonment, exile, surveillance, or violence.

Respect for that courage should not become hero worship.

Some independence leaders expanded education, health care, infrastructure, and international cooperation. Some built durable national identities across diverse populations. Some also concentrated power, weakened opposition, censored critics, or treated the ruling party as if it were the nation. A number of governments were overthrown by coups; others adopted one-party systems in the name of unity or development. The causes varied, and the next chapter examines them more closely.

Two truths can stand together. The struggle against colonial domination was legitimate. Governments created by that struggle still had to be accountable for what they did with power.

This distinction protects history from both cynicism and nostalgia. It rejects the claim that later failures made independence meaningless, but it also rejects the idea that a liberation record excuses every decision made afterward.

What the New States Inherited—and What They Chose

The colonial state became the starting point of the independent state. Its territory, administrative habits, export patterns, and coercive institutions could not be remade overnight. Foreign companies retained influence in important sectors. Former colonial powers maintained commercial, military, linguistic, and diplomatic relationships. The United States, Soviet Union, China, and other powers also competed for influence.

This international environment constrained choices, but it did not eliminate them. African governments made decisions about political competition, education, land, industry, public finance, and regional cooperation. Citizens organized for or against those choices. Countries with similar colonial inheritances often followed different paths; countries with different colonial histories sometimes confronted comparable problems.

That is why neither of two simple explanations is adequate. Colonialism cannot be blamed for every post-independence outcome, as if Africans ceased to possess agency once they gained power. But colonial history cannot be dismissed as though institutions, borders, and economic structures were reset on independence day.

Inheritance creates conditions. It does not write the entire future.

Political independence and economic self-determination were also different tasks. A government could control its flag and foreign policy while depending on a narrow export base, imported machinery, foreign credit, or decisions made in distant markets. Nkrumah understood this problem in Ghana, as did leaders elsewhere who pursued industrialization, nationalization, regional integration, or African socialism. Their programs produced varied and often contested results.

The question of how African states can convert sovereignty into productive capacity will return in later chapters on institutions, trade, industry, infrastructure, and economic power. It should not be confused with the question of whether independence itself mattered. Political freedom has value in its own right. It also creates responsibility.

What Is Independence For?

The liberation generation gave a clear answer to the first question of self-determination: Africans should govern themselves. The more difficult question concerned the purpose of that authority.

Was independence chiefly about national sovereignty, democratic citizenship, economic transformation, cultural recovery, social equality, continental unity, or security? In practice, it carried all these hopes, but governments ranked them differently. Some argued that national unity required limits on political opposition. Others treated rapid development as the first priority. Some pursued close ties with former colonial powers; others sought nonalignment, socialist partnership, or stronger continental institutions.

No government could meet every expectation at once. But limited capacity did not remove the obligation to govern honestly, protect citizens, and build institutions able to survive a change of leadership.

The achievement of independence remains fundamental. It rejected the claim that foreign empires had a right to rule African societies without equal consent. It transformed the United Nations, created the basis for African diplomacy, and placed public authority—formally, at least—in African hands.

It did not guarantee wise leadership, social justice, prosperity, or peace. Freedom is not the same as performance. Yet without freedom, Africans would not possess the political authority to demand better performance from governments acting in their name.

Chapter 3 explained how the colonial state was imposed. This chapter has followed the many struggles that transferred its authority to African governments. The next chapter asks what happened when liberation movements became governing parties and the promise of independence met the daily work of building a state.

Lowering the colonial flag ended one struggle. Deciding how to use sovereignty began another.

Evidence Note

African decolonization was neither a single event nor the work of a few famous leaders. The cases in this chapter are selected examples, not a complete record. Negotiation, elections, labor action, international diplomacy, civil resistance, and armed struggle often operated together. The Congo crisis involved Congolese conflict as well as documented Belgian, American, Soviet, and United Nations intervention. The historical importance of leaders such as Nkrumah, Lumumba, Nyerere, and Mandela does not require treating them as flawless or attributing collective achievements to them alone. South Africa's 1994 transition is included because formal sovereignty without equal citizenship did not constitute self-determination for the majority. Throughout the chapter, political independence is distinguished from the longer work of building accountable institutions and economic capacity.

CHAPTER 5

After Independence

Building Nations Under Pressure

Chapter 4 ended with a simple but demanding question. Once the colonial flag had been lowered, what would Africans do with sovereignty?

Independence transferred legal authority, but it did not deliver a finished nation. The new governments inherited borders, ministries, armies, courts, roads, and export economies built for colonial purposes. They also inherited public expectations that had grown during the struggle for freedom. Citizens wanted dignity, certainly, but they also wanted schools, clinics, jobs, land, electricity, and a government that treated them as members of the nation rather than subjects of an empire.

The work began under intense pressure. Administrative experience was scarce in some countries and more developed in others. Economies often depended on one or two export commodities whose prices were set abroad. The Cold War turned local disputes into international contests. Political leaders had to hold together populations with different languages, faiths, regional loyalties, and memories of colonial rule, while deciding what kind of economy and political system the new state should build.

Some countries preserved constitutional continuity. Others endured military coups, civil wars, personal rule, or economic collapse. Many achieved progress in one area and disappointment in another. Tanzania strengthened national cohesion but struggled with parts of its socialist economic program. Botswana used diamond revenue more effectively than many resource-rich states, yet remained dependent on mining and marked by inequality. Nigeria survived a devastating civil war and remained a federation, but its early republic was broken by coups and violence.

There was no single post-independence African experience. There were dozens of national histories, each shaped by a different mixture of inheritance, leadership, institutions, resources, conflict, and chance. What joined them was the difficulty of turning the right to govern into the capacity to govern well.

A State Was Not Yet a Nation

Colonial territories became internationally recognized states at independence. A state has borders, laws, public institutions, and a government that claims authority over a territory. A nation is something less mechanical: a political community whose members believe they share a future and owe one another certain obligations.

The two did not automatically arrive together.

As Chapter 3 explained, most colonial borders had not been designed to create democratic communities. They reflected conquest, imperial bargaining, and administrative convenience. Inside them lived people with varied identities and political traditions. That diversity was not itself a defect. Countries around the world contain regional, religious, linguistic, or ethnic differences. The danger arose when institutions distributed power and security so unevenly that losing an election could feel like exclusion from the state itself (Herbst, 2000; Young, 1994).

This was especially important because the state was often the largest source of formal employment, licenses, contracts, education, and investment. In countries dependent on mineral or agricultural exports, control of government could also mean control of a large share of national revenue. Political competition was therefore rarely about policy alone. It could determine which region received a road, who entered the civil service, which language was used in schools, and whose community felt protected by the army.

The central nation-building problem was not that Africans were too diverse to live together. It was whether public institutions could make citizenship more valuable than access to power through a particular leader, party, or community.

Governments tried to answer that question in different ways. Some promoted a national language or expanded boarding schools and national service so that young people would meet citizens from other regions. Some used federalism to divide authority. Others centralized power in the presidency or declared that a single party represented the whole nation. These choices grew from real fears of fragmentation, but they carried very different consequences.

Why Power Moved Toward the Center

Many independence leaders distrusted the political competition they had inherited. Colonial governments had restricted African organization, manipulated local authorities, and often encouraged regional or communal rivalry. Nationalist movements, by contrast, had won legitimacy by presenting themselves as broad coalitions against foreign rule. Once independence arrived, leaders could easily begin to treat the movement, the ruling party, and the nation as if they were the same thing.

The argument for centralization was not always cynical. Leaders feared secession, foreign interference, and the use of ethnicity by political rivals. They also believed rapid development required unity and long-term planning. In that setting, opposition parties could be described not merely as competitors but as threats to national survival. One-party systems spread across parts of the continent during the 1960s and 1970s (Cooper, 2002).

Yet a system designed to protect unity could weaken the institutions needed to preserve it. When courts, parliaments, newspapers, and opposition parties could not check executive power, presidents became harder to replace peacefully. Political disagreement moved outside constitutional channels. Public office became more dependent on loyalty, and succession became dangerous because too much authority had been concentrated in one person.

Military officers then presented themselves as rescuers. They promised order, discipline, and an end to corruption. In practice, military rule often reproduced the same problems in uniform. Armies contained their own factions and regional rivalries. A coup could remove a government in a day, but it could not create legitimacy, economic competence, or trusted institutions. Across the continent, the causes of military intervention varied, and no single explanation fits every country. Weak civilian institutions, personal ambition, political violence, economic crisis, and Cold War alliances all mattered in different combinations (Decalo, 1990).

The Congo offered an early warning. Joseph Mobutu first intervened in the political crisis of September 1960 and then seized power outright on 25 November 1965. He removed President Joseph Kasa-Vubu and Prime Minister Évariste Kimba, later renamed the country Zaire, and remained in power for more than three decades. His regime received extensive Western support because it was considered strategically useful against Soviet influence (U.S. Department of State, Office of the Historian, n.d.-b).

Uganda showed another form of the danger. Idi Amin overthrew Milton Obote in January 1971. The new government did not restore accountable rule; it presided over mass violence, purges, economic disruption, and fear. The lesson was larger than either country. Soldiers could seize the state, but military command was not a substitute for public institutions.

Nigeria: When Fear Broke the Federation

Nigeria entered independence in 1960 as a federation with a large population, significant economic potential, and strong regional political parties. Its size and diversity could have been sources of strength. They also made the terms of power-sharing unusually important.

The First Republic struggled with disputed elections, regional rivalry, and arguments over the distribution of federal authority. In January 1966, military officers carried out a coup in which Prime Minister Abubakar Tafawa Balewa, Northern Region premier Ahmadu Bello, and other political and military leaders were killed. Major General Johnson Aguiyi-Ironsi became head of state. A counter-coup followed in July, bringing Lieutenant Colonel Yakubu Gowon to power. Because the first coup's leading plotters were largely Igbo while many of its most prominent victims were northern, it was widely interpreted through a communal lens, even though the motives and participants were more complicated than that description suggests (Falola & Heaton, 2008).

The consequences were catastrophic. Mass killings of Igbo and other easterners in northern Nigeria drove large numbers of people toward the Eastern Region and deepened the belief that they could no longer be safe inside the federation. Negotiations over regional autonomy and security failed. On 30 May 1967, the Eastern Region, led by Chukwuemeka Odumegwu Ojukwu, declared the Republic of Biafra. The federal government rejected the secession, and war began in July.

The conflict lasted until January 1970. Federal forces fought to preserve Nigeria; Biafra fought to secure the independence it had declared. The war devastated the east, and the blockade and breakdown of food production produced a humanitarian disaster that became one of the defining international images of the period. Foreign governments and organizations supplied arms, diplomacy, or relief, but the war was rooted in Nigeria's own political crisis as well as in outside involvement (U.S. Department of State, Office of the Historian, n.d.-a).

Nigeria remained one country. Gowon's government announced a policy of reconciliation and rejected formal collective punishment, although the experience of reintegration was far more uneven than the slogan suggested. The federation was reorganized into more states, partly to reduce the dominance of the old regions. Oil later gave the federal government much greater revenue, but it also raised the stakes of controlling the center.

The Nigerian Civil War should not be reduced to the claim that "tribalism" made conflict inevitable. That explanation turns a sequence of political decisions into an ancient instinct. Coups, assassinations, massacres, fear, failed negotiations, military choices, and the structure of federal power all mattered. Diversity became dangerous when people lost confidence that the state could protect them and that political defeat would remain temporary.

Tanzania: Unity, Ujamaa, and Coercion

Tanzania followed a different path. Tanganyika became independent in 1961 and united with Zanzibar in 1964. The union brought together societies with distinct histories, while the mainland itself contained many linguistic communities. Under Julius Nyerere, the government deliberately cultivated a national identity that did not depend on one dominant ethnic group. The wider use of Kiswahili, the expansion of national education, and a political culture that emphasized common citizenship helped Tanzania avoid some of the regional polarization experienced elsewhere (Bjerk, 2015).

Political stability, however, came within a one-party system. Opposition was restricted, and the state did not meet contemporary standards of multiparty democracy. Tanzania therefore resists a simple verdict. Its record of national cohesion was important, but cohesion and political freedom were not identical.

Economic policy was equally ambitious. The Arusha Declaration of 1967 committed Tanzania to socialism and self-reliance. Nyerere argued that development should be built around equality, rural communities, public leadership, and the productive effort of Tanzanians themselves rather than permanent dependence on foreign capital. Major enterprises were nationalized, and *ujamaa*—a term associated with familyhood—became the language of a distinct postcolonial project (Nyerere, 1968).

The program addressed a genuine problem. Most citizens lived in rural areas, public services were scarce, and the colonial economy had not produced balanced national development. Concentrating settlement in villages appeared to offer a practical way to provide schools, clinics, water, and agricultural support. Some people moved voluntarily, but the villagization campaign became increasingly compulsory in the 1970s. Officials relocated rural families, sometimes with little regard for local knowledge, existing farms, or consent (Lal, 2015).

The results were mixed. Tanzania made meaningful gains in national identity, literacy, and access to basic services. At the same time, agricultural production, incentives, state enterprises, and public finance suffered serious difficulties. External shocks, including oil-price increases and war with Uganda, added pressure, but domestic policy failures cannot be ignored.

Ujamaa should therefore be neither romanticized as a complete success nor dismissed as an irrational failure. It was a serious attempt to define development on postcolonial terms. Its social purposes deserve to be understood; its coercion and economic weaknesses deserve to be judged. Good intentions do not erase harmful results, and poor results do not prove that the problems a policy tried to solve were imaginary.

Botswana: Resources Met Institutions

Botswana provides another useful contrast. At independence in 1966, the country had a small population, limited infrastructure, and little formal administrative capacity. Large diamond deposits were identified soon afterward, including at Orapa in 1967. Those discoveries transformed the country's economic prospects, but geology alone does not explain what followed.

Botswana's government negotiated a substantial public role in the diamond industry through its partnership with De Beers, later known as Debswana. It directed mineral revenue into public investment and maintained greater continuity in economic management and constitutional government than many contemporary states. Scholars have connected that performance to political institutions, prudent macroeconomic choices, and relationships between elected leaders and established local authorities, while also debating how inclusive those institutions have been (Acemoglu et al., 2003; Ndlovu & Vandome, 2024).

The comparison should be kept within limits. Botswana is not a flawless model. Its economy remained heavily dependent on diamonds. Mining generated revenue more readily than employment, while inequality, unemployment, and the treatment of minority communities remained serious concerns. Nor could every country reproduce its circumstances: population size, the timing and quality of mineral discoveries, regional security, and historical institutions all differed.

The lesson is narrower and more useful. **Natural resources do not govern themselves. Contracts, taxation, auditing, budgeting, and political restraint determine whether mineral wealth strengthens public capacity or finances private power. Resources create an opportunity; institutions decide how much of that opportunity reaches the nation.**

The Cold War Entered the Room

Post-independence governments did not make choices in isolation. The United States and Soviet Union competed for allies, military access, diplomatic support, and ideological influence. Former colonial powers defended commercial and strategic interests. China, Cuba, apartheid South Africa, and regional governments also intervened in African politics.

Outside support could help a government survive without becoming more accountable to its citizens. Mobutu's anticommunist value helped him secure Western assistance despite authoritarian rule and corruption. Governments aligned with the Soviet bloc could receive similar protection from criticism when they served strategic purposes. In both camps, the language of ideology often covered an ordinary calculation: an unreliable ally was still preferable to an opponent's ally.

Angola became one of the clearest examples. As Chapter 4 noted, Portugal's withdrawal in 1975 did not produce a settled transfer of power. The MPLA, FNLA, and UNITA competed to control the new state. The Soviet Union armed the MPLA, Cuba sent troops, the United States supported the FNLA and UNITA, and South African forces entered from the south. These interventions altered the military balance and enlarged a conflict whose local actors had their own histories and ambitions. The civil war continued, in changing forms, until 2002 (U.S. Department of State, Office of the Historian, n.d.-c).

The Horn of Africa showed how quickly alliances could reverse. Ethiopia had been a close partner of the United States under Emperor Haile Selassie. In 1974, the military committee that became known as the Derg removed the emperor, ended the monarchy, nationalized major property, and eventually aligned the country with the Soviet bloc. Political repression intensified, while existing wars in Eritrea and elsewhere continued (Clapham, 1988; Zewde, 2001).

Somalia, ruled by Mohamed Siad Barre after a 1969 coup, had initially developed a close military relationship with the Soviet Union. When Somali forces invaded Ethiopia's Ogaden region in 1977, Moscow shifted decisively toward Ethiopia, and Cuban forces fought on the Ethiopian side. Somalia broke with the Soviet Union and later drew closer to the United States. The rapid reversal revealed the limits of ideological labels: local territorial aims and superpower strategy could matter more than yesterday's declared friendship (U.S. Department of State, 2016).

It would be equally misleading to say that the Cold War created every African conflict or that foreign intervention was secondary. African leaders, parties, armies, and liberation movements retained agency; they made choices with real consequences. External powers supplied weapons, money, training, and diplomatic cover that could make conflicts longer and deadlier. Both levels of responsibility belong in the same history.

The State Also Built

The first decades of independence cannot be remembered only through coups and wars. African governments also undertook an enormous expansion of public life. They opened schools and universities, trained civil servants, built hospitals and clinics, extended roads and electricity, created national broadcasting systems, and established diplomatic services. People who had been deliberately excluded from senior positions under colonial rule entered professions needed to operate the state.

Education became a continental priority because it served several purposes at once. It was a right long denied to much of the population, a path to individual opportunity, and a practical necessity for governments that needed teachers, nurses, engineers, accountants, and administrators. At the 1961 Conference of African States on the Development of Education in Africa, governments gathered in Addis Ababa with UNESCO to plan a major expansion of education and relate it directly to economic and social development (UNESCO, 1961).

The scale of ambition frequently exceeded available money and trained personnel. Rural areas remained underserved, rapid enrollment placed pressure on quality, and universities could not produce every skill as quickly as governments required. Still, the political expectation changed. A colonial state had been built chiefly to maintain order and organize extraction. An independent government was increasingly judged by whether it could improve the lives of its own citizens.

Health policy carried the same promise. Clinics, vaccination campaigns, sanitation programs, and professional training expanded unevenly across the continent. War and fiscal crisis later damaged many systems, and access remained unequal. Yet these institutions mattered. They were not decorative achievements; they formed part of the social foundation on which later generations would build.

When Development Models Met Economic Crisis

Most new governments believed the state had to lead economic transformation. Domestic private capital was limited, foreign companies controlled important sectors, and markets alone were unlikely to build roads, power systems, or heavy industry at the speed citizens expected. Governments established public enterprises, protected new industries, regulated trade, and borrowed to finance development. Some projects created lasting capacity. Others were poorly chosen, politically managed, or too costly to sustain.

During the 1970s and 1980s, the environment became harsher. Oil-price shocks increased costs for importers. Commodity prices fluctuated, drought affected several regions, global interest rates rose, and debt-service burdens grew. Domestic choices also mattered: overvalued exchange rates, inefficient public enterprises, uncontrolled spending, conflict, and corruption weakened a number of economies. No honest explanation can assign all responsibility either to the international system or to African governments.

By the 1980s, many states were negotiating structural-adjustment programs with the International Monetary Fund and World Bank. These programs commonly sought fiscal restraint, exchange-rate reform, trade liberalization, reduced subsidies, and the restructuring or sale of state enterprises. Supporters argued that existing policies had become financially impossible and were discouraging production. Critics argued that austerity reduced public services, shifted costs onto vulnerable citizens, and treated institutional and social problems as if they could be solved through prices alone.

The record varied by country and remains contested. The World Bank's own later assessment emphasized that macroeconomic reform was more likely to endure when accompanied by credible institutions, public investment, and country ownership, while African scholars challenged both the assumptions and social costs of externally designed adjustment (Mkandawire & Soludo, 1999; World Bank, 1994). It is therefore unhelpful to describe adjustment either as the policy that rescued Africa or as the single cause of the continent's economic difficulties.

The deeper lesson concerns capacity. A government can nationalize an industry without knowing how to run it. It can privatize the same industry without creating competition or effective regulation. It can borrow for a dam, a school system, or an unproductive prestige project. The label attached to a policy matters less than whether institutions can design it well, implement it honestly, learn from failure, and protect the public interest.

From Sovereignty to Responsibility

The Organization of African Unity reflected the priorities of the independence era. Its 1963 Charter defended sovereign equality, territorial integrity, and non-interference. Those principles were understandable protections for states emerging from colonial domination. They also helped African governments support liberation movements and resist attempts by outside powers to decide the continent's future (Organization of African Unity, 1963).

But strong protection for governments could leave citizens weakly protected from their own rulers. The OAU was often reluctant to challenge abuses presented as domestic affairs. Its caution did not mean Africans were indifferent to human rights; lawyers, journalists, religious leaders, trade unionists, women's organizations, and opposition movements continued to demand accountability. The institutional balance, however, favored sovereignty over intervention.

By the end of the twentieth century, the continent's central diplomatic problems had changed. Most formal colonial rule had ended, apartheid had fallen, and the Cold War was over. Civil conflict, unconstitutional changes of government, economic integration, and human rights had moved closer to the center of the continental agenda.

The African Union, launched in 2002, embodied part of that shift. Its Constitutive Act retained respect for sovereignty but also rejected unconstitutional changes of government; Article 30 bars governments that come to power through unconstitutional means from participating in the Union's activities (African Union, 2000). The rule has not always been applied with equal speed or consistency. Even so, its existence records an important lesson: the manner in which power is acquired is not merely a private concern of the state where it happens.

Political independence answered who had the right to govern African countries. It did not settle how that authority should be limited, transferred, or judged. Sovereignty was essential, but it could not be the final measure of government.

What Independence Made Possible

It is tempting to summarize the early post-independence era with one word: triumph, failure, crisis, or betrayal. None is adequate.

These decades contained civil wars and peaceful transfers, one-party states and constitutional continuity, failed projects and durable public institutions. Governments expanded education and health care, built infrastructure, and strengthened African diplomacy. Some also censored critics, mismanaged resources, or made the state serve a ruler rather than the public. Foreign powers constrained choices and intensified conflicts, but African leaders and citizens were never without agency.

Colonialism created powerful starting conditions. It did not write every later decision. Leadership mattered, but no leader acted outside institutions, markets, geography, and international pressure. Resources mattered, but Botswana and other cases showed that the political management of resources mattered too. Ideology mattered, but the quality of implementation often mattered more than the name of the model.

Perhaps the most useful distinction is between gaining power and building capacity. A movement may win a liberation struggle. An army may take the presidential palace. A government may nationalize a mine. None of those acts, by itself, creates a court that people trust, a school in which children learn, a professional civil service, or a budget that can survive a fall in export prices.

Freedom did not remove the work. It made Africans responsible for directing it and gave citizens the standing to demand better from governments acting in their name.

The first five chapters have carried the story from human origins and early civilizations through conquest, resistance, liberation, and the first difficult decades of sovereignty. The chapters that follow turn toward Africa's present: its people, resources, economies, institutions, and possibilities. The history remains essential, but it should serve as context rather than an excuse.

Lowering the colonial flag made self-government possible. Building a state worthy of its citizens was the harder test.

Evidence Note

The post-independence era is especially vulnerable to ideological storytelling. The countries discussed here are comparative examples, not a representative sample of every African state. Military coups did not share one cause. The Nigerian Civil War cannot be explained as an automatic product of ethnic diversity. Tanzania's Ujamaa program combined important nation-building and social aims with coercive implementation and serious economic weaknesses. Botswana's institutional and resource-management record is instructive without making the country a perfect or universally reproducible model. Cold War intervention materially shaped African conflicts, but African governments and movements retained agency. Structural adjustment differed across countries and remains debated. Throughout the chapter, inherited constraints are distinguished from later choices, and political sovereignty from accountable government.

CHAPTER 6

A Future Defined from Within

From Potential to Practice and the Quiet Revolution Already Underway

Chapter 5 ended with the harder test of independence: building a state worthy of its citizens. That work did not end with the first generation of African leaders. It continues in ministries and municipal offices, classrooms and clinics, farms and factories, laboratories and small businesses. It is visible in crowded cities, border posts, power lines, courtrooms, and family decisions about education, work, and migration.

To see Africa clearly today, we must resist two familiar stories. The first presents the continent as a permanent emergency, defined by war, poverty, corruption, and dependence. The second offers an equally misleading celebration in which a young population, valuable minerals, new technology, and economic growth make progress seem inevitable. Each story selects real evidence. Neither is large enough to hold the truth.

Africa is not one condition moving in one direction. The African Union has 55 member states, grouped into five geographic regions, and those states differ profoundly in population, political institutions, economic structure, geography, language, religion, infrastructure, and security (African Union, n.d.-a). A continental average can reveal a broad pattern, but it can also hide the circumstances in which people actually live.

This chapter is therefore not a verdict on Africa. It is a way of looking. Before we discuss what the continent can build, we must distinguish potential from capacity, policy from performance, and an announced ambition from a result that citizens can use.

One Continent, Many Conditions

South Africa has major financial, industrial, mining, and service sectors. Nigeria combines a vast domestic market with petroleum production, agriculture, manufacturing, and a large service economy. Botswana's modern economy has been shaped heavily by diamonds. Ethiopia is landlocked and depends on neighboring ports for much of its international trade. Djibouti's location near the Bab el-Mandeb gives ports and logistics unusual importance. Mauritius, a small island state, has an economic structure very different from that of the mineral-rich Democratic Republic of the Congo.

These countries share continental institutions and many historical experiences. They do not share one economic model. The same is true of politics. Some African states have sustained repeated elections and peaceful transfers of power. Others have experienced dominant-party rule, military coups, disputed elections, or armed conflict. Constitutional monarchies exist alongside republics; federal systems alongside highly centralized states. Conflict is a devastating reality in some countries, but it is not the daily political condition of the whole continent.

This diversity makes broad statements dangerous. "Africa is growing" means little without a period, a measure, and a set of countries. "Africa is poor" may point to genuine deprivation, but it says nothing about who is poor, how poverty is measured, or why living conditions differ so sharply within and between states. Even the categories used by international institutions require care. Africa, North Africa, sub-Saharan Africa, and the membership of the African Union are related but not interchangeable.

Difference does not make continental thinking useless. It makes precision necessary. A regional pattern can identify a shared pressure, while national evidence shows how governments and societies respond to it. The purpose of comparison is not to rank countries for pride or humiliation. It is to discover why similar challenges produce different outcomes.

Demography Is a Deadline, Not a Destiny

The scale of Africa's demographic change will shape almost every subject in the chapters ahead. The United Nations projects that the population of sub-Saharan Africa will increase by about 79 percent between 2024 and 2054, reaching roughly 2.2 billion. Nine countries in the region are projected to double in population during that period (United Nations Department of Economic and Social Affairs, Population Division, 2024).

Those numbers are projections, not promises. They depend on assumptions about fertility, mortality, migration, health, and policy. Their importance lies less in the exact total than in the pressure they reveal. More children will need schools. More households will need food, water, electricity, health care, and housing. More young adults will seek work, land, credit, and a meaningful place in public life.

Africa's youth is often described as an economic advantage. It can be, but age alone creates no dividend. A young person without a functioning school, reliable health care, useful skills, or access to productive work is not a statistic waiting to become prosperity. Potential becomes capability only through institutions and investment.

The employment challenge makes the distinction plain. The World Bank projects that sub-Saharan Africa's working-age population will grow by more than 620 million between 2025 and 2050. Its 2025 jobs report also found that only about 24 percent of new workers were entering wage-paying employment; many others relied on own-account, family-run, or otherwise insecure work (World Bank, 2025). Informal work is not the same as idleness. It includes farmers, traders, transport operators, craftspeople, repairers, and countless small businesses that keep economies moving. The problem is that much of this work remains low in productivity, unstable in income, and poorly protected.

The demographic question is therefore practical. Can education systems teach at the scale required? Can firms grow beyond survival and hire more people? Can women enter economic life without legal and social barriers that keep their talent from productive use? Can governments provide basic services while the number of citizens grows? A large generation can expand production, creativity, and public revenue. If institutions fail to keep pace, the same generation may face deep frustration. Demography sets the deadline; choices determine the outcome.

Cities Will Carry More of the Future

Africa is becoming more urban, although the pace and level of urbanization differ widely by country. The United Nations' 2025 urbanization revision shows especially rapid growth in the urban populations of sub-Saharan Africa and emphasizes the continuing importance of small and medium-sized cities, not only megacities (United Nations Department of Economic and Social Affairs, Population Division, 2025).

Urban growth can bring workers, customers, universities, hospitals, finance, and infrastructure closer together. A business can reach a larger market. A specialized clinic can serve more patients. A factory can draw on a deeper pool of skills and suppliers. These are among the reasons cities can raise productivity.

But density does not organize itself. When housing, roads, drainage, public transport, sanitation, and electricity grow more slowly than the population, proximity becomes congestion. Long journeys reduce the time people can work or care for their families. Informal settlements expand because formal housing is too scarce or expensive. Floods become more destructive when building outruns drainage and land-use planning. A city can collect talent while still making daily life exhausting.

Lagos is not Addis Ababa. Johannesburg is not Kigali. Cairo is not Nairobi, and Casablanca is not Kinshasa. Their histories, economies, climates, and systems of local government differ. Yet each illustrates the same principle: the quality of urbanization depends on decisions made before a neighborhood is fully built. Streets, transit corridors, water systems, and land records are difficult and costly to repair after settlement has spread.

Rural Africa remains equally important. Urban families depend on rural producers for food. Manufacturers depend on agricultural inputs. Rural communities need roads, storage, irrigation, finance, market information, and reliable energy if farming is to become more productive and less vulnerable. Development is not a choice between a modern city and an abandoned countryside. A successful economy connects them.

Growth Must Reach the Household

Economic growth matters. Without a larger productive base, governments struggle to finance schools, health systems, infrastructure, and public administration. Businesses cannot hire at scale if markets remain small and uncertain. But gross domestic product is a total, not a description of how every citizen is living.

An economy may grow because the price of one export rises. The benefit may be concentrated in a small sector that creates relatively few jobs. National income can increase while population growth limits gains per person. A new mine can strengthen public revenue while leaving nearby communities with displacement, pollution, or little employment. A technology company can become valuable while most firms remain small and unable to obtain credit.

This is why the useful question is not simply whether an economy is growing. We must ask what is becoming more productive, who is finding better work, where income is going, and whether public revenue is being converted into services and durable assets. Growth becomes development when it expands people's real capabilities: to learn, stay healthy, travel safely, earn a living, start a business, and participate in public life.

The difference is visible in ordinary budgets. A percentage point in a national account means little to a parent if food prices rise faster than wages, a clinic lacks medicine, or a child attends school without learning. At the same time, hardship at the household level should not lead us to dismiss growth altogether. The point is to connect national performance to lived improvement, not to choose one measure and ignore the other.

This standard also protects the discussion from spectacle. A skyline, railway, conference center, or industrial park may be useful. Its presence does not prove that a wider transformation has occurred. The serious questions come afterward. Is the asset maintained? Do people and firms use it? Does it reduce costs, improve services, or create productive work? Construction is an event. Development is what the investment continues to make possible.

Resources Do Not Organize Themselves

Africa possesses important mineral, energy, agricultural, and environmental resources. The earlier chapters showed why possession should never be confused with power. A resource becomes economically useful through knowledge, finance, extraction or cultivation, transport, processing, regulation, taxation, and investment. Weakness at any point can transfer much of the value elsewhere.

The familiar demand for "value addition" is directionally sound but should be applied with care. Processing more commodities within African countries can build skills, suppliers, and industrial capacity when energy, logistics, technology, markets, and finance make the activity competitive. It is not automatically sensible to process every raw material in the country where it is extracted. The better question is where African firms and workers can capture more value on sustainable terms.

Agriculture demonstrates the same principle. Farming remains central to livelihoods and food security in many countries, but its future is not a return to an unchanged past. Productive agriculture depends increasingly on research, soil and water management, reliable inputs, storage, cold chains, roads, digital information, insurance, and access to buyers. It is both a rural activity and part of a wider system that includes transport, finance, manufacturing, and trade.

Energy sits beneath nearly every productive ambition. The International Energy Agency estimated that about 600 million people in sub-Saharan Africa lacked access to electricity in 2024, roughly 47 percent of the region's population (International Energy Agency, 2025). That figure is not only about household lighting. Electricity affects irrigation, refrigeration, hospitals, schools, digital networks, factories, and the cost of running a small business.

Africa has substantial renewable-energy potential as well as fossil-fuel resources, but potential is not a power supply. A solar resource must become a financed project, a functioning grid or local system, a dependable connection, and a bill households and firms can afford. Announced generation capacity is not the same as power delivered. Once again, the distance between possession and performance is filled by institutions.

Technology Is Already Changing Daily Life

It is no longer credible to speak of technology in Africa only in the future tense. Mobile communications and digital payments have changed how many people send money, pay bills, find customers, receive information, and manage small businesses. Governments are digitizing some services.

African developers, researchers, and entrepreneurs are building products for local markets as well as global ones. Mobile money, in particular, has become part of ordinary economic life in many countries rather than a novelty (GSMA, 2025).

The change is significant, but it is uneven. The International Telecommunication Union estimated that 36 percent of Africa's population used the Internet in 2025. It also reported that the continent's urban-rural gap remained the widest of any region, with urban residents about 2.6 times as likely as rural residents to be online (International Telecommunication Union, 2025). Coverage, device cost, data prices, electricity, language, skills, and trust all affect whether a person can make meaningful use of a connection.

It is tempting to call every digital advance "leapfrogging." Sometimes a new system does bypass an older one. Mobile payments can reach people who never had a conventional bank branch nearby. Yet a phone cannot carry produce over a washed-out road, refrigerate a vaccine without electricity, or replace a teacher who understands the child in front of her. Technology works best when it strengthens physical and human systems rather than serving as a slogan for avoiding them.

Ownership matters too. If African countries remain mainly consumers of platforms, equipment, and knowledge designed elsewhere, digital growth can deepen dependence even as it improves convenience. Greater capability requires engineers, researchers, technicians, investors, regulators, data systems, and firms able to create and maintain technology. It also requires rules that protect citizens without preventing useful innovation.

The relevant divide is therefore not between an "old" Africa and a "modern" one. Both can exist on the same street: a trader using a digital wallet while working without reliable power, or a student accessing a global lecture on a phone while studying in an overcrowded classroom. The task is to turn isolated tools into dependable systems.

Connection Changes the Scale of What Is Possible

Many African economies are small when considered separately. Landlocked states depend on transport routes through their neighbors. Rivers, electricity networks, disease outbreaks, digital platforms, and supply chains do not stop neatly at political borders. National development and regional cooperation therefore cannot be treated as separate projects.

The African Continental Free Trade Area expresses this recognition. The agreement entered into force in 2019, formal trading began in 2021, and the Guided Trade Initiative launched in 2022 to test and expand implementation. These dates mark genuine institutional progress. They do not mean that a fully integrated continental market already exists. Tariff schedules, rules of origin, customs systems, transport costs, payment arrangements, and national implementation still determine whether a firm can actually trade across a border (United Nations Economic Commission for Africa, 2024).

A treaty can create legal possibility. Businesses experience integration only when a truck crosses a border without unpredictable delay, a payment can be settled, a product standard is recognized, and a dispute can be resolved. The same distinction applies to regional power pools, transport corridors, and freedom-of-movement agreements. An initiative under implementation should not be reported as a completed system.

Regional cooperation also does not erase national sovereignty or identity. A Kenyan remains Kenyan; a Senegalese remains Senegalese. People may identify through language, ethnicity, faith, locality, profession, and nation while also seeing themselves as African. Cooperation does not require cultural sameness. It requires enough trust and institutional discipline to pursue shared interests across difference.

The African Union's Agenda 2063 places integration, infrastructure, capable institutions, peace, human development, and a stronger global role within one continental framework (African Union, n.d.-b). Its second ten-year implementation plan, covering 2024 to 2033, was launched as a "decade of acceleration" (African Union, 2024). The language is ambitious. The results must still be judged by implementation. In 2026, the AU Assembly itself acknowledged that the pace and depth of transformation remained insufficient in areas including structural change, human capital, productive employment, domestic resource mobilization, peace, and climate resilience (African Union, 2026).

That acknowledgment is not a reason for cynicism. It is evidence of a more mature standard. A plan should be measured against what it delivers, and an institution should be able to report where it is falling short.

The Quiet Revolution Is Built in Ordinary Places

Headlines favor extremes: a coup, a war, a famine, a disputed election, a spectacular investment, or a celebrated start-up. Necessary reporting on crisis can make instability appear universal. Promotional reporting creates the opposite distortion, selecting a handful of success stories and treating them as proof that transformation has already arrived.

Most development is quieter. A nurse adopts a safer procedure. A farmer gains dependable storage and stops selling immediately after harvest at the weakest price. A local manufacturer improves quality enough to supply a larger firm. A municipal office reduces the time needed to register property. A researcher produces evidence that changes a health program. A repair business hires three apprentices and survives long enough to become a stable employer.

None of these acts can transform a continent by itself. Together, repeated across institutions and over time, they create capacity. They are also more difficult to photograph than a ribbon-cutting ceremony. A new building is visible in a day; a trustworthy institution may require years of consistent decisions.

This quiet revolution is already underway in uneven forms. It can be found in citizens who refuse to treat poor service as normal, in professionals who improve systems from within, in women whose businesses sustain families and employ others, and in young people who create work where formal opportunities are scarce. But praise should not become romanticism. Citizens cannot compensate indefinitely for unreliable institutions, and entrepreneurship should not be used as an excuse for governments to neglect infrastructure, education, law, and public administration.

The most hopeful evidence is not that Africans can endure almost anything. They have had to endure too much already. It is that capability grows when effort is joined to institutions that work. The aim is not heroic survival. It is an ordinary life in which systems are reliable enough that heroism is not required.

Self-Determination Now Means Capability

For the independence generation, self-determination meant ending foreign colonial government. That achievement remains fundamental. Yet political sovereignty does not answer every modern question of power.

A country may have a flag and a seat at the United Nations while depending heavily on others for finance, technical expertise, medicines, data infrastructure, security, or the processing of its exports. Dependence is never absolute, and interdependence is normal in the modern world. The issue is whether a society can define priorities, negotiate from knowledge, maintain essential institutions, and refuse terms that undermine its long-term interests.

Self-determination today includes the ability to educate citizens well, collect and manage public revenue, produce scientific knowledge, regulate markets, maintain infrastructure, and transfer political authority without violence. It includes the capacity to choose partners rather than merely receive instructions. It also includes accountability, because a government acting without foreign control can still fail its own people.

This understanding avoids two errors. The first blames every present weakness on colonial history and leaves African choices beyond criticism. The second ignores inherited structures and treats unequal starting points as irrelevant. History shapes the field on which decisions are made; it does not make those decisions in advance.

The phrase "defined from within" should not imply isolation. Africa's countries will continue to trade, borrow, learn, invest, and cooperate across the world. They should. The deeper question is whether external relationships strengthen African capability or substitute for it. A partnership is most valuable when it leaves people and institutions better able to act after the project, loan, or adviser has gone.

Measure First, Then Imagine

The chapters ahead turn from historical foundations toward population, resources, economies, infrastructure, education, health, institutions, and continental cooperation. Evidence will become more quantitative, but numbers must be used with discipline. A forecast is not an outcome. A national average can hide regional and household inequality. A continental total may combine countries with radically different conditions. A policy announcement records intention, not performance.

Africa does not need invented resource percentages, exaggerated population claims, or the promise that one mineral, technology, or trade agreement will make it prosperous. Neither does it need a permanent crisis narrative that treats every setback as proof that improvement is impossible.

The responsible position is more demanding. It recognizes resources and constraints at the same time. It celebrates a result only after identifying what was achieved, for whom, and at what cost. It admits failure without turning failure into identity. It asks the same question of a government plan, a private investment, an international partnership, and a continental institution: what changed in people's actual ability to live, work, learn, and build?

Africa's future will not emerge from potential alone. It will be shaped in the difficult passage from promise to practice, where ideas meet budgets, institutions, skill, maintenance, and public judgment. That passage is already being made in thousands of ordinary places. Its progress is uneven, sometimes reversed, and rarely dramatic enough for a headline.

The future is not guaranteed. It is being built, and the most important question is who has the knowledge, authority, and persistence to build it well.

Evidence Note

This chapter treats Africa as a continent of diverse states rather than a single statistical unit. Figures for Africa, sub-Saharan Africa, North Africa, and African Union membership are not used interchangeably. Population numbers are identified as projections, and current employment, electricity, Internet, and urbanization estimates may be revised as institutions update their data and methods. Continental plans and treaties are distinguished from completed implementation. The chapter's examples illustrate differences and common pressures; they do not represent every country. Its central argument is interpretive but testable: potential matters only when people and institutions convert it into durable capability.

CHAPTER 7

The African Mind

Identity, Knowledge, and the Confidence to Build

Chapter 6 ended with a question about the people who will build Africa's future. This chapter asks what those builders must believe, know, and be willing to examine. Roads, laboratories, power systems, businesses, and public institutions are physical or organizational achievements, but each begins in the mind of someone who can identify a problem, test an idea, and carry useful knowledge into practice.

The phrase *the African mind* does not describe one way of thinking. The African Union includes 55 member states across five regions, and their people speak from different histories, languages, faiths, professions, and political experiences (African Union, n.d.). No serious account can compress that variety into a single personality. Here, the phrase refers to a shared intellectual responsibility: the confidence to study Africa honestly, learn from the wider world, and make informed choices without assuming that wisdom must arrive from somewhere else.

Confidence matters because people rarely build what they have already accepted as beyond their ability. Yet confidence alone is not enough. It can become vanity, denial, or a refuge from difficult evidence. The more durable form is quieter. It does not claim that Africans are superior, that the continent's past was flawless, or that every African-made product deserves support regardless of quality. It begins with a simpler conviction: Africans are fully capable of understanding their circumstances, producing knowledge, setting standards, correcting mistakes, and contributing to human progress.

That conviction carries a burden. If a society claims the authority to define its future, it also accepts responsibility for the quality of its thinking. It must learn to separate pride from myth, respect from obedience, education from certification, and borrowing from imitation. Intellectual independence is not the rejection of the world. It is the ability to meet the world as a participant.

The Work of Intellectual Independence

Political independence transferred formal authority from colonial governments to African states. That achievement was indispensable, but sovereignty did not instantly produce the technical knowledge, research institutions, administrative systems, or economic power required to exercise freedom well. A country can govern itself while depending heavily on imported machinery, external finance, foreign consultants, overseas laboratories, or technologies it cannot maintain.

Dependence of some kind is normal. Every modern society relies on knowledge and goods produced elsewhere. Scientists collaborate across borders, universities exchange ideas, companies license technology, and governments study one another's policies. The problem begins when exchange becomes a one-way habit and borrowed knowledge is treated as beyond local examination.

Intellectual independence means being able to judge what one receives. What problem was this policy designed to solve? What evidence supports it? Which conditions allowed it to work? What would have to change before it could serve a different population? Who bears the cost if it fails? Those questions turn a recipient into a decision-maker.

This kind of independence cannot be declared at a ceremony. It grows through functioning schools, serious universities, skilled professions, reliable public data, open debate, and institutions willing to learn from results. It also grows in ordinary life. A farmer who compares methods across seasons, a mechanic who understands a machine well enough to modify it, and a teacher who changes an approach after seeing that students are not learning are all practicing intellectual agency.

The aim is not national self-sufficiency in every field. That would be neither practical nor desirable. It is sufficient capability to choose partners wisely, negotiate from knowledge, adapt what is borrowed, and create where local needs demand something different. Political authority gives a society the right to decide. Intellectual capability gives that right substance.

Rooted and Open

Africa has no reason to isolate itself from the world's knowledge. An engineer should study reliable infrastructure wherever it exists. A physician should use the best available medical evidence. A business owner can learn from companies on several continents. Governments should examine public institutions that deliver services well, and African students should be able to enter global scholarship without apology.

Openness becomes a weakness only when it is joined to self-erasure. A foreign accent is not evidence of intelligence. An imported product is not automatically better. A consultant who has worked in many countries may still misunderstand the place in front of him. A respected international university may possess great expertise while lacking the local relationships or language needed to frame a particular African research question well.

The reverse is also true. An African origin does not make an idea correct. A familiar practice can be unjust. A locally made product can fail. A celebrated leader can be wrong. Knowledge deserves judgment, not loyalty based on birthplace.

A healthy intellectual position is therefore rooted and open. It knows where it stands without refusing to move. It studies local history and geography, listens to communities, and takes African experience seriously. At the same time, it accepts that useful ideas can come from any society and that evidence may challenge what people most want to believe.

This balance is harder than either defensiveness or imitation. Defensiveness dismisses criticism by asking who made it. Imitation accepts advice by asking who delivered it. Both avoid the real work of evaluation. A confident society asks whether the claim is true, whether the method is sound, and whether the proposed solution fits the conditions in which people actually live.

Pride Without Myth

Many Africans have encountered accounts of the continent that begin with deficiency and rarely move beyond it. Colonial writing often placed European institutions, languages, and knowledge at the top of a racial and cultural hierarchy, part of the historical imbalance that contemporary work on African knowledge systems continues to address (UNESCO, 2025b). Later public narratives frequently reduced Africa to famine, war, corruption, or helplessness. Recovering neglected histories and achievements is a necessary response.

But repair cannot be built on another distortion. Replacing the claim that Africa contributed nothing with the claim that Africans invented everything preserves the same careless relationship with evidence. The emotional direction changes; the intellectual weakness remains.

Pride that depends on exaggeration is fragile. One disputed story can make a reader doubt ten well-documented achievements beside it. False statistics spread quickly because they seem to defend the continent, yet they teach people that a worthy cause excuses weak evidence. It does not.

The historical record is rich enough to stand without invention. Earlier chapters examined African states, trade networks, systems of learning, political institutions, and intellectual traditions in their particular settings. Those histories contain creativity and violence, wise adaptation and costly failure. Treating the past honestly is not disrespect. It is a sign that African history deserves the same disciplined study expected of any other history.

The same standard applies to tradition. The Oromo Gada system, discussed earlier in the book, is worth studying for the questions it raises about authority, generational responsibility, social organization, and the transfer of leadership. Serious study does not require turning a historical institution into a perfect model for a modern state. It asks what the institution was, how it changed, whom it served, where its limits lay, and which principles might still illuminate a present problem.

Pride and self-criticism can live together. A person who respects a culture can still challenge practices that deny dignity or opportunity. A citizen who loves a country can demand better government. The opposite of contempt is not mythology. It is truthful regard.

Education That Produces Understanding

The clearest test of a society's relationship with knowledge is its education system. Enrollment, examinations, certificates, and degrees matter. They represent access, effort, and completed study. None, by itself, proves what a learner understands or can do.

The World Bank and UNESCO Institute for Statistics developed the term *learning poverty* to describe children who cannot read and understand a simple text by age ten, while also accounting for children who are out of school (World Bank, 2021). The measure is limited to foundational reading, but the distinction behind it is important: attendance and learning are connected, not identical.

A child may spend years in a classroom and still struggle to explain a paragraph, use numbers in daily life, or ask a question without fear. A graduate may know how to pass an examination yet have little practice applying knowledge to an unfamiliar problem. When credentials become the goal rather than evidence of learning, families and governments can invest heavily while capability remains thin.

Education should enlarge what a person can notice and do. At the foundational level, that means literacy, numeracy, communication, curiosity, and the habit of reasoning from evidence. Later education should deepen those capacities and add specialized skill. An engineer must eventually apply engineering. A teacher must be able to help different students learn. A medical professional must unite scientific knowledge with sound clinical judgment. A researcher must know how to frame a question, choose a method, examine evidence, and acknowledge uncertainty.

Practical skill deserves equal dignity. Universities are essential, but an economy also depends on electricians, machinists, welders, builders, laboratory technicians, equipment operators, software specialists, and maintenance workers. A new hospital cannot function through physicians alone. A factory with advanced machinery becomes an expensive shell if no one can operate, repair, and improve it.

The African Union's Continental Education Strategy for Africa 2026-2035 places education within the continent's wider goals for inclusive development, and the AU's education agenda connects learning with skills, technical and vocational education, entrepreneurship, science, technology, and workforce readiness (African Union, 2025). This is a continental framework, not proof that every national system has achieved those goals. Its value lies in naming the right test: education should develop people who can continue learning and contribute usefully in the conditions they face.

That test also protects education from becoming narrowly commercial. Schools and universities do more than prepare workers. They preserve culture, advance science, train citizens, develop judgment, and give people access to intellectual lives larger than their immediate employment. The proper question is not whether education should serve the economy or the human person. Good education should equip people to earn, think, participate, create, and live with greater freedom.

Learn Without Copying

Borrowing a successful idea is sensible. Copying it without understanding can be expensive.

Every policy works inside a particular history and set of institutions. Population density, climate, public revenue, administrative capacity, settlement patterns, law, and political trust shape what implementation requires. A transport system designed for a compact, densely settled country cannot simply be placed across a vast and sparsely populated one. A farming method suited to Morocco's water conditions may not fit tropical Central Africa. A social program that depends on reliable civil records will struggle where many residents are missing from official systems.

Context does not mean that every country is so unique that comparison becomes useless. That excuse can protect failure. It means comparison should go deeper than appearance. If a policy worked elsewhere, decision-makers should identify the mechanism that produced the result. Was success driven by stable financing, local authority, staff training, public trust, or a particular technology? Which of those conditions exists locally, and which must be built first?

The same discipline applies within Africa. Mauritius cannot be copied by the Democratic Republic of the Congo. Rwanda cannot be copied by Namibia. A reform that succeeds in one province may fail in another. African examples are valuable because they can reveal solutions developed under more comparable constraints, but proximity does not eliminate difference.

Learning is an active process. It studies, tests, adapts, measures, and revises. Copying is passive. It imports the visible form of a solution and often leaves behind the less visible institutions that made it work. The best question is rarely, "Which country should we become?" It is, "What can their experience teach us about our own problem?"

Language Is Access, Not Rank

Language carries memory, humor, technical knowledge, family history, and ways of describing the world. It also determines who can enter a classroom discussion, understand a public notice, use a digital service, or speak to an institution without feeling diminished.

Africa's multilingual reality cannot be resolved by choosing between local languages and languages of wider communication. English, French, Arabic, Portuguese, Swahili, and other widely used languages connect people across borders and provide access to scholarship, commerce, diplomacy, and technology. African languages connect learning to homes, communities, histories, and forms of knowledge that may not be fully represented elsewhere. Both kinds of access matter.

UNESCO's global guidance treats multilingualism as a normal human condition and encourages education policy that allows learners to study in languages they understand while building additional language skills (UNESCO, 2025a). Implementing that principle is difficult. It requires teachers, books, agreed terminology, assessment systems, and sustained public support. In some communities, several home languages may share one classroom. Parents may prefer a former colonial language because they associate it with mobility and employment. Policy must take those realities seriously rather than pretending that language choice is simple.

Still, one principle should be clear: proficiency in a prestigious language is a skill, not a measure of intelligence or human worth. Accent should not be confused with knowledge. A person who speaks excellent English may reason poorly; a farmer who has limited formal schooling may possess exact knowledge of soil, weather, livestock, or local markets. Respecting that knowledge does not mean refusing scientific testing. It means recognizing where useful questions and observations may begin.

The digital world makes language policy more urgent. If African languages are weakly represented in software, public information, research databases, and artificial intelligence systems, many people will encounter technology through an additional barrier. Expanding language resources is therefore not only cultural preservation. It is part of widening access to modern knowledge.

The goal is additive. A child should not have to abandon a familiar language in order to become educated, nor should education trap that child within one linguistic community. The strongest outcome is the ability to move between worlds without being taught that one of them is intellectually inferior.

Producing Knowledge at Home

African universities cannot exist only as classrooms for knowledge produced elsewhere. Teaching established scholarship is essential; so is creating new knowledge. The questions are close at hand. How can a city provide affordable housing as its population grows? Which crops and storage systems best reduce food loss under local conditions? How can medical technologies be made more accessible? What forms of public transport fit the way people actually move? How should water be governed where rainfall is becoming less predictable? How can African languages be represented more accurately in digital tools?

These are not exclusively African questions, and researchers from anywhere may contribute to them. International collaboration can bring laboratories, finance, comparative experience, data, and specialized expertise. But partnership is incomplete when African researchers enter only after the problem has been defined, the method chosen, or the data removed.

Who frames a question influence what will be seen. Who speaks the relevant languages affects which testimony can be heard. Who controls data shapes what can be studied later. Who receives authorship, funding, and mentorship helps determine where the next generation of expertise will grow.

The African Union created the Pan African University as a continental network for postgraduate training, research, and innovation linked to Africa's development needs. Its design joins regional mobility and collaboration with research on shared challenges (African Union, 2019). The institution is one example, not a measure of the continent's entire research system. Its premise is the important part: Africa's integration requires networks of people who produce knowledge together, not only markets that exchange goods.

UNESCO's 2025 work on transforming knowledge for Africa similarly calls for stronger research ecosystems, better infrastructure and governance, collaborative capacity, and serious engagement with Indigenous and local knowledge (UNESCO, 2025b). Such engagement must be careful. Community knowledge should not be romanticized, extracted without consent, or treated as automatically proven. It should be documented with respect, investigated with suitable methods, and connected to the people who have preserved it.

Research capacity takes time. It depends on libraries, laboratories, stable electricity, data access, ethical review, academic freedom, mentoring, and careers that allow skilled people to remain productive. It also depends on a public culture that can tolerate inconvenient findings. A university that must reach a predetermined political conclusion is not producing knowledge. It is decorating authority.

The goal is neither to place a border around African scholarship nor to ask outsiders for permission. It is to ensure that African scholars, institutions, and communities are full participants in deciding what is studied, how it is understood, and how the results are used.

Knowing One Another

Continental cooperation is difficult when Africans know the capitals of distant powers better than the countries next door. A student may learn European history in detail while leaving school with only a thin understanding of Africa's regions, trade routes, political institutions, writers, and contemporary economies.

No national curriculum can teach the complete history of 55 states. Nor should continental education become propaganda or a parade of heroes. The purpose is practical literacy. An educated African should be able to locate major countries and regions, understand why landlocked states depend on coastal corridors, recognize the diversity of the continent's languages and political systems, and know enough history to resist both crude stereotypes and invented glory.

That knowledge changes cooperation. A business owner considering a new market can ask better questions. A voter can understand why a regional agreement matters. A journalist can report a crisis without treating one country as the whole continent. A traveler can arrive with curiosity rather than assumption.

Chapters ahead will examine trade, resources, population, infrastructure, education, and institutions in greater detail. Those subjects are connected by a simple human fact: people cooperate more intelligently when they know something about one another. Continental integration begins in treaties and border systems, but it also begins in the imagination. People must be able to see neighboring societies as real places with their own histories and interests, not as blank spaces on a map.

Criticism Is a Form of Care

Respect for parents, elders, teachers, and community leaders is important in many African societies. It can preserve experience and hold communities together. Yet respect becomes intellectually dangerous when it means that a younger person may not ask why, an employee may not identify a failing method, or a citizen may not question a public decision.

Questioning is not the same as contempt. A student can listen carefully and still ask for evidence. A professional can honor a predecessor while improving the system inherited from that person. A citizen can criticize a government because public institutions matter too much to be protected from scrutiny.

The distinction is especially important where criticism is treated as betrayal. Institutions become brittle when bad news cannot travel upward. A clinic manager who punishes a nurse for reporting an error may preserve authority for a day and endanger patients for years. A ministry that rewards agreeable numbers can make its own plans less reliable. A family that never allows children to explain disagreement may produce silence, not wisdom.

Critical thinking should also turn inward. It is easy to detect prejudice in an outsider and harder to examine favoritism, ethnic suspicion, sexism, or contempt for manual work within one's own community. Intellectual freedom is not merely the right to challenge foreign claims about Africa. It is the discipline to challenge comforting African claims when evidence does not support them.

A mature culture does not choose between continuity and change once and for all. It asks what should be preserved, what should be repaired, and what should be left behind. That conversation requires humility from the young and the old, from citizens and leaders, and from experts and communities.

Confidence Must Become Standards

Calls to buy African products, trust African professionals, and support African businesses can strengthen local capability. Loyalty, however, cannot carry a weak product forever. Consumers have the right to expect medicine that is safe, buildings that stand, airlines that operate reliably, universities that protect academic standards, and public offices that keep their promises.

The strongest form of pride is not asking people to overlook poor performance because the producer is African. It is doing the patient work that makes quality unmistakable. That work is rarely glamorous. It includes measurement, training, maintenance, honest accounting, customer service, safety checks, and the willingness to correct a defect before defending a reputation.

This is where mindset must meet institution. Inspirational language can encourage effort, but it cannot replace a working process. A capable engineer inside a procurement system that rewards political connections may be unable to deliver a safe bridge. A talented teacher without books, time, or administrative support cannot repair an education system alone. Personal responsibility matters, and so do the rules and organizations that shape what responsible people can accomplish.

Leadership, in this sense, is not confined to political office. A laboratory director who insists on accurate results is leading. So is a mechanic who trains apprentices carefully, a civil servant who simplifies a needlessly difficult procedure, and a business owner who pays workers on time. Their influence becomes durable when they build standards that survive their departure.

The practical meaning of confidence is therefore responsibility for something that can be improved. It replaces the question "When will someone fix Africa?" with a more exact one: "What lies within my authority, and what larger institution must change for this work to endure?" That shift avoids two extremes. Individuals are not blamed for structural failures beyond their control, and structure is not used as an excuse for neglecting the work close at hand.

Africa needs more than celebrated leaders. It needs millions of people who can perform useful work well, judge results honestly, and build organizations stronger than any one personality. Civilizations are sustained in that ordinary discipline.

From Conviction to Evidence

The African mind described here is neither a slogan nor a personality shared by every African. It is an intellectual posture: rooted enough to know its history, open enough to learn, confident enough to create, and disciplined enough to correct itself.

It does not ask Africa to reject the world or copy it. It asks Africans to enter global exchange with judgment. It does not defend tradition from every question or treat modernity as automatically wise. It measures each by human dignity, evidence, and practical consequence. It does not confuse a certificate with learning, a resource with capability, or pride with quality.

This chapter has stayed largely at the level of principle. The next chapter changes the method. It begins testing familiar claims about Africa with population figures, geographic definitions, economic measures, and carefully identified sources. That transition matters because confidence should survive contact with numbers. Africa's possibilities are too important to be defended with evidence that cannot withstand examination.

The task is not to prove that Africa is superior. It is to understand the continent well enough to make better choices within it, and to build with the seriousness that such knowledge demands.

Evidence Note

This chapter is interpretive rather than statistical. "The African mind" is used as a statement of shared intellectual responsibility, not as a claim that Africans think alike. References to colonial influence describe broad historical patterns whose form and intensity differed across territories, institutions, classes, and generations. African traditions and Indigenous knowledge are presented as subjects for serious, ethical study, not as automatically valid alternatives to tested evidence. Policy frameworks from the African Union and UNESCO identify continental or international goals; they do not demonstrate uniform implementation within individual countries. Detailed quantitative evidence on education, research capacity, language, technology, and human capital is reserved for later chapters, where dates, geographic definitions, methods, and data limitations can be examined directly.

CHAPTER 8

Africa by the Numbers

People, Land, Economy, Resources, and the Scale of the Continent

The previous chapter argued that confidence should survive contact with evidence. This chapter puts that principle to work. Africa is often described with large numbers: a vast continent, a young population, abundant land, immense resources, and a market of more than a billion people. Some of those statements are well supported. Others are repeated so often that their source, date, or meaning disappears.

Numbers can correct an impression, but they can also create one. A figure may refer to Africa, sub-Saharan Africa, the African Union, or an institutional region that uses different boundaries. It may be a census observation, a modelled estimate, or a projection. A number can be accurate and still mislead when its category is changed, its year is hidden, or it is asked to prove more than it measures.

The aim here is not to bury Africa beneath statistics. It is to build a factual outline of the continent and then ask what the outline reveals. Population, land, employment, energy access, digital connection, and trade do not tell the whole story of African life. Together, however, they give us a firmer place from which to think.

What a Number Can and Can not Say

Official statistics are not photographs of reality. They are organized measurements. Producing a continental total requires national data, common definitions, estimation where records are incomplete, and decisions about which countries or territories belong in a region. The result can be enormously useful, but it must be read with its notes attached.

This is especially important with large aggregates. A continental average may describe no individual country well. A high figure in one country can pull the average upward; a low figure in another can pull it down. The average also conceals differences within countries, including differences between urban and rural communities, women and men, income groups, and regions.

Dates matter just as much. The UNData profile for Africa displays several indicators beneath a column headed 2025. Its footnotes show that the population and age figures are 2025 projections, while GDP and employment figures in the same column refer to 2023. Trade values refer to 2024, and several environmental indicators refer to 2022 (United Nations Statistics Division, 2025a). Without the footnotes, numbers that describe different years appear to belong to the same moment.

None of this makes the data useless. It shows how to use the data honestly. A careful reader asks four questions: What is being measured? Which geographic area is included? What is the reference year? Is the figure observed, estimated, calculated, or projected? Those questions will guide the chapter.

A Continent of About 1.55 Billion People

The United Nations Statistics Division places Africa's population at about 1.55 billion in 2025. More precisely, the UNData profile reports 1,549,868,000 people. This is a medium-fertility projection, not a single census count taken across the continent on one day. The same profile reports a projected population density of 52.4 people per square kilometre and a surface area of 29,648,481 square kilometres (United Nations Statistics Division, 2025a).

Even the surface-area figure needs context. Readers may encounter totals closer to 30.3 million square kilometres in other sources. Differences can arise from the treatment of inland water, territories, coastlines, and institutional geographic definitions. The useful conclusion is not that only one rounded total may ever be printed. It is that the definition should travel with the number.

Scale is easier to feel when the political map is added. The African Union has 55 member states, grouped into five geographic regions:

Central, Eastern, Northern, Southern, and Western Africa (African Union, n.d.). Those states vary enormously. Nigeria has a population measured in hundreds of millions, while several island states have fewer than one million residents. Algeria and the Democratic Republic of the Congo stretch across immense territories; countries such as Rwanda and Burundi contain far more people per square kilometre. Some states have long coastlines. Others depend on neighbours for access to a port.

The continental population total therefore represents neither a single society nor a single market already functioning as one. It describes people living under different governments, currencies, legal systems, languages, climates, and levels of infrastructure. The number matters because of its scale, but political and economic organization determines what that scale can accomplish.

Population density illustrates the same point. An average of 52.4 people per square kilometre does not mean people are spread evenly across Africa. Settlement is shaped by water, soil, climate, employment, transport, history, and security. The Nile Valley, the Gulf of Guinea, the Ethiopian highlands, the Great Lakes region, and major metropolitan areas hold dense populations. Large parts of the Sahara and other arid regions are sparsely populated. A continental average cannot tell a government where to build a school, a road, or an electricity line. Planning requires much more local information.

Yet the continental total still changes the frame. Africa cannot be treated as a marginal part of the human story. Decisions about African education, public health, cities, food systems, employment, energy, and trade affect not only Africa's future but a substantial share of the world's population.

A Young Population Is a Demand on the Present

The same UNData profile estimates that 38.8 percent of Africa's population was between birth and age fourteen in 2025, while 5.8 percent was aged sixty or older (United Nations Statistics Division, 2025a). Applying those percentages to the projected population produces rough totals of 601 million children aged fourteen or younger and 90 million people aged sixty or older. These are calculations from the published percentages, not separate counts issued by the United Nations.

The word *young* is often followed quickly by *opportunity*. There is good reason for hope. A large generation entering adulthood can enlarge the workforce, create businesses, expand markets, and bring new skill and energy into public life. But age structure does not create those outcomes by itself. Children require nutrition, healthcare, safety, schools, trained teachers, and places to learn. Young adults need pathways into productive work, whether through employment, farming, skilled trades, professions, public service, or entrepreneurship. If these systems fail to expand at the same pace as the population, demographic promise can become frustration.

The distinction between a condition and an outcome is central. A young population is a documented condition. A demographic dividend is a possible outcome under particular conditions. It depends on health, education, gender equality, economic growth, job creation, institutions, and the ability of families to plan their lives. Calling youth an asset may express confidence, but the asset is developed through years of investment before it appears in national accounts.

The age figures also remind us not to make youth the only demographic story. Ninety million people aged sixty or older is itself a large population. Families and governments must consider pensions, healthcare, housing, mobility, and care. African societies will have to expand opportunities for the young while building systems that allow older people to live with dignity. These are not competing responsibilities. They are part of the same social contract.

The projected sex ratio is close to numerical balance, at 99.8 males for every 100 females. Economic participation is less balanced. UNData estimates labour-force participation at 55.2 percent for females and 73.7 percent for males (United Nations Statistics Division, 2025a). That indicator records whether people are working or actively seeking work under the statistical definition. It does not measure wages, hours, security, productivity, unpaid care, business ownership, or the quality of a job.

The gap is still important. It signals that a large share of women's economic activity and potential may not enter the measured labour force on the same terms as men's. The reasons differ by country and household. They can include care responsibilities, safety, law, social expectations, education, transport, access to finance, and the availability of suitable work. The continental estimate identifies a pattern. Explaining and changing that pattern requires national and local evidence.

Land Is Not One Statistic

Africa's physical scale encourages grand claims about agriculture. A sentence may begin with the size of the continent and end by asserting that Africa could feed the world. Between those two ideas lie rainfall, soil, water, tenure, roads, storage, finance, conflict, markets, technology, and the decisions of millions of farmers. Land area alone does not settle the question.

The vocabulary must be correct first. The Food and Agriculture Organization distinguishes agricultural land, cropland, and arable land. Agricultural land is the broad category. It includes cropland as well as permanent meadows and pastures. Cropland includes arable land and land under permanent crops. Arable land is narrower and generally refers to land under temporary crops, temporary meadows and pastures, and temporary fallow. Substituting one term for another can turn a valid statistic into a false claim (Food and Agriculture Organization of the United Nations, 2025).

Recent FAOSTAT reporting shows why these categories matter. In 2024, agricultural land worldwide was about 4.6 billion hectares. Between 2001 and 2024, global cropland expanded by 92 million hectares even as permanent meadows and pastures declined. FAO identified Africa as the main regional driver of cropland expansion during that period (Food and Agriculture Organization of the United Nations, 2026).

Expansion can mean that more land is available for crop production, but it is not automatically evidence of progress. New cropland may support food production and livelihoods. It may also replace forest or other ecosystems, expose fragile soils, or extend cultivation without raising yields or farm income. FAO reports that cropland expansion accounted for much of global forest loss over the period. The environmental and economic result depends on where expansion occurs, how land is managed, and who benefits.

Nor is unused land necessarily idle land waiting for a project. It may support pastoral movement, wildlife, forests, water systems, community use, or customary rights that are poorly represented in formal records. A map that marks land as available can miss the people whose lives already depend on it. This is why responsible agricultural planning needs more than hectares. It needs information about soils, water, climate, tenure, ecology, infrastructure, and local use.

Africa clearly has major agricultural capacity. Agriculture also remains a central source of work, as the employment figures later in this chapter show. The serious question is not whether the continent possesses land. It is whether farmers, businesses, communities, and governments can raise productivity and income while protecting soil, water, forests, and legitimate land rights. Precision does not weaken the argument for African agriculture. It reveals the work required to make that argument real.

A Large Economy, Unevenly Lived

UNData reports Africa's gross domestic product at about $2.807 trillion in current United States dollars, GDP per person at about $1,898, and real annual growth at 3.1 percent. Although these values appear in the profile's 2025 column, the footnote identifies 2023 as the reference year (United Nations Statistics Division, 2025a). This is a small detail with a large consequence. Repeating the figures as 2025 data would make the chapter sound current while quietly changing what the source says.

GDP measures the value of goods and services produced within an economy. It is indispensable for understanding economic scale and change. It does not measure how income is distributed, how much unpaid work sustains households, whether people feel secure, or whether public services function well. GDP per person divides output by population; it is not the amount received by a typical person. Current-dollar comparisons are also affected by exchange rates, which can cause the dollar value of an economy to rise or fall even when domestic production changes less dramatically.

The continental total is particularly uneven. Africa contains upper-middle-income economies, low-income economies, major oil exporters, service centres, agricultural economies, manufacturing hubs, and small island states. A rise in commodity prices can lift output in one group while doing little for another. Drought, conflict, debt costs, currency changes, or a tourism shock can affect countries in very different ways. The total matters, but it does not erase the structure beneath it.

Employment offers another view. For 2023, UNData estimates that 45.5 percent of employed Africans worked in agriculture, 14.3 percent in industry, and 40.3 percent in services (United Nations Statistics Division, 2025a). The figures add to 100.1 percent because of rounding. Their broad message is clear: agriculture remained a major employer, services accounted for a large and growing share, and industry employed a much smaller share than either.

These shares do not tell us how productive or well paid the work is. A service job may be in a bank, hospital, restaurant, transport business, government office, software company, or informal street enterprise. Agricultural work may range from highly capitalized commercial production to small-scale farming with limited irrigation and market access. Industry includes mining, manufacturing, construction, and utilities, activities with very different wages and technological demands.

Still, the distribution raises an important development question. When nearly half of employed people work in agriculture, improvements in farm productivity, storage, processing, transport, and market access can affect a large part of the population. At the same time, the smaller industrial employment share points to the limited depth of manufacturing and other industrial activity across much of the continent. Transformation is not simply moving people out of farming.

It is increasing the value and security of work within agriculture and creating productive choices beyond it.

The numbers also warn against treating population as economic power by itself. A market of 1.55 billion people includes immense demand, but demand is shaped by income, transport, payment systems, regulation, and the ability of producers to reach consumers. People are not an economic opportunity merely because they can be counted. Their health, knowledge, purchasing power, and freedom to participate determine what the number can become.

Africa Is Not Sub-Saharan Africa

The geographic distinction most often lost in writing about Africa is the difference between the whole continent and sub-Saharan Africa. The terms are not interchangeable. North African countries are part of Africa, and their inclusion changes continental totals and averages.

UNData projects the population of sub-Saharan Africa at about 1.274 billion in 2025, compared with about 1.550 billion for Africa as a whole. Its economic profile reports sub-Saharan GDP at about $1.957 trillion and GDP per person at about $1,616. Those economic figures refer to 2023, despite their position in the 2025 column. It estimates agriculture's share of employment at 49 percent in sub-Saharan Africa, compared with 45.5 percent for the entire continent (United Nations Statistics Division, 2025a, 2025b).

The distinction is not merely technical. It affects statements about religion, language, income, health, energy, education, and demography. A study may exclude North Africa because a particular institution groups it with the Middle East. That may be reasonable for the purpose of the study, but its findings cannot then be presented as a complete account of Africa.

The reverse error also occurs. A continental average may hide conditions concentrated in sub-Saharan Africa and give a misleading impression of individual countries. Good writing names the region actually measured. It does not expand a result because the larger label sounds more powerful.

Regional definitions can differ even among respected institutions. The African Union, the United Nations, the World Bank, the International Energy Agency, and the International Telecommunication Union do not always organize countries in exactly the same way. Readers should therefore pay attention not only to the institution but to the definition attached to its data.

Resource Strength and Energy Poverty

Few contrasts are repeated more often than Africa's energy abundance and its shortage of modern energy services. The contrast is real, but its components must remain separate.

In its *Africa Energy Outlook 2022*, the International Energy Agency reported that Africa holds 60 percent of the world's best solar resources and more than 40 percent of global reserves of cobalt, manganese, and platinum, minerals used in several energy technologies. In the same report, the agency noted that Africa then held only about 1 percent of installed global solar photovoltaic capacity (International Energy Agency, 2022). The capacity comparison is a 2022 statement, not a current 2026 measurement. Its value is historical: it shows how little resource quality alone reveals about installed infrastructure.

Sunlight is not electricity. A mineral deposit is not a battery, a processing plant, a skilled job, or public revenue. Conversion requires finance, engineering, roads, grids, institutions, maintenance, markets, and agreements that distribute risk and reward. Reserve estimates can also change with exploration, prices, technology, and the economic definition of what can be extracted. Resource endowment is a starting condition, not a development result.

The access figures show the human side of that distinction. *Tracking SDG 7: The Energy Progress Report 2026*, using new 2023 and 2024 data, reported that 655 million people worldwide still lacked electricity. More than 560 million of them lived in sub-Saharan Africa. The report also placed the sub-Saharan population without access to clean cooking at about 970 million (World Bank, 2026).

Those figures refer specifically to sub-Saharan Africa. They should not be relabelled as continent-wide totals. Even with that limitation, their scale is difficult to overstate. Lack of electricity affects evening study, refrigeration, medical services, communication, business hours, irrigation, manufacturing, and the cost of nearly every modern service. Reliance on polluting cooking fuels affects health and often places a heavy burden of fuel collection and household labour on women and girls.

The geography within the regional total also matters. National access rates differ, and urban communities are generally easier to connect than remote rural settlements. A dense neighbourhood near a grid presents a different engineering and financial problem from scattered households far from transmission infrastructure. Grid expansion, mini-grids, and stand-alone systems may all have roles, depending on local conditions.

The honest conclusion holds both sides together. Africa has exceptional solar resources and important mineral reserves. Sub-Saharan Africa also contains most of the world's population without electricity access. The first fact does not cancel the second, and the second does not make the first meaningless. Together they define a conversion problem:

how to turn physical resources into reliable, affordable energy and wider productive capacity.

Connected, but Not Equally

Mobile phones have changed commerce, communication, finance, and access to information across Africa. Yet a phone in the hand does not necessarily mean a person is connected to the Internet.

The International Telecommunication Union estimated in 2025 that 66 percent of people in its Africa region owned a mobile phone, while 36 percent used the Internet. That 30-percentage-point gap was the largest among the ITU's regions (International Telecommunication Union, 2025a). Some owners use basic phones. Others face expensive data, weak coverage, unreliable electricity, limited digital skills, or devices shared within a household. Ownership and meaningful use are different measurements.

Connection is also uneven by place. The ITU estimated that the rate of Internet use among urban residents in Africa was 2.6 times the rural rate in 2025 (International Telecommunication Union, 2025b). A continental Internet-use percentage therefore hides a large geographic divide. It also hides differences in speed, affordability, device quality, language, safety, and the ability to use a connection for education or work.

The distinction matters because digital systems increasingly mediate ordinary life. A government may put an application online and call the service accessible. For someone without affordable data, a suitable device, identification, electricity, or confidence in the platform, the service has moved farther away. Digital expansion succeeds when it reduces a barrier for the user, not simply when an institution launches a website.

At the same time, the ownership figure shows a foundation on which more can be built. Mobile networks already reach deeply into societies where fixed infrastructure is limited. Expanding affordable broadband, reliable power, locally useful content, digital skills, and consumer protection could turn that physical reach into broader participation. The figure is neither proof of a digital revolution completed nor evidence of failure. It identifies the gap between access to a device and effective connection.

Trade Reveals Fragmentation

A continent of 1.55 billion people is often called a vast market. Demographically, that is true. Economically, the market remains divided by borders, regulations, currencies, transport costs, payment systems, product standards, and uneven infrastructure.

UN Trade and Development's *Economic Development in Africa Report 2024*, published in 2025, states that intra-African trade accounts for only about 16 percent of Africa's total trade (UN Trade and Development, 2025). The exact share can vary by year, dataset, and denominator. Some summaries use exports; others use total merchandise trade. Informal cross-border exchange is also difficult to capture fully. The careful conclusion is that recorded trade within Africa remains a minority of the continent's recorded trade.

That pattern has consequences. When producers face high costs moving goods to a neighbouring country, they lose access to nearby consumers and suppliers. A manufacturer may import an input from outside Africa because regional transport, customs, finance, or standards make the closer option harder to use. A farmer may be near a food-deficit market across a border yet unable to reach it reliably. Landlocked countries depend especially on transport corridors and ports located in other states.

It is tempting to compare Africa's intra-African trade share with trade inside the United States, China, or India. The comparison is not direct. Commerce between two provinces or states inside one country is domestic trade, while trade between Kenya and Ethiopia or Ghana and Côte d'Ivoire crosses an international border. The European Union offers a closer comparison because sovereign states participate in an integrated market, but its institutions and history remain different from Africa's.

The central issue is not that African countries should become identical. Their differences create reasons to trade. Coastal and landlocked economies, energy exporters and importers, agricultural producers and urban markets, large manufacturing centres and smaller specialized economies can complement one another. The problem is that too many practical barriers prevent those differences from becoming exchange.

The African Continental Free Trade Area is an attempt to reduce some of those barriers and build a more connected market. It should not be described as though full integration already exists. Agreements, tariff schedules, customs systems, transport links, payment mechanisms, and rules of origin must work in practice. Projections about what the agreement could achieve are scenarios, not completed results.

The next chapter examines that implementation in detail. The 16 percent figure provides the reason for the discussion. It does not prove what policy will succeed, but it shows how far the continent remains from operating as a coherent economic space.

What the Numbers Establish

The evidence in this chapter does not produce one simple verdict. Africa is vast, but its markets remain fragmented. Its population is young overall, yet about 90 million people are already sixty or older. It holds major physical resources, yet often lacks the systems required to turn them into widely shared services and income. Agriculture employs a large share of workers, while the land itself must be described with greater care than popular claims usually allow. Mobile ownership is widespread, while Internet use remains much lower. The continent has some of the world's strongest solar resources, while hundreds of millions of people in sub-Saharan Africa still live without electricity.

These are not contradictions to be explained away. They are conditions that exist together.

The numbers also show why slogans fail. Population does not equal purchasing power. Land does not equal food security. Mineral reserves do not equal industrial strength. A mobile phone does not equal meaningful digital access. A trade agreement does not equal an integrated market. In each case, the gap between possession and outcome is filled by institutions, infrastructure, skill, investment, maintenance, and public choices.

Nor do the figures justify pessimism. A constraint measured clearly is a problem that can be addressed more intelligently. The purpose of evidence is not to reduce a continent to its deficits. It is to distinguish the resources that exist, the systems that are missing, and the scale at which action is required.

Africa's future cannot be read directly from a table. Statistics describe conditions already observed or estimated; projections describe what may happen under stated assumptions. Neither can guarantee how governments, businesses, communities, or citizens will act. The future remains open to decisions.

What the figures provide is discipline. They tell us to invest in children long before they enter the workforce, to treat women's participation as an economic and social question, to distinguish land area from productive agriculture, to build energy systems rather than celebrate sunlight, and to connect people to useful digital services rather than count devices alone. Above all, they show that Africa's continental scale remains only partly converted into economic connection.

Chapter 9 turns to that unfinished work: how African markets can connect across borders, and what must happen before continental trade becomes an everyday reality rather than an institutional ambition.

Evidence Note

This chapter preserves the geographic and temporal definitions used by each source. “Africa,” “sub-Saharan Africa,” “African Union member states,” and the ITU's “Africa region” are not assumed to contain identical country groupings. The 2025 population, density, sex-ratio, and age figures from UNData are medium-fertility projections. Approximate child and older-person totals are the author's calculations from those published figures. UNData's GDP and employment values displayed in its 2025 column refer to 2023; trade values on that profile refer to 2024. Energy-access figures come from the 2026 SDG 7 report and refer to sub-Saharan Africa. Trade shares vary by reference year and denominator, and official statistics may not capture all informal cross-border trade. Rounded totals should not be treated as more precise than their underlying sources.

CHAPTER 9

What If Africa Operated More Like One Economic Market?

Chapter 8 established the scale of Africa's population, land, economy, and resources. It also established a necessary caution: scale is not the same as connection. A continent can contain an immense number of people and still make it difficult for a producer in one country to reach a customer in the next.

That difficulty is easy to miss when Africa is described as a market of about 1.55 billion people. The phrase is true in a demographic sense, but it can sound more complete than the economic reality. A market is not created by counting potential customers. It depends on whether those customers can be reached, whether they have purchasing power, whether goods can move at a reasonable cost, whether payments can be settled, and whether rules remain predictable long enough for a business to invest.

The central question of this chapter is therefore practical. What would change if African economies became easier to trade across, invest across, and produce across? The answer does not require Africa to become one country, erase national identities, or copy another region. It requires a clearer understanding of what economic integration can accomplish, what it cannot accomplish, and why implementation matters more than declarations.

A Large Population Is Not Yet One Market

Consider a small food processor in Ghana. At home, the company learns one tax system, one set of product rules, and one commercial environment. If it wants to sell in nearby countries, the distance may be manageable, yet the transaction can become much more complicated. The company may need different registrations, labels, certificates, agents, payment arrangements, and customs documents. It must understand the rules of another sovereign state and find a reliable way to move goods across a border.

None of these requirements is automatically unreasonable. Governments have legitimate responsibilities to collect revenue, protect consumers, enforce health standards, and know what enters their territories. The problem arises when procedures are duplicated, unclear, slow, incompatible, or applied unpredictably. A shipment delayed for a day may inconvenience a manufacturer of durable goods. The same delay can destroy the value of fresh produce.

This is why the number of people on a map is only a beginning. For a business, the relevant market is the portion it can serve at a price customers can afford. Roads, ports, railways, warehouses, electricity, credit, insurance, digital networks, exchange arrangements, and law determine how much of the continental population is commercially reachable.

Income matters as well. A large population with limited purchasing power is not equivalent to a smaller but wealthier consumer market. Nor is demand uniform. Rural households, growing cities, established industrial centres, fragile states, and tourism-dependent islands require different products and distribution systems. Integration cannot erase these differences. It can make it easier for firms to discover them and respond to them.

The right claim is therefore more modest and more useful than the slogan. Africa possesses continental scale, but much of that scale remains divided among national markets. Greater integration could allow more African producers and consumers to benefit from proximity to one another.

The Border Changes the Calculation

Comparisons with the United States, China, and India require care. Commerce between Texas and California, or between provinces in China, takes place inside one sovereign state. It is generally recorded as domestic commerce, not international trade. A sale from Kenya to Uganda or from Ghana to Côte d'Ivoire crosses an international border, even when the journey is shorter than many domestic routes in larger countries.

This distinction makes simple internal-trade percentages misleading. There is no directly comparable official figure showing what share of American, Chinese, or Indian trade occurs internally and matching it neatly against intra-African trade. The statistical systems classify the transactions differently because the political structures are different.

The structural comparison is still valuable. A firm expanding across a large national market usually does not meet a new customs territory at every state or provincial boundary. Across Africa, a company may encounter tariffs, border inspections, product standards, licensing rules, transport regulations, currency conversion, and legal uncertainty each time it enters another country. The cost is not only the fee paid at the border. It includes staff time, spoilage, storage, missed delivery dates, idle vehicles, working capital tied up in transit, and the risk that a rule will be interpreted differently from one crossing to the next.

Removing tariffs alone cannot solve all of this. A product with a low tariff can remain uncompetitive if the truck carrying it spends days waiting, if the exporter cannot prove that it qualifies for preferential treatment, or if the receiving country does not accept its certification. A market becomes usable when the physical and institutional parts work together.

This point changes the meaning of integration. It is not simply an agreement among trade ministries. It reaches customs agencies, standards bodies, central banks, transport regulators, courts, port authorities, electricity utilities, and the officials who meet traders at a border post. The quality of those everyday systems determines whether a continental rule becomes a commercial reality.

What the Trade Record Shows

Chapter 8 noted that recorded intra-African trade accounts for only about 16 percent of Africa's total trade. A more recent calculation by the United Nations Economic Commission for Africa placed intra-African merchandise trade at $101.7 billion in 2024, equal to 15.1 percent of the continent's total merchandise trade. The calculation used the average of recorded intra-African exports and imports (Economic Commission for Africa, 2025).

The two figures are not contradictory. Trade shares vary with the year, source, denominator, and treatment of imports and exports. Merchandise trade also excludes services, and official records do not capture every informal transaction. A trader carrying food, textiles, or household goods through an unofficial channel may participate in a real regional economy without appearing fully in continental customs data.

The careful conclusion is that recorded trade among African countries remains a minority of the continent's recorded trade. That finding should not be interpreted as a call to withdraw from global markets. African economies need trade within the continent and with the wider world. The concern is that nearby suppliers and customers are often harder to reach than geography alone would suggest.

Trade composition matters as much as the percentage. Selling an unprocessed commodity abroad and importing a finished product creates a different economic relationship from exchanging components, processed foods, machinery, business services, and technology within a regional production network. A higher intra-African trade share would be most valuable if it reflected wider productive capacity, stronger firms, and goods and services with more value added.

The headline percentage therefore diagnoses fragmentation, but it does not prescribe a single remedy. Some trade barriers are at the border. Others begin far from it, in unreliable electricity, weak roads, limited finance, inconsistent standards, insecurity, or low production capacity. A customs reform cannot fill a pothole, and a new highway cannot correct an arbitrary licensing system. Both may be necessary.

What Europe Shows, and What It Does Not

The European Union offers a closer comparison than a single country because its members remain sovereign states. The EU has 27 member countries, while Norway, Iceland, and Liechtenstein participate in the single market through the European Economic Area. Within that framework, common rules support the movement of goods, services, capital, and people (European Commission, 2026).

The difference in trade depth is substantial. Eurostat reported that the value of goods traded within the EU in 2024 was 1.6 times the value of the EU's goods trade with non-member countries. It also noted that the removal of customs formalities among EU members required a separate statistical system for recording internal goods movements (Eurostat, 2025). In other words, national borders remain, but they interfere far less with ordinary commerce than they once did.

This comparison must not be turned into a blueprint. European integration developed over decades under conditions different from Africa's. The EU has stronger average infrastructure, larger fiscal resources, and institutions with powers that African governments have not necessarily chosen to share. Its single market is also unfinished in some sectors and remains the subject of political disagreement.

Africa's geography and political economy require their own solutions. Many African countries are landlocked. Infrastructure inherited from colonial economies often connected mines or farms to overseas ports more effectively than it connected neighbouring African markets. Regional organizations overlap, national capacities vary, and conflict makes integration especially difficult in some corridors. A system designed without these realities would look impressive on paper and fail in use.

Europe demonstrates a narrower point. Sovereign states can reduce the economic cost of crossing their borders without surrendering their national identities. They can agree on rules, recognize standards, coordinate infrastructure, and give firms access to a market larger than any one member. Africa can learn from that principle without reproducing Europe's institutions or history.

What Integration Changes for a Business

Return to the Ghanaian food processor. In a fragmented market, expansion may require rebuilding the business country by country. Packaging accepted at home may need alteration abroad. A payment may move through an outside currency and several correspondent banks. A vehicle may meet different axle-load rules along one route. A certificate issued by one laboratory may not be recognized by another country. Each problem looks small in isolation. Together they can make regional expansion too expensive for a modest firm.

In a more integrated market, the company would still need to compete. It would still have to meet safety standards, understand customers, manage exchange-rate risk, and build distribution. Integration does not guarantee profit. What it can do is remove unnecessary duplication and make the remaining requirements clearer.

That difference is especially important for smaller enterprises. A multinational corporation can hire lawyers, customs specialists, and local representatives in several countries. A young African company may not be able to absorb those fixed costs. Simplified procedures, transparent tariff schedules, compatible digital systems, and mutual recognition of appropriate standards can lower the threshold for regional trade.

Consumers may benefit from a wider choice of suppliers and more competition. Producers may gain access to inputs that are unavailable or costly at home. Investors may be more willing to finance a factory designed to serve several countries than one confined to a small domestic market. Governments may also gain when formal trade expands, because transparent and efficient systems make compliance more attractive than avoidance.

There are risks. Larger firms can dominate weaker competitors. Benefits can concentrate around established ports, cities, and industrial centres. Governments can lose tariff revenue before other tax systems are ready to replace it. Workers and businesses in exposed sectors may face painful adjustment. Integration should therefore include competition policy, support for productive capacity, infrastructure beyond major hubs, and credible measures for countries and communities bearing disproportionate costs.

The aim is not movement for its own sake. It is a market in which a productive business has a fairer chance to reach regional customers and in which integration does not become another name for concentration.

Regional Value Chains Need Predictable Borders

Manufacturing shows why predictability is as important as speed. Consider a refrigerator assembled in one African country. Its metal panels, compressor, insulation, electronic controls, plastic fittings, packaging, and design services do not have to originate in the same place. Different firms can specialize in different stages of production.

Such a value chain becomes difficult when an intermediate component crosses several unpredictable borders. A factory cannot run efficiently if a missing part stops the production line for an unknown period. The manufacturer may respond by importing a finished refrigerator through one established route, even when African firms could supply some of its components. Fragmentation then discourages the very specialization that could deepen industrial capacity.

Reliable cross-border systems change the calculation. If firms can know the tariff treatment, prove origin, meet recognized standards, settle payment, and estimate delivery time, regional sourcing becomes more realistic. One country does not need to produce every input. The value lies in the network.

This is the serious meaning behind the phrase *made in Africa*. It should not be a label attached to an aspiration. It should describe a product whose design, inputs, processing, assembly, logistics, finance, or marketing create substantial value within African economies. Rules of origin matter because they determine which goods qualify for preferential treatment and how much regional production a product must contain.

The same logic applies beyond factories. A film may combine writers, actors, finance, locations, editing, and distribution from several countries. A software firm may develop a product in one city, host services elsewhere, and sell across a region. A tourism route may depend on coordinated visas, airlines, roads, and conservation policies. Modern production networks include services as well as physical goods.

Chapter 10 will examine the value-addition challenge directly. The connection begins here. Processing more African resources is difficult when every national market must carry an entire industry alone. Integration can give processors access to regional inputs and customers, making investment in larger and more specialized facilities more practical.

Food, Power, and Payments

Agriculture makes the human stakes visible. Food can be scarce in one area while producers elsewhere struggle to find a profitable market. Better regional trade can help connect surplus and deficit areas, but only when transport is reliable, information is timely, and health and plant-safety rules are scientifically justified and consistently applied.

Perishable goods reveal the weakest link. A farmer may produce enough to sell, yet lose the opportunity because there is no cold storage, the road is impassable, or a border delay consumes the product's remaining shelf life. Integration in this setting is not an abstract reduction in tariffs. It is the combined work of rural roads, storage, testing, customs, market information, finance, and trustworthy contracts.

Regional electricity trade offers another example. Energy resources are unevenly distributed, and national demand changes by season and hour. Interconnected systems can allow one country to sell available power to another rather than requiring every country to meet every moment of demand alone. In January 2025, the World Bank approved the first phase of the West Africa Regional Electricity Market Program. Among its planned investments was the Ghana-Côte d'Ivoire interconnection, intended to strengthen transmission and electricity trade within the West African Power Pool (World Bank, 2025).

The project is not proof that a fully functional regional market already exists. It shows what integration looks like in concrete form: transmission lines, market rules, regulators, utilities, and payment obligations that must work together. Electricity cannot wait at customs, but it still depends on institutions crossing borders.

Payments create a similar challenge for ordinary trade. A buyer and seller may agree on a price yet struggle to transfer money quickly and affordably between their banking systems. The Pan-African Payment and Settlement System, developed by the African Export-Import Bank in collaboration with African institutions, is designed to support real-time cross-border payments in local currencies through participating central banks, commercial banks, payment providers, and financial intermediaries (Pan-African Payment and Settlement System, n.d.).

PAPSS addresses a practical bottleneck, but it is not a universal switch that instantly integrates every currency and bank. Participation, foreign-exchange liquidity, regulatory compliance, cybersecurity, consumer protection, and trust still matter. Its significance lies in the problem it is trying to solve: African trade should not always need an external currency and distant intermediaries simply because the buyer and seller live in different African countries.

Food corridors, power pools, and payment systems make the same point in different ways. Integration becomes meaningful when a farmer can deliver, a factory can keep running, and a seller can receive payment. Institutions matter because they make these ordinary transactions possible.

AfCFTA Is a Framework, Not a Finished Market

The African Continental Free Trade Area is the most ambitious continental attempt to reduce these divisions. The agreement was signed in Kigali on 21 March 2018, entered into force on 30 May 2019, and began trading under its framework on 1 January 2021. Its objectives include creating a single market for goods and services, improving competitiveness, and supporting industrial development, diversification, regional value chains, agriculture, and food security (African Union, n.d.).

These dates mark legal and institutional milestones. They do not mean that one fully integrated market appeared on the first day of trading. Tariff schedules must be implemented. Customs authorities need usable procedures. Rules of origin must be completed and understood. Businesses need information about how to claim preferences. Standards, services regulation, transit systems, payments, competition rules, and dispute settlement all have to function beyond conference rooms.

An Economic Commission for Africa assessment issued in December 2025 illustrates the distance between negotiation and outcome. It recorded considerable progress in tariff offers, rules of origin, national implementation strategies, and services commitments. Yet it also concluded that the projected expansion of intra-African trade had not yet been realized, with the 2024 merchandise share standing at 15.1 percent (Economic Commission for Africa, 2025).

That is not a reason to dismiss the agreement. Major trade systems take time to build, and businesses invest only after rules become credible. It is a reason to describe the AfCFTA accurately. The agreement creates a framework through which governments can reduce barriers. It cannot substitute for national reforms, productive firms, secure transport corridors, or competent administration.

Nor does the AfCFTA require political unification. African countries retain their governments, borders, languages, cultures, and legal identities. The practical goal is to make those borders less disruptive to legitimate economic activity while preserving the public purposes that border administration serves.

The distinction protects the idea from two opposite errors. One is to present integration as a loss of national identity. The other is to celebrate the agreement as though implementation were complete. A functioning continental market will be built through thousands of specific decisions about documents, standards, roads, data, payments, competition, and enforcement.

Projections Are Not Outcomes

Economic modelling helps estimate what deeper integration might achieve, but model results must be labelled as scenarios. They are not observations and they are not promises.

A 2022 World Bank study examined the AfCFTA alongside trade facilitation, investment, competition, e-commerce, and intellectual-property reforms. Under its deeper-integration scenario, the model estimated that African incomes could be 9 percent higher by 2035, an increase of about $571 billion. It also estimated almost 18 million additional jobs and up to 50 million fewer people living in extreme poverty than under the study's baseline (World Bank, 2022).

Those figures are substantial, but the conditional language carries the argument. The results depend on assumptions about implementation, investment, the response of firms, the movement of workers and capital, and future economic conditions. A model compares possible paths. It does not report gains already delivered by the agreement.

Continental totals also conceal distribution. A rise in overall income does not guarantee that every country, sector, household, or worker gains at the same time. Some firms will expand. Others may close or adapt. Transport hubs may benefit sooner than remote districts. Skilled workers may capture opportunities before people who lack education, finance, land rights, or digital access.

Policy must therefore ask two questions together: how can integration increase productive opportunity, and how can more people participate in that opportunity? Education, reliable energy, finance for smaller firms, worker adjustment, social protection, competition policy, and investments in lagging regions are not separate from integration. They influence who can use the larger market.

The projections are best understood as evidence that the potential gains are large enough to justify serious implementation. They are not permission to replace practical work with optimistic numbers.

From Scale to Connection

Africa does not need to choose between national development and continental integration. Stronger national institutions make regional agreements more credible, while a larger regional market can make national investment more productive. Roads inside one country may serve a cross-border corridor. A national standards laboratory may help local firms qualify for regional trade. A reliable domestic electricity system may become part of a power pool. The two levels reinforce each other when policy is coherent.

Governments carry much of the responsibility because they write and administer the rules. Businesses also shape the outcome through investment, competition, compliance, and their willingness to build regional partnerships. Banks, universities, professional associations, logistics companies, standards bodies, farmers' organizations, and technology providers all connect parts of the market that treaties alone cannot join.

The most useful comparison is not Africa against Europe, China, India, or the United States. It is Africa as it operates now compared with Africa after more of its practical barriers have been reduced.

The people would be the same. The land, sunlight, ports, farms, cities, skills, and minerals would still be there. What would change is the ability to combine them. A producer could reach more customers. A manufacturer could source from more suppliers. A country facing an electricity shortage could draw more effectively on regional generation. A farmer's harvest could reach a market before it spoiled. An African payment could travel through African financial infrastructure.

None of this is automatic. Integration can widen opportunity, but only production creates goods to trade, skill raises productivity, and public institutions protect fairness. A larger market magnifies what its members bring to it, including their strengths and their weaknesses.

That is the chapter's central economic lesson. We do not have to create the continent's scale. We already have it. We have to connect it.

Connection, however, is only useful if African economies have more to exchange than raw materials and imported finished goods. Chapter

10 turns to that next challenge: how countries can retain more value through processing, production, and diversification.

Evidence Note

This chapter distinguishes demographic scale from an economically accessible market. The 2024 intra-African figure refers to recorded merchandise trade and uses the average of intra-African exports and imports; it does not include services and may not capture all informal cross-border exchange. The Eurostat comparison uses total goods trade within and beyond the European Union and is not presented as a statistically identical measure. Commerce among states or provinces inside the United States, China, and India is generally domestic commerce, so this chapter does not invent directly comparable internal-trade percentages for those countries. AfCFTA dates describe legal and operational milestones, not the completion of a continental market. The World Bank figures for 2035 are results from a modelled deeper-integration scenario and should not be read as observed gains, forecasts guaranteed to occur, or benefits distributed equally across countries and households.

CHAPTER 10

Africa's Resources and the Value-Addition Challenge

From Commodity Dependence to Production, Processing, and Diversification

Chapter 9 asked what could change if African economies operated more like a connected market. A larger accessible market can make regional production more practical, but connection alone does not determine what a continent produces or how much value it retains. That depends on what happens between the first extraction of a resource and the final sale of a product.

Africa is often described as rich in natural resources. The description can be accurate, but it is economically incomplete. A country may export large quantities of minerals, fuels, or agricultural commodities and capture only part of the activity associated with the final product. Extraction and cultivation are important stages. So are refining, processing, component production, manufacturing, logistics, finance, research, design, branding, distribution, repair, and recycling.

The problem is therefore not that commodities have no value. They generate export earnings, employment, public revenue, and investment. The problem is excessive dependence on a narrow range of commodities, especially when too few other productive activities develop around them.

The more useful question is not simply, What does Africa have? It is, What do African economies do with what they have, and what capabilities do they build in the process?

What Commodity Dependence Actually Measures

Commodity dependence has a specific statistical meaning in the work of UN Trade and Development. A country is classified as commodity dependent when commodities account for more than 60 percent of its merchandise exports. These commodities include agricultural products, minerals, ores, metals, and fuels.

Using that threshold, the *Economic Development in Africa Report 2022* classified 45 of the 54 African countries in its dataset as commodity dependent. That was about 83 percent of the countries measured (UN Trade and Development, 2022).

The statistic concerns the composition of merchandise exports. It does not mean that 83 percent of African economies produce nothing except commodities. A country may have active construction, retail, transport, public services, tourism, telecommunications, and finance while still earning most of its merchandise-export revenue from oil, copper, cocoa, coffee, or another primary product.

This distinction matters because export concentration describes exposure. If a large share of foreign earnings comes from one or two products, a change in international prices can quickly affect the exchange rate, government revenue, investment, employment, and the ability to pay for imports. The shock can spread far beyond the mine, oil field, or farm where the commodity originated.

Commodity dependence also differs across Africa. A petroleum exporter faces a different market from a cocoa producer. A country exporting copper and cobalt has different processing options from one exporting tea, fish, cotton, or timber. Even countries selling the same commodity may differ in energy costs, transport access, technical skill, environmental regulation, and bargaining power. A continental percentage identifies a pattern; but it does not provide one policy for every country.

The 54-country statistical group must not be confused with the African Union's 55-member political membership (African Union, n.d.). Naming the denominator prevents a valid statistic from becoming a misleading one.

When a Global Price Becomes a Domestic Shock

Commodity prices move for reasons that no single producing country controls. Global demand rises or falls. New sources of supply enter the market. Technology changes the quantity of a material required. Weather affects harvests. Conflict interrupts shipping. Producers or governments alter output. Financial expectations can amplify a movement already under way.

For a diversified economy, the effect of one falling export price may be partly absorbed elsewhere. For a highly concentrated exporter, the same decline can weaken the public budget and the wider economy at once. A government may postpone infrastructure. A company may cancel investment. Foreign-exchange shortages may raise the domestic cost of machinery, medicine, or fuel. Households that never worked in the export industry can still feel the result.

The reverse is also true. A price boom can improve earnings and create fiscal room. Yet temporary revenue can make long-term planning harder if spending rises as though the price will remain high. When the cycle turns, commitments remain while revenue falls.

UN Trade and Development's 2024 Africa report, published in 2025, links the continent's economic performance during parts of the period since 2000 to commodity-price cycles. It identifies the 2014 commodity downturn and the COVID-19 shock as examples of the vulnerability created by concentrated external dependence (UN Trade and Development, 2025).

Diversification is one way to reduce that vulnerability. It does not prevent every shock, and it cannot stabilize all prices. It gives an economy more than one source of earnings, skill, employment, and public revenue. The point is resilience, not the abandonment of successful commodity industries.

Where Value Is Added

Value addition is sometimes presented as though a raw material enters a factory and automatically becomes prosperity. The real process is more demanding.

Consider a mineral used in an energy technology. Its chain may include geological exploration, extraction, concentration, smelting, refining, chemical processing, component production, equipment manufacturing, distribution, use, recovery, and recycling. Each stage has its own economics. Some require enormous capital and continuous electricity. Others depend on chemical expertise, precision engineering, intellectual property, market access, or reliable supplies of several materials that no one country possesses.

Agricultural chains are equally layered. Cocoa begins with cultivation, but the quality and value of the bean are affected by harvesting, fermentation, drying, storage, aggregation, transport, and testing. Further stages can include grinding, the production of cocoa liquor, butter, cake, and powder, chocolate manufacturing, packaging, branding, distribution, and retail.

The final retail price is not divided according to who performed the hardest physical labor. It reflects bargaining power, risk, capital, productivity, technology, market structure, brand value, and control over distribution. A farmer or miner may perform indispensable work without receiving a large share of what the final consumer pays.

This does not mean that every later stage is automatically more profitable. A refinery can lose money. A poorly located factory can become an expensive monument. A branded product can fail to attract buyers. The phrase *move up the value chain* is useful only when it is connected to demand, cost, capability, and competition.

The sound objective is to identify stages that African firms and economies can perform competitively, then build the systems those stages require. That may mean improving quality at the farm, processing an intermediate material, producing a component, providing engineering services, financing trade, or developing a consumer brand. Value can be added in many places, not only at the final assembly line.

Critical Minerals Make the Gap Visible

Minerals used in batteries, electricity networks, renewable-energy equipment, and other technologies provide a clear example of the difference between resource supply and industrial participation.

The International Energy Agency reported in 2025 that Africa supplied about 75 percent of global manganese, 70 percent of cobalt, and nearly 20 percent of copper. At the same time, the continent captured less than 1 percent of the value generated by manufacturing clean-energy technologies and their components (International Energy Agency, 2025).

These figures describe different parts of the same chain. The mineral shares concern supply of key unprocessed materials. The manufacturing figure concerns technologies and components such as batteries, electric vehicles, solar equipment, wind equipment, electrolysers, and heat pumps. The comparison does not imply that mineral production and technology manufacturing are technically interchangeable. It shows how far apart upstream resource strength and downstream industrial activity can be.

The Democratic Republic of the Congo illustrates both the opportunity and the danger of imprecise storytelling. UN Trade and Development reported that the country produced about 68 percent of the world's cobalt and held about 48 percent of estimated global reserves in 2022 (UN Trade and Development, 2023). Those figures were tied to a specific year. Production shares and reserve estimates can change with new mines, discoveries, prices, technology, and reporting methods.

Cobalt itself does not become a battery through national determination alone. Depending on the battery chemistry, the chain can require refined chemicals, precursor materials, cathode production, cells, battery-management systems, packs, vehicle or equipment assembly, software, testing, and recycling. Copper, lithium, nickel, manganese, graphite, aluminum, and other materials may enter the same industrial system.

The IEA identified possible African opportunities in several intermediate stages. Its examples included spherical graphite for battery anodes in East Africa, high-purity manganese sulfate in South Africa and

Gabon, purified phosphoric acid in Morocco, and further cobalt and copper processing in the Democratic Republic of the Congo and Zambia (International Energy Agency, 2025).

These are assessed opportunities, not investments guaranteed to happen. Commercial feasibility depends on energy, transport, water, finance, technical performance, environmental management, regulation, market demand, and long-term agreements with buyers. A deposit is an asset. A competitive industrial system must be built.

Processing Must Be Economically and Environmentally Real

The call to stop exporting raw materials sounds decisive, but it can hide the sequence required to replace an export market. Processing capacity cannot be created by prohibition alone.

A plant needs reliable inputs in the right quantity and quality. It needs equipment, power, water where the process requires it, skilled operators, maintenance, finance, safety systems, waste management, transport, and customers. It must operate at a scale that allows its output to compete with established suppliers. If one link fails repeatedly, the whole investment becomes fragile.

Energy is especially important. Smelting, refining, fertilizer production, cold storage, and many forms of manufacturing require power that is not merely connected but reliable and competitively priced. Chapter 8 showed the scale of the electricity-access gap in sub-Saharan Africa. Household access and industrial supply are different measures, yet both point to the need for investment in generation, transmission, distribution, and system reliability.

Transport matters before and after production. Machinery and replacement parts must reach the facility. Raw material must arrive on schedule. Finished output must reach regional or global customers without losing its price advantage to delay and logistics costs. A factory located near a resource may still be commercially distant from its market.

Environmental and social costs belong inside the calculation. Mineral processing can require substantial energy and water and can generate hazardous waste. Agricultural processing can place pressure on water, land, and forests. Workers need safe conditions, and communities need credible protection from pollution, displacement, and uncompensated loss. A higher domestic share of value does not justify shifting a larger share of harm onto local people.

Good industrial policy therefore asks more than whether processing is possible. It asks whether the activity can remain competitive, whether benefits are broadly shared, whether public support is proportionate, and whether environmental obligations can be enforced. A plant that survives only through permanent protection, unreliable subsidies, or unpriced damage may add less national value than its output suggests.

Cocoa Shows That Value Addition Is Not Only About Mining

Agriculture brings the discussion closer to the lives of millions of producers. Cocoa from West and Central Africa moves through a long chain before it appears as chocolate, cocoa powder, cosmetics, beverages, or other consumer goods.

The first stages already involve knowledge. Farmers choose varieties, manage soil and disease, harvest ripe pods, and oversee fermentation and drying. Poor handling at any point can reduce quality. Aggregators, warehouses, testing systems, traders, processors, manufacturers, logistics providers, brands, and retailers then shape the product and its price.

African countries already perform some of these downstream activities. Ghana, for example, has substantial installed cocoa-processing capacity, even though its facilities have not always operated at full capacity (Ghana Cocoa Board, 2025). Food manufacturers in several African countries also produce cocoa-based goods. The honest argument is not that every bean leaves Africa untouched or that no chocolate is made on the continent. It is that the chain contains many stages and that producing countries do not yet capture as much processing, manufacturing, branding, and distribution activity as they could under competitive conditions.

The cocoa example also shows why a raw-export ban can be too simple. If grinding capacity expands faster than reliable bean supply, electricity, finance, shipping, or demand, factories may operate below capacity. If policy favors large processors but leaves farmers with low prices and high risk, the value chain may grow without improving the position of its foundation.

Adding value can begin before a factory. Better fermentation, traceability, storage, farmer organization, quality differentiation, and direct market relationships can raise the value of an agricultural product. Processing and branding can then build on that foundation. The best strategy depends on the country, product, market, and people expected to benefit.

Not Every Country Must Manufacture Everything

No serious diversification strategy should require every African country to refine every mineral, process every crop, and manufacture every final product it consumes. That would reproduce fragmentation under the language of self-reliance.

Industries benefit from scale, specialized suppliers, skilled labor, infrastructure, and accumulated knowledge. A small national market may not support every stage efficiently. Some activities are viable only when a plant can serve several countries. Others may cluster where energy, ports, mineral deposits, engineering skill, or existing industrial firms create an advantage.

Regional specialization offers a more practical path. One country may supply a mineral. Another may refine or process it. Firms elsewhere may produce components, assemble equipment, provide software, finance transactions, or handle distribution. More stages can occur within African economies without every stage occurring inside one border.

This is where Chapter 9 and Chapter 10 meet. A regional value chain depends on predictable movement of inputs, services, payments, and people. A component delayed at customs can stop an assembly line. A standard accepted in one country but rejected in another can make regional sourcing too risky. A payment system that relies on slow and costly external intermediation can erase a supplier's price advantage.

UN Trade and Development reported in 2025 that only 16 of the 54 African countries studied sourced more than 0.5 percent of their intermediate goods from within Africa. The same report identified regional networks in which countries including Kenya, Nigeria, and South Africa already acted as suppliers and users of value-added goods (UN Trade and Development, 2025).

The finding holds two realities together. Regional production networks already exist, so integration is not an imaginary starting point. Yet regional sourcing remains limited and concentrated. The AfCFTA can improve the conditions for those networks by reducing unnecessary trade barriers and clarifying rules of origin. It cannot create competitive suppliers where energy, finance, skills, logistics, and production capacity are missing.

The phrase *made in Africa* can therefore describe a product made across Africa. Its value may come from several countries and several kinds of work. What matters is whether African firms, workers, and institutions perform more economically significant stages and gain capability from doing so.

Diversification Is Larger Than Manufacturing

Manufacturing is central to this chapter, but it is not the only path away from commodity dependence. Modern production relies on services at almost every stage.

A mine uses geological analysis, engineering, finance, insurance, security, transport, environmental monitoring, data systems, and equipment maintenance. A food-processing company depends on laboratories, packaging, cold storage, banking, marketing, and distribution. A manufacturer needs design, software, accounting, legal advice, telecommunications, and logistics.

UN Trade and Development's 2022 report emphasized the role of knowledge-intensive services, including information and communication technology, business services, and digital financial services, in export diversification and productivity (UN Trade and Development, 2022). These services can be exported directly, but they also make agriculture and industry more competitive.

Tourism, creative industries, transport, professional services, finance, technology, and renewable-energy services can all broaden an economy's sources of income. Diversification may involve new products, new markets, more complex tasks, or greater productivity within an existing industry. It should not be reduced to counting factories.

Existing African industrial bases also deserve recognition. The IEA's 2025 assessment cited established automotive industries in Morocco and South Africa, cement, fertilizer, and petrochemical production in

Nigeria, and electronic and electrical-component production in Egypt and Tunisia (International Energy Agency, 2025). These examples do not represent the whole continent, and they do not prove that every industrial strategy has succeeded. They show that Africa is not beginning from zero.

The challenge is to deepen capability, widen participation, and create stronger links among firms. A vehicle assembly plant adds more lasting value when local and regional suppliers can meet its standards, workers gain transferable skills, engineers solve production problems, and related firms emerge. The number of units produced matters. So does what the economy learns to do.

Resource Revenue Can Finance Capability, but It Does Not Guarantee It

The IEA estimated that mineral production accounted for about 8 percent of government revenue in resource-rich African countries at the time of its 2025 report (International Energy Agency, 2025). The geographic qualifier is essential. This is not an average for all African governments, and it does not describe every mineral producer in the same way.

Resource revenue can help finance electricity, transport, schools, technical training, health systems, research, and public administration. Those investments can raise productivity beyond the resource sector. Revenue can also be lost through poor contracts, tax avoidance, corruption, weak public investment, or spending that becomes unsustainable when prices fall.

The resource itself does not decide between those outcomes. Institutions do. Governments determine licensing, taxation, local-content rules, environmental enforcement, and the use of public revenue. Companies make investment, technology, employment, and procurement decisions. Communities, workers, courts, journalists, and civil-society organizations influence whether agreements are transparent and obligations are respected.

Local-content requirements can help firms and workers enter a value chain, but poorly designed rules can become box-ticking exercises or protect politically connected intermediaries. Tax incentives can attract an investment, but they can also transfer public value to a project that would have proceeded anyway. State participation can build capacity, or it can accumulate risk without adequate oversight.

There is no automatic route from resource wealth to diversification. There are choices, capabilities, and institutions that can make the connection stronger or weaker.

Industrial Strategy Must Be Specific

The preliminary question is not, "Should Africa add value?" Almost everyone can agree with that ambition. The harder questions concern which activity, in which location, for which market, using what inputs, at what cost, and with what public risk.

Cobalt is not cocoa. Copper is not coffee. Petroleum is not cotton. Lithium is not livestock. Each product has its own technology, market structure, environmental demands, transport needs, and competitive landscape. A policy suitable for cocoa grinding may be irrelevant to battery materials. A strategy viable in a country with abundant low-cost electricity may fail where firms depend on expensive diesel generation.

Sector-specific analysis should begin with the market. Who will buy the output? What quality is required? Which competitors already supply it? How large must a plant be? What would electricity, transport, finance, and compliance cost? Which inputs are available locally or regionally? What skills can be developed within a realistic period? What environmental and social risks must be managed?

The answer may support a new processing industry. It may instead point toward better farm quality, a specialized service, a component, a logistics hub, or a regional partnership. Rejecting an uncompetitive factory is not a rejection of industrialization. It can protect resources for an opportunity with a stronger foundation.

Public policy still has a necessary role. Markets do not automatically build cross-border power lines, technical colleges, standards laboratories, ports, or research institutions. Governments can coordinate infrastructure, finance early capability, enforce competition, negotiate fair contracts, and reduce risks that no single firm can manage. The discipline is to connect support to measurable goals, time limits, transparency, learning, and the willingness to change course.

The IEA made the same caution in its 2025 report. Its identified opportunities were not prescriptions. It called for market analysis, attention to project economics, skilled workers, technological expertise, suitable regulation, partnerships, and strategies capable of correction as evidence changes (International Energy Agency, 2025).

From Resource Ownership to Productive Capability

Africa's resources matter. They can support livelihoods, earn foreign exchange, supply global industries, and finance public investment. But ownership of a resource and mastery of a value chain are different achievements.

Mastery grows when workers gain skill, firms learn to meet demanding standards, engineers maintain and improve equipment, banks understand industrial risk, universities support research, regulators enforce credible rules, and producers reach customers at home and abroad. It appears in the ability to solve problems repeatedly, not merely in the announcement of a project.

This is why diversification should be understood as capability building. A country becomes less vulnerable not simply because it exports another product, but because more people and institutions can perform more complex and productive work. The result may be a processed mineral, a branded food, an electrical component, a logistics service, a software product, or an industry that combines several of them.

The evidence supports a clear but measured conclusion. Many African economies remain heavily dependent on commodity exports. Africa supplies large shares of several minerals essential to modern energy technologies while capturing a much smaller share of related technology manufacturing. Regional sourcing of intermediate goods remains limited. At the same time, processing, manufacturing, and sophisticated services already exist in a number of African economies.

The continent is therefore neither empty of industry nor guaranteed an industrial future by its resources. It has a base to deepen and a structural gap to close.

Chapter 11 turns from the gap to the conditions of transformation. Education, infrastructure, institutions, energy, trade, investment, technology, and leadership are not separate topics. Together, they determine whether resources become productive capability and whether that capability improves people's lives.

Evidence Note

Commodity dependence in this chapter uses UN Trade and Development's threshold of commodities exceeding 60 percent of merchandise exports. The figure of 45 out of 54 countries describes the dataset and period used in the 2022 report; it does not imply that those economies produce no other goods or services. The 54-country UN statistical group is not interchangeable with the African Union's 55-member political membership. Mineral production and reserve shares are dated because they change with output, exploration, prices, technology, and revised estimates. The International Energy Agency's identified processing and manufacturing opportunities are assessments, not committed investments or guaranteed outcomes. References to value addition do not assume that every commodity should be processed domestically or that all later stages are automatically more profitable. Continental statements should not be read as descriptions of every African country or industry.

CHAPTER 11

Paths Toward Transformation

From Constraints to Solutions

The previous chapters described a difficult but familiar contradiction. African countries possess large reserves of minerals, extensive agricultural land, a young population, growing cities, and expanding markets. Yet possession alone does not create prosperity. A resource becomes economically valuable only when people can extract or cultivate it responsibly, process it competitively, move it efficiently, finance the work, and sell the result. A large population becomes an advantage only when people are healthy, educated, skilled, and able to find productive work.

Chapter 10 examined the distance between producing raw materials and capturing more value through processing, manufacturing, and knowledge-intensive services. That distance cannot be closed by announcing an industrial policy or building one factory. A processor needs steady electricity. A manufacturer needs technicians, spare parts, finance, predictable rules, transport, and customers. A farmer may raise a good harvest, but without storage, roads, refrigeration, information, and reliable buyers, much of its value can still be lost.

This chapter turns from constraints to the conditions that make transformation possible. Its central argument is simple: development depends on connected capabilities. Infrastructure, energy, education, institutions, finance, productive firms, and regional markets reinforce one another when they function well. When one of them fails, the weakness often travels through the rest of the system.

That is why there is no single lever that can transform an entire country, much less a continent as diverse as Africa. The work is more demanding. It involves building institutions that can carry out decisions, infrastructure that remains usable after the opening ceremony, schools that produce learning, firms that can invest and compete, and regional arrangements that work at the border as well as on paper.

Transformation Is a Systems Problem

Public debate often reduces development to one preferred solution. Some argue that education comes first. Others emphasize infrastructure, industrialization, foreign investment, entrepreneurship, technology, or governance. Each points to something important. The problem begins when one part is presented as a substitute for all the others.

Consider a new industrial park. The buildings may be completed, but firms will struggle if electricity is unreliable, customs clearance is slow, imported machinery is delayed, or local suppliers cannot meet technical standards. Training programs may produce capable graduates, but their skills can go unused if firms are not investing. A new road may shorten a journey, yet poor maintenance, expensive border procedures, or insecurity can weaken its commercial value. Even a sound policy can remain largely symbolic when the agency responsible for it lacks staff, data, authority, or money.

These are not arguments against factories, schools, roads, or reforms. They show why connections matter. Development is less like completing a checklist and more like making many parts work together. Progress in one area creates possibilities, but complementary capabilities determine whether those possibilities become results.

The scale of the infrastructure challenge illustrates the point. The African Development Bank has repeatedly cited estimated annual infrastructure needs of about $130 billion to $170 billion and an annual financing gap of roughly $68 billion to $108 billion. These figures are continental planning estimates, not a bill that applies equally to every country or every year. They nevertheless indicate the magnitude of the investment under discussion (African Development Bank Group, 2024).

Money alone does not settle the matter. A project must be selected for a defensible reason, designed well, financed on manageable terms, built to an appropriate standard, connected to other systems, and maintained throughout its useful life. A country can spend heavily and still receive poor infrastructure. It can also improve the value of limited resources through careful project selection, transparent procurement, competent management, and routine maintenance.

Infrastructure Must Function

Infrastructure is sometimes counted as a collection of physical objects: kilometers of road, megawatts of generation, railway tracks, fiber-optic cable, classrooms, ports, or water systems. Those measures are useful, but they do not tell the whole story. The economic value of infrastructure lies in the service it provides.

A road is valuable when it allows people and goods to travel more safely, quickly, and affordably. A port depends on roads or railways, storage, customs, security, digital systems, and efficient handling. A power plant is useful only when transmission and distribution networks can deliver electricity. Internet cable does little for a rural clinic if the clinic lacks power, equipment, trained staff, and affordable service. Construction creates an asset; operation turns the asset into a capability.

The East Africa Regional Transport, Trade and Development Facilitation Project offers a concrete example. According to World Bank results reported in 2023, more than 320 kilometers of road were built and communications infrastructure was expanded. Between selected locations on the Kenya and South Sudan corridor, travel time fell from about forty-eight hours to six, while passenger transport costs fell by about half (World Bank, 2023). These are project-specific results, not a measure of transport performance across East Africa. Their value is that they show what a functioning connection can change: time, cost, and access.

The same lesson applies to corridors elsewhere. A corridor is not merely a paved line between two points. It links farms, mines, factories, towns, borders, ports, and markets. This is especially significant for landlocked countries, whose access to global trade depends heavily on infrastructure and procedures beyond their own borders. If a truck moves quickly along a highway but waits for days at a crossing, the corridor is not functioning as one system.

Maintenance is part of that system, although it attracts less attention than construction. Political credit often comes from launching something new. The quieter work of repairing surfaces, clearing drains, replacing equipment, inspecting bridges, and funding operations receives fewer headlines. Yet deferred maintenance raises future costs and can erase earlier gains. A serious infrastructure strategy therefore asks not only what should be built, but who will operate it, how performance will be measured, and how maintenance will be financed.

Reliable Energy Expands What an Economy Can Do

Electricity shows the difference between access and capability particularly clearly. A household connection matters, but so do the hours of service, voltage quality, affordability, and the cost of backup generation. For a small business, an unreliable connection can damage equipment and interrupt production. For a mine, smelter, cold-storage facility, hospital, or data center, the consequences are larger.

The relationship to value addition is direct. Minerals cannot be processed at scale without energy. Agricultural products often require milling, refrigeration, packaging, or drying. Manufacturing depends on powered machinery and quality control. Digital services need telecommunications networks, servers, and dependable electricity. When energy is scarce or expensive, countries may still export resources, but it becomes harder to build the activities that capture more value from them.

Regional electricity trade is one-way countries can use different endowments more efficiently. The West African Power Pool connects national systems so that electricity can move across borders. A World Bank report published in May 2026 stated that more than 4,000 kilometers of high-voltage transmission lines had been built to connect the grids of fifteen West African countries. It also reported that about 8 percent of regional electricity was being traded and that transmission and distribution investments between 2019 and 2025 had extended service to more than 3 million people in Burkina Faso, Guinea, Liberia, Senegal, Sierra Leone, and The Gambia (World Bank, 2026).

Those results did not come from transmission towers alone. The program also involved contracts, grid codes, operator agreements, pricing rules, distribution upgrades, and institutional coordination. Physical connection made trade possible; common operating arrangements made it usable. The example captures the chapter's argument in practical form.

Eastern Africa provides another illustration. The Eastern Electricity Highway between Ethiopia and Kenya became operational in December 2022. The 1,065-kilometer, 500-kilovolt high-voltage direct-current line allows bidirectional transfers of up to 2,000 megawatts, according to the World Bank. It enables Kenya to import renewable electricity from Ethiopia and supports power exchange within the Eastern African Power Pool (World Bank, 2025a).

Neither example means that regional power integration has solved electricity shortages. Millions of households and firms still lack adequate service, and utilities in several countries face financial and operational difficulties. The evidence supports a narrower conclusion: cross-border infrastructure can move electricity from places with available generation to places that need it, but doing so requires engineering, regulation, finance, and trust among participating countries.

Schooling Must Produce Learning and Useful Skills

Physical infrastructure expands what people and firms can do. Human capability determines whether they can do it well. Education is therefore central to transformation, but enrollment cannot be treated as a complete measure of progress.

Africa has enrolled many more children in school, yet access and learning have not advanced at the same pace. A joint continental assessment by UNESCO, UNICEF, and the African Union reported in 2025 that 75 million more African children were enrolled than in 2015, while the number out of school had also increased as the school-age population grew. The report found persistently weak learning outcomes and serious shortages in teachers, facilities, and resources (African Union, UNESCO, & UNICEF, 2025). The figures describe a continental pattern; outcomes vary widely among and within countries.

The distinction matters. A child can attend school for years without mastering literacy or numeracy. A graduate can hold a credential that is poorly matched to available work. A firm can have vacancies while qualified applicants remain scarce. Expanding access remains necessary, especially for children excluded by poverty, geography, disability, conflict, or discrimination. But access must be joined to capable teachers, suitable materials, safe schools, early childhood foundations, reliable assessment, and curricula that develop real understanding.

Education must also connect to the structure of an economy without becoming narrowly vocational. Agricultural modernization needs agronomists, veterinary professionals, irrigation specialists, mechanics, food scientists, and extension workers. Manufacturing needs technicians, machinists, electricians, engineers, managers, and quality-control specialists. Healthcare requires nurses, physicians, pharmacists, therapists, laboratory staff, and public-health professionals. Digital sectors need software, data, communications, and cybersecurity skills.

Universities are essential to this work, but they cannot carry it alone. Technical and vocational education and training can prepare people to install, operate, repair, and maintain the equipment on which modern economies depend. A country needs researchers and engineers, but it also needs skilled tradespeople and technicians. The sensible question is not whether university education or vocational training is superior. It is whether the education system develops a balanced range of capabilities and whether employers, schools, training institutions, and students can respond to changing needs.

At the same time, education should not be reduced to immediate labor-market demand. Reading, mathematics, science, history, civic knowledge, and the ability to reason remain valuable beyond a first job. Technologies and industries change. People need foundations strong enough to learn again. An education system serves the economy, but it also serves individuals and society.

Institutions Turn Decisions into Results

Infrastructure and education do not operate outside institutions. Public agencies plan and procure projects. Utilities manage networks. Customs services determine how goods cross borders. Courts resolve disputes. Regulators set rules. Statistical offices produce information. Schools, hospitals, and local governments translate national policy into daily services.

The word *governance* is often used so broadly that it becomes a label instead of an explanation. It is more useful to ask specific questions. Can a business obtain a license without unpredictable delay? Are procurement decisions open to scrutiny? Can a court resolve a commercial dispute within a reasonable period? Are public accounts audited? Do customs agencies use clear procedures? Are regulations stable enough for a firm to plan an investment? Can citizens obtain reliable public services?

These questions focus attention on performance. They also avoid dividing countries into simplistic categories of "good" and "bad" governance. Institutional strength is not uniform within a country. A revenue authority may be capable while a municipal planning office is weak. A sector regulator may be technically strong but lack political independence. A well-written law may be undermined by inconsistent enforcement.

The World Bank's 2025 report *21st-Century Africa: Governance and Growth* places accountable and capable government, human capital, structural transformation, and well-functioning markets among the conditions for inclusive growth. It highlights the rule of law, regulatory quality, accountability, and control of corruption (World Bank, 2025b). These dimensions shape the environment in which investment and public services operate. They do not, by themselves, guarantee a particular rate of growth.

Institutional reform is difficult because it concerns incentives, authority, professional capacity, and public trust, not only organizational charts. Creating a new agency may accomplish little if its responsibilities overlap with others or its budget is inadequate. Passing a rule may have little effect if enforcement is selective. Durable improvement usually requires the less dramatic work of clarifying responsibilities, training staff, improving data, protecting professional standards, and allowing citizens and oversight bodies to examine performance.

Public Systems and Productive Firms Need Each Other

Governments cannot produce economic transformation alone. Private firms make investments, employ workers, organize production, test ideas, respond to customers, and enter supply chains. Farmers, cooperatives, household enterprises, and larger companies all participate in this process. Universities and research institutes develop knowledge. Financial institutions allocate capital. Workers supply labor and skills.

The opposite claim, that government should simply step aside, is equally incomplete. A private factory still depends on roads, power, trained workers, contract enforcement, public health, financial rules, and access to markets. Firms rarely build an entire national electricity grid or education system for themselves. Governments, in turn, depend on productive households and businesses for much of the tax base that finances public services.

The relationship is complementary, although the division of responsibility differs by country and sector. Government may finance an asset, regulate a private provider, operate a public utility, or combine these roles. Private investment may bring capital and expertise, but investors also expect a return. Neither public ownership nor private participation is automatically efficient. Performance depends on the design of the arrangement, the competence of the institutions involved, the distribution of risk, and the ability to hold decision-makers accountable.

This matters for the diversification discussed in Chapter 10. A government can identify promising industries, but firms must still develop products, manage costs, meet standards, and find customers.

Public policy can help solve coordination problems, support research, improve logistics, or build skills. It can also waste resources when projects are chosen for political influence rather than economic value. The challenge is not to choose between the state and the market as slogans. It is to build rules and capabilities that allow both public institutions and productive firms to perform their proper work.

Financing Is About Quality as Well as Quantity

Infrastructure, education, energy, industry, and climate resilience all require financing. Sources can include tax revenue, domestic banks, pension funds, capital markets, development banks, foreign direct investment, concessional lending, commercial borrowing, and public-private partnerships. Each source carries different costs, time horizons, conditions, and risks.

Borrowing can allow a country to build useful assets sooner, but debt must be repaid. Foreign-currency debt creates additional exposure when exchange rates move. Private investors can contribute capital and operating expertise, but they require a return. Public-private partnerships can distribute responsibilities across parties, yet poorly designed contracts may leave governments carrying risks they did not fully understand. Concessional finance may lower borrowing costs, but it is limited and often tied to particular purposes.

The essential question is not simply how much money can be mobilized. It is whether the investment is worth its full cost, whether the financing terms are manageable, whether implementation can be supervised, and whether funds exist for operation and maintenance. A prestigious project with weak demand can become a burden. A smaller investment that removes a critical bottleneck may deliver more value.

Domestic resource mobilization also matters, but it should not be discussed as though all governments can raise the same amount with equal ease. Economic structures, income levels, informality, administrative capacity, and public trust differ. Improving tax systems may increase revenue and fairness, but reform must also consider the burden on households and firms. Better public spending is as important as collecting more.

Finance is therefore a discipline of choice. Scarce funds require governments, lenders, and investors to compare alternatives, disclose risks, and learn from performance. The quality of selection and execution can matter as much as the headline value of a financing package.

Regional Markets Make Scale More Practical

Chapter 9 explained why fragmented markets restrict commerce. Many African economies are individually small, and several are landlocked. A firm that can sell efficiently across borders has a larger potential customer base and may be better able to justify investment in machinery, standards, marketing, and distribution. Regional integration can therefore support the diversification described in Chapter 10.

But a trade agreement does not move a shipment. Businesses still encounter customs forms, product standards, payments, transport costs, border delays, licensing rules, and disputes. The practical value of the African Continental Free Trade Area will depend on how steadily its commitments are translated into those everyday systems.

Transport corridors show how physical and institutional integration meet. In 2023, the World Bank reported more than $3.5 billion in International Development Association financing for selected regional corridors involving East Africa, Malawi, Cameroon and Chad, Togo,

Burkina Faso and Niger, and the Central African Republic and Republic of the Congo (World Bank, 2023). The figure describes a portfolio of financed projects, not a complete estimate of Africa's corridor needs.

Regional power pools make a similar point. Their purpose is not to erase national responsibility, but to solve problems that do not fit neatly within national borders. The same logic applies to transport, disease surveillance, river basins, digital networks, payment systems, and research. Cooperation is most valuable when it produces a service that countries could not provide as efficiently on their own.

Regional integration also requires trust. Countries must believe that agreements will be honored, payments made, rules applied, and shared infrastructure protected. That trust grows from repeated performance rather than declarations. The strongest evidence for integration will therefore be found in lower costs, shorter delays, more reliable services, and increasing use by households and firms.

Demography Creates Possibility, Not Destiny

Africa's young and growing population is often described either as a guaranteed dividend or an approaching crisis. Neither description is adequate. Age structure creates conditions; it does not predetermine an outcome.

A demographic dividend becomes possible when a larger working-age population is healthy, educated, productively employed, and supported by institutions that enable saving and investment. If job creation and productivity do not keep pace, the same demographic change can intensify pressure on households, schools, housing, public services, and labor markets. The result depends partly on choices made over many years.

Women's participation is central to this question. A development strategy cannot discuss the continent's workforce while treating roughly half the population as an afterthought. Girls' education, health, safety, property rights, access to finance, childcare, transport, and workplace rules can all affect women's opportunities. The barriers and appropriate policies vary across countries and communities, but the economic principle is consistent: talent that is excluded or underused reduces productive capacity.

Young people also need more than encouragement to become entrepreneurs. Some will build businesses, but many will seek dependable paid work. Entrepreneurship cannot substitute for functioning labor markets, capable firms, and public services. A realistic strategy values initiative without transferring the responsibility for structural problems onto individuals who have little capital or power.

Climate Resilience Belongs Inside Development Planning

Climate change is sometimes treated as an environmental issue separate from economic transformation. In practice, the two are intertwined. Rainfall and temperature affect agriculture and hydropower. Flooding can damage homes, roads, railways, schools, and drainage systems. Drought can weaken food production, water supplies, and electricity generation. Heat can reduce labor productivity and increase health risks.

The Intergovernmental Panel on Climate Change's assessment of Africa describes widespread risks to food and water security, ecosystems, health, settlements, infrastructure, and economies, with vulnerability shaped by poverty, inequality, governance, and limited adaptive capacity (Intergovernmental Panel on Climate Change, 2022). These risks differ sharply by location. A coastal city, a dryland farming community, and a highland power system do not face the same hazards.

Adaptation should therefore be built into ordinary development decisions. A road designed for future flood risk is both transport infrastructure and climate-resilient infrastructure. Efficient irrigation, soil management, early-warning systems, heat-aware urban planning, water storage, and more resilient electricity networks can protect earlier investments as well as future growth.

This does not mean labeling every project "climate" guarantees good results. As with other investments, plans must be tested against local evidence, cost, maintenance needs, and the people most exposed to harm. Climate resilience strengthens development when it improves the durability and fairness of the systems on which communities depend.

There Is No Single African Model

The systems described in this chapter are broadly relevant, but their design cannot be identical everywhere. Africa is not one economy. Botswana is not Ethiopia. Nigeria is not Mauritius. Morocco is not Rwanda. Egypt is not Ghana. Kenya is not Angola. Countries differ in geography, population, resources, institutions, history, income, infrastructure, and relations with neighboring markets.

A landlocked agricultural economy will make different choices from a coastal mineral exporter. A small island state cannot pursue the same industrial scale as a country with a population of more than 100 million. A nation with abundant hydropower faces a different energy problem from one dependent on imported fuel. Conflict-affected regions must often rebuild security and basic administration while other places are deciding how to regulate advanced digital services.

Experience can still travel. One country may offer useful lessons in power auctions, agricultural extension, port management, mobile finance, school reform, or public procurement. But a lesson is not a template. Policymakers must ask why an intervention worked, what institutions supported it, which costs were hidden, and whether the relevant conditions exist elsewhere.

The same caution applies to "success stories." A country may improve one indicator while struggling on another. Growth can rise without creating enough decent work. Exports can expand while domestic linkages remain weak. School enrollment can improve while learning stagnates. A new railway can increase capacity yet fail to cover operating costs. Honest analysis should recognize progress without turning it into mythology.

From Potential to Capability

Across Chapters 8 through 11, one distinction has become increasingly important. Population is not the same as human capital. Minerals are not the same as industry. Sunlight is not the same as electricity. Cultivable land is not the same as agricultural productivity. A trade agreement is not the same as trade. A road is not the same as a functioning transport system. School attendance is not the same as learning. Investment is not automatically productive investment.

Potential describes what may be possible. Capability describes what people, firms, and institutions can reliably do.

Building capability requires coordination, but not perfect coordination. Countries do not have to repair every weakness before progress can begin. They can identify binding constraints, improve them, measure the results, and adjust. A reliable power connection may allow firms to expand. Better customs procedures may make a corridor more valuable. Stronger foundational learning may improve later training. Transparent procurement may increase the value obtained from infrastructure spending. Each improvement can create room for the next.

The sequence will differ from place to place, and setbacks are inevitable. What matters is whether policies produce services and institutions that continue to function after the initial funding, political attention, or public ceremony has passed. Transformation is not a moment. It is the accumulation of productive capabilities and the widening of access to them.

Some of this work is already visible. Electricity is being traded across regional grids, and selected transport corridors have reduced travel time and costs. Governments and regional institutions are putting new trade and infrastructure arrangements into operation. These developments should not be inflated into a claim that transformation is complete. They do establish that change can be observed where institutions and systems are actually implemented.

Chapter 12 turns to that evidence. Where can measurable change already be seen across the continent? Which outcomes represent durable improvement, which remain early or uneven, and what does the available evidence allow us to conclude?

Evidence Note

This chapter distinguishes observed results from plans, projections, and continental estimates. Infrastructure-cost figures are presented as planning ranges rather than fixed annual requirements. Project results are dated and geographically specific; they should not be generalized to Africa as a whole. The discussion also avoids treating education, governance, trade, finance, demography, or infrastructure as single-cause explanations for development. The cited evidence supports relationships among capabilities and economic conditions, but outcomes remain dependent on local institutions, implementation, geography, distribution, and external events.

CHAPTER 12

Africa in Motion

Evidence of Measurable Change Across the Continent

Chapter 11 argued that transformation depends on connected capabilities. Electricity must reach the factory, training must match the work, roads must connect to ports, and agreements must be carried out by institutions that people and businesses can rely on. That argument raises a practical question: where can such change already be seen?

The answer cannot be reduced to a list of new projects. A dam may be enormous without supplying reliable power to every household. A trade agreement may enter into force while businesses still face delays at borders. An export industry may grow while many workers remain excluded from opportunity. Announcements tell us what governments and institutions intend to do. Evidence tells us what has actually changed, where it changed, and for whom.

Across Africa, the record is mixed, but it is not empty. Manufacturing networks have taken root in places once known mainly for primary exports. Mobile finance has changed how millions of people move money. Countries have developed energy systems around their own natural advantages. Long-term diversification has altered the structure of some economies. Regional institutions are building the practical machinery needed for electricity trade, payments, public health coordination, and continental commerce.

None of these developments proves that Africa has completed an economic transformation. They show something more useful: change becomes measurable when policy, infrastructure, institutions, skills, and firms begin to work together. The strongest examples are not miracles and should not be treated as templates. They are evidence from which other societies can learn.

How to Read Evidence of Change

The language of development often moves faster than the evidence. A project is announced and immediately described as transformative. A target is repeated until it begins to sound like an achievement. A single success is presented as the story of an entire country. These habits create excitement, but they weaken understanding.

Measurable change requires a clearer sequence. First, establish the condition being examined. Then identify an observed result, such as export earnings, electricity generated, travel time reduced, or a service actually used. Next, ask how policy and institutions contributed. Finally, examine the limitations. This approach does not drain hope from the story. It protects hope from exaggeration.

The date matters. So does the geographic scale. A result measured in one corridor cannot describe a whole region. A figure for sub-Saharan Africa does not automatically apply to North Africa, and a program involving African Union member states should not be described as though every country has implemented it in the same way. Even familiar words such as *access*, *capacity*, and *trade* require care. Installed generating capacity is not the same as electricity delivered. Legal access to a market is not the same as a shipment crossing a border.

With those cautions in place, it becomes possible to recognize progress without turning it into mythology.

Morocco: Manufacturing as a Network

Morocco's automotive industry shows how productive capacity can emerge from a connected system rather than a single factory. Vehicle assembly attracted public attention, but assembly alone does not explain the industry's growth. The wider network includes component suppliers, industrial zones, port and road logistics, vocational training, export procedures, and relationships with European and African markets. Renault and Stellantis operate plants in the country, while suppliers manufacture wiring, seats, batteries, and other components. Tanger Med gives producers access to a major logistics platform near important shipping routes.

The result is visible in trade data. Morocco's Office des Changes reported automotive exports of 157.6 billion Moroccan dirhams in 2024, an increase of 6.3 percent from the previous year. Automotive products remained the country's largest export category, well ahead of phosphate and derivative exports at 87.1 billion dirhams (Office des Changes, 2025). These figures do not show how much value remains in Morocco after imported inputs and foreign-owned firms are considered. They do establish that automotive manufacturing has become a major part of the country's export economy.

The lesson is not that every African country should manufacture cars. Automotive production demands scale, precise quality standards, reliable logistics, trained labor, and access to large markets. The lesson is about coordination. Investors were not responding only to low wages or a tax incentive. They were responding to a production environment in which several necessary pieces had been assembled over time.

Morocco's energy strategy offers a related example of ambition joined to physical investment. The Noor-Ouarzazate solar complex has a capacity of 580 megawatts. The World Bank described it as part of a national plan to obtain 52 percent of installed electricity capacity from renewable sources by 2030 (World Bank, 2018). That 52 percent is a target, not a completed result. The complex itself is real infrastructure, but its broader significance depends on grid integration, cost, operation, and the performance of the energy system around it.

Taken together, manufacturing and energy illustrate the difference between an isolated asset and a productive network. A port does not create an export industry by itself. A solar complex does not settle every energy problem. Their value grows when they are connected to firms, skills, finance, regulation, and markets.

Kenya: Innovation Built Around Daily Needs

Kenya's M-PESA is often described as a technological success, but technology alone is an incomplete explanation. Safaricom launched the service in March 2007, allowing users to send and store small amounts of money through ordinary mobile phones. The service spread rapidly because it addressed a common problem: many people needed a safe and convenient way to transfer money, including between cities and rural communities, without depending on a nearby bank branch (Mas & Radcliffe, 2010).

The phone was only one part of the system. M-PESA also depended on an agent network that allowed customers to convert cash into electronic value and back again. Brand recognition, regulation, pricing, customer trust, and the usefulness of the service to families and small businesses all mattered. The innovation succeeded because the commercial model was adapted to conditions in Kenya rather than copied from a banking system designed for another setting.

Its wider influence is clear. Mobile money expanded across African markets, although no two systems followed exactly the same path. In some countries, competition among providers drove adoption. Elsewhere, regulation, limited agent coverage, low trust, or weak telecommunications constrained growth. Kenya's experience therefore offers a principle, not a formula: innovation becomes transformative when it solves a real problem and is supported by a network people can actually use.

Kenya's power sector shows the same attention to local conditions in a different field. The country has developed geothermal resources in and around the Rift Valley, including the Olkaria fields. In 2023, nearly 90 percent of Kenya's electricity generation came from renewable sources. Geothermal supplied 47 percent, hydropower 21 percent, wind 16 percent, and solar 4 percent, according to the International Energy Agency (2024). The country's installed geothermal capacity was about 950 megawatts.

Geothermal power is especially valuable because it can generate continuously rather than only when the sun shines or the wind blows. It is not universally available, however, and exploration and drilling require technical skill and capital. Kenya's achievement rests partly on geology, but geology became productive capacity only through investment, expertise, institutions, and a grid capable of using the power.

These two Kenyan examples may appear unrelated. One concerns digital payments and the other electricity. Yet both reveal the same discipline: begin with an actual need, work with the conditions that exist, and build the surrounding system required for the solution to endure.

Ethiopia: The Power and Limits of Scale

Few recent African infrastructure projects match the scale or political significance of Ethiopia's Grand Ethiopian Renaissance Dam. Built on the Blue Nile near the Sudanese border, the project has an installed generating capacity of 5,150 megawatts. Ethiopia officially inaugurated the dam on September 9, 2025 (Reuters, 2025; Webuild, n.d.). Its financing relied heavily on domestic public resources and bond purchases, a feature that gave the project unusual national significance. For a country seeking to expand electricity supply and exports, the dam represents engineering capability, sustained financing, and an investment carried across many years.

Scale, however, must be interpreted carefully. Installed capacity indicates what the generating units are designed to produce under suitable conditions. It does not mean that 5,150 megawatts will be delivered continuously, nor does it measure how quickly households and firms will receive reliable service. Transmission networks, distribution systems, utility finances, maintenance, rainfall, and demand all affect the economic result.

The dam also exists within a shared river system. Egypt and Sudan have raised concerns about water security, reservoir filling, and rules for drought periods. Ethiopia has emphasized its need for development and electricity. These positions cannot be understood responsibly by describing the project only as a national triumph or only as a regional threat. The Blue Nile crosses political borders, so durable management requires data, negotiation, and arrangements that participating countries consider credible.

The evidence supports two conclusions at once. Ethiopia has completed infrastructure of continental significance, and the full developmental value of that infrastructure will depend on systems beyond the dam wall. Recognizing both is not indecision. It is a more honest account of what large projects can and cannot accomplish.

Botswana and Mauritius: Change Across Decades

Some of the clearest evidence of transformation appears not in a recent announcement but across several decades. Botswana and Mauritius followed different paths, yet both show how policy and institutions can alter an economy's possibilities over time.

At independence in 1966, Botswana had limited infrastructure and a small formal economy. Diamond discoveries changed its fiscal position, but minerals did not govern themselves. The country used diamond revenue to finance public services and infrastructure while maintaining a long period of political stability and comparatively strong public institutions. The World Bank's 2023 systematic country diagnostic describes the combination of natural resource wealth and institutions as central to Botswana's rise to upper-middle-income status (World Bank, 2023).

This record deserves recognition, but it should not be romanticized. Botswana remains highly dependent on diamonds. That dependence leaves growth and public revenue exposed to changing global demand, while unemployment, inequality, limited private-sector development, and the need for deeper diversification remain serious concerns. The country's success in managing resource revenue does not mean it has escaped the problem of economic concentration.

Mauritius began from a different position. Its small size, distance from major markets, limited natural resources, and dependence on sugar once appeared to offer little room for development. Over time, it expanded into textile manufacturing, tourism, financial and professional services, real estate, and other activities. The World Bank now describes Mauritius as an upper-middle-income economy with a diversified base rather than the low-income sugar producer it once was (World Bank, 2026a).

Diversification did not eliminate vulnerability. As a small island state, Mauritius remains exposed to external demand, import dependence, cyclones, rising seas, and other climate risks. The World Bank has also argued that the state-led model that supported earlier gains has reached limits and requires renewal. Again, two truths can coexist: economic structure changed substantially, and the next stage of development presents new constraints.

Botswana and Mauritius are often discussed together, but their value as examples lies precisely in their differences. Botswana's path was shaped by diamonds, public revenue management, and a landlocked geography. Mauritius used trade preferences, manufacturing, services, and its island position. Neither path can be transferred whole to another country. What can travel is the habit of using today's advantage to build capabilities that remain useful when conditions change.

South Africa: Capability Without Broad Inclusion

Evidence of productive capacity does not always amount to evidence of shared progress. South Africa has one of the continent's most diversified industrial and service bases. It has major financial institutions, universities, mines, manufacturers, farms, ports, and technology firms. Its companies operate across African markets, and its scientific and professional communities possess considerable expertise.

At the same time, exclusion remains severe. Statistics South Africa reported an official unemployment rate of 33.6 percent in the second quarter of 2026, with 8.5 million people unemployed. The broader measure that includes the potential labor force was 43.8 percent (Statistics South Africa, 2026). Those national figures also conceal sharp differences by age, sex, race, education, and location.

The contrast is important. South Africa does not lack every capability; it struggles to translate substantial capability into sufficiently broad employment, reliable services, and rising living standards. Weak growth, electricity and logistics problems, spatial inequality, and the continuing effects of apartheid all shape that outcome. The World Bank reported in 2025 that real gross domestic product per person was near its 2007 level after a decade of average annual economic growth of only 0.7 percent (World Bank, 2025b).

This is a warning against reading development from a skyline, stock exchange, or group of successful firms. An economy may contain advanced sectors while large numbers of people remain outside them. Transformation must be judged not only by what a country can produce, but by how widely people can participate in productive life.

From National Examples to Regional Systems

National capability matters, but many African problems cross borders. Electricity networks, transport corridors, river basins, payments, disease surveillance, and trade all depend on cooperation among governments and institutions. Chapter 11 examined how power pools and cross-border transmission can turn separate national grids into a more useful regional system. The evidence is already visible. More than 4,000 kilometers of high-voltage lines now connect grids across fifteen West African countries, while the Ethiopia-Kenya electricity highway allows bidirectional transfers of up to 2,000 megawatts (World Bank, 2025a, 2026b).

These links do not end national power shortages. They make an additional capability possible: electricity can move across a border when systems, contracts, and operators are aligned. That distinction applies equally to other forms of integration.

The Pan-African Payment and Settlement System, known as PAPSS, was commercially launched in Accra on January 13, 2022. It provides infrastructure through which participating banks and payment providers can settle eligible cross-border transactions in national currencies (PAPSS, 2022). The system is not a single African currency, and its launch did not place every bank or every transaction on one platform. Its significance is practical. Traders should not always have to route an intra-African payment through a third currency and distant correspondent banks.

The African Continental Free Trade Area provides a broader legal framework. The agreement entered into force on May 30, 2019, and trading under its rules formally commenced on January 1, 2021 (African Union, n.d.). Those dates mark institutional progress. They do not mean that Africa instantly became one frictionless market. The gap between legal commitment and daily commercial practice remains substantial, and Chapter 13 will examine that work more closely.

Regional cooperation is not limited to commerce. Africa Centres for Disease Control and Prevention was established by the African Union Assembly in January 2016 and officially launched in January 2017. Its mandate includes disease surveillance, laboratory capacity, emergency preparedness, and coordination among member states (Africa CDC, n.d.). Epidemics do not stop at customs posts. Shared surveillance and rapid exchange of information therefore provide a regional public good even when national health systems remain responsible for care.

These institutions are at different stages and should not be measured by the same indicator. A power line can be assessed through electricity flows. A payment platform can be assessed through participation and transactions. A trade area must ultimately be judged through business use, reduced barriers, and changing trade patterns. A public health body is tested by surveillance, coordination, and response. What connects them is the movement from continental intention toward an operating system.

Learning Across African Borders

African countries often look beyond the continent for policy ideas, finance, technology, and training. There is value in doing so. No region has a monopoly on useful knowledge. Yet the examples in this chapter show why learning within Africa deserves equal seriousness.

Kenya's mobile-money experience can help other regulators and providers think about agents, trust, and practical access, but it cannot be copied without regard to market structure. Morocco's automotive network can inform discussions of industrial coordination, but countries without similar logistics or market access will need a different strategy. Botswana's management of mineral revenue offers lessons in public institutions, yet a country facing conflict or weak revenue administration begins elsewhere. Mauritius shows the value of moving into new activities, but island tourism and financial services cannot employ every continent-sized population.

Responsible learning asks why a result occurred. Which institutions carried the work? What incentives shaped behavior? What did the project cost? Who benefited and who did not? Which conditions were unique, and which can be created elsewhere? It also asks what went wrong. A polished success narrative can be dangerous if it hides debt, environmental damage, displacement, inequality, or dependence on favorable external conditions.

Learning should move in more than one direction. National governments can study cities and provinces within their own borders. Larger economies can learn from smaller states that have developed capable specialist institutions. Anglophone, Francophone, Lusophone, Arabic-speaking, and other African communities can exchange evidence without assuming that administrative traditions make their experiences incomparable. Regional organizations can help preserve and spread this knowledge, but only if they evaluate performance honestly.

The purpose is not to discover an African formula. It is to deepen the continent's capacity to compare experience, adapt ideas, and correct mistakes without waiting for outside institutions to define what counts as knowledge.

Progress Is Real, Uneven, and Reversible

The examples in this chapter do not add up to one verdict on Africa. They cannot. Morocco's export manufacturing, Kenya's digital finance and geothermal power, Ethiopia's dam, Botswana's resource management, Mauritius's diversification, and South Africa's industrial depth emerged from different histories and face different limits. Continental institutions add another layer, linking countries that do not share the same capacities or pace of implementation.

What the evidence permits is a set of narrower conclusions. Productive change is possible when assets are joined to institutions and skills. Local conditions can become advantages when people invest in the systems needed to use them. Diversification is usually cumulative and takes time. Large projects can expand national capability while creating new financial, environmental, or diplomatic responsibilities. Regional agreements matter most when they alter the practical experience of households, firms, and public institutions.

Progress can also reverse. Infrastructure deteriorates when maintenance is postponed. Skills are lost when trained people cannot find meaningful work. Firms close when electricity, finance, or logistics fail. Institutional trust can weaken quickly under corruption, political interference, or selective enforcement. A successful export sector can suffer when global demand changes. Climate shocks can damage gains accumulated over decades.

This is why measurable change should produce neither complacency nor cynicism. Celebration without scrutiny turns projects into symbols. Cynicism dismisses evidence simply because it is incomplete. A more useful position is disciplined confidence: recognize what has worked, specify what remains uncertain, and keep testing whether benefits are durable and widely shared.

Africa is in motion, but motion is not the same as direction. The continent's future will depend on whether separate advances become connected systems. A factory needs markets beyond one border. A power plant becomes more valuable when electricity can be traded. A payment platform matters when businesses can use it alongside workable customs and transport. Public health coordination depends on national institutions that can detect and report threats.

Chapter 13 turns to that next challenge. It examines what it would take to connect Africa more fully, moving from a continental vision toward a functioning market in which goods, services, people, payments, energy, and ideas can travel with fewer unnecessary barriers.

Evidence Note

This chapter distinguishes observed outcomes from installed capacity, policy targets, formal launch dates, and intended benefits. Country examples are dated and specific; none is presented as representative of Africa as a whole. Export totals do not measure domestic value retained, installed megawatts do not measure continuous delivery, and the entry into force of an agreement does not establish full implementation. The discussion identifies documented relationships among policy, institutions, infrastructure, and economic activity, while recognizing that causation is rarely attributable to a single intervention. Statistics may be revised after publication, and conditions can change.

CHAPTER 13

Connecting Africa

From Continental Vision to a Functioning Market

Chapter 12 examined evidence of change already visible across Africa. Factories, power projects, payment systems, transport corridors, and regional institutions show that transformation is not merely an idea. Yet separate advances do not automatically form a continental economy.

A manufacturer can produce a good product and still be unable to reach customers across a nearby border. A farmer can live closer to a market in another country than to the capital of her own, yet face more difficulty selling across that border. A software company may serve clients online but struggle to receive payment from another African market. In each case, production is only part of the problem. The connections are missing, expensive, or unpredictable.

This is the practical meaning of African integration. It is not the disappearance of countries, nor does it require every government to adopt identical policies. It means reducing unnecessary barriers so that goods, services, payments, electricity, investment, people, and ideas can move more easily where agreements permit them to move.

The African Continental Free Trade Area is the most ambitious legal framework yet created for that purpose. Its importance is difficult to overstate, but it is also easy to exaggerate. A signed agreement can establish rules and direction. It cannot clear a delayed truck, build a railway, settle a payment, certify a product, or make a business competitive. Those results depend on implementation.

The central question of this chapter is therefore not whether Africa has a continental vision. It does. The harder question is whether that vision can become an ordinary commercial experience for the people who produce, transport, sell, buy, finance, and regulate African goods and services.

What the AfCFTA Is, and What It Is Not

The Agreement Establishing the African Continental Free Trade Area was adopted in Kigali, Rwanda, on 21 March 2018. It entered into force on 30 May 2019. The operational phase was launched in Niamey, Niger, in July 2019, and trading under the AfCFTA regime formally began on 1 January 2021 (African Union, n.d.-a).

The agreement is often described as a free-trade agreement, but its architecture reaches beyond tariffs on physical goods. It includes trade in services, customs cooperation, trade facilitation, dispute settlement, and rules of origin. Later protocols address investment, competition policy, intellectual property rights, digital trade, and women and youth in trade. The stated direction is a progressively more integrated African market, not an instant borderless economy (African Union, 2018, 2024).

That word *progressively* matters. Countries do not eliminate every tariff on the same day. Product exclusions and sensitive categories exist. Services commitments are negotiated by sector. Domestic laws, customs systems, tariff schedules, and administrative practices must be aligned. Businesses then have to learn the rules and decide whether using them is commercially worthwhile.

Participation also has more than one meaning. A government may sign an agreement, approve ratification through its domestic process, deposit an instrument of ratification with the African Union, publish the necessary tariff schedule, and begin preferential trade at different times. These stages should not be collapsed into a single number.

The African Union's depositary status list dated 22 May 2026 recorded 54 signatures and 49 deposited ratifications among its 55 member states (African Union, 2026). Some public statements use a higher ratification count because they include domestic approvals that had not yet been deposited. Neither count proves that all participating countries are implementing every part of the agreement. The honest description is that legal participation is broad, while operational readiness remains uneven.

That gap should not be treated as evidence that the project has failed. Large trade agreements take time to negotiate and apply. But it should prevent us from confusing institutional progress with a completed market.

The Product Needs a Passport

Tariff preferences cannot work until customs officials can answer a basic question: where did this product come from?

Consider a company that imports a finished appliance from outside Africa, replaces the packaging in an African country, and sends it to a second African country. If repackaging alone qualified the appliance for tariff-free treatment, businesses could route outside goods through whichever country offered the easiest entry and claim African preferences without creating meaningful production on the continent.

Rules of origin are designed to prevent that outcome. They set the conditions a product must satisfy to be treated as originating within the free-trade area. Depending on the product, the test may involve where it was wholly obtained, how its tariff classification changed, how much local or regional value was added, or whether specified production processes occurred (African Union, 2022).

The rules also allow forms of cumulation. In practical terms, qualifying inputs from one participating African country can contribute to the originating status of a product completed in another. A clothing producer, for example, should not have to grow cotton, spin yarn, weave fabric, design garments, and sew them all within one national border for regional production to count. Properly designed rules can encourage firms in several countries to form a supply chain.

Rules of origin therefore serve two purposes that can pull in different directions. They protect the preference from simple transshipment, and they must remain workable enough for legitimate producers to use. If the rules are too weak, they may fail to support African production. If they are too complex or costly to prove, smaller firms may avoid the preference altogether.

This is where a technical provision becomes a business question. Can a producer identify the correct rule? Can it document its inputs? Can the relevant authority issue a certificate without unreasonable delay? Will customs officials on the other side interpret the rule consistently? A preference that exists only on paper has little value to a firm trying to deliver an order on time.

The Cost of Friction

Tariffs are visible because they appear as a charge. Many other trade costs are less visible but just as real.

A shipment may require duplicate documents from several agencies. A food product may pass one country's safety test and then need another test across the border. A truck may wait while officials repeat an inspection already completed at the departure point. A trader may not know which rule applies until the goods arrive. A payment may pass through correspondent banks outside Africa before reaching a seller in a neighboring country.

None of these problems is solved simply by reducing a customs duty to zero.

UN Trade and Development reported that intra-African trade accounted for about 16 percent of Africa's total recorded trade in its *Economic Development in Africa Report 2024*. The figure depends on the reporting period and denominator, and some informal cross-border exchange is not fully captured. The broad conclusion is nevertheless clear: most of Africa's recorded international trade still takes place with economies outside the continent (UN Trade and Development, 2024).

This pattern has historical, geographic, and economic causes. Colonial transport networks often connected mines and plantations to ports rather than neighboring African markets. Many economies continue to export commodities while importing manufactured goods. Production structures can be similar rather than complementary. Small national markets limit scale. Conflict and political mistrust disrupt routes. High transport costs make a nearby country commercially distant.

An agreement can change incentives, but it does not erase these conditions. Its value will be determined by whether countries lower the combined cost of crossing a border: money, time, paperwork, uncertainty, and risk.

Predictability deserves special attention. A business can plan around a known fee or a reliable two-hour process. It is much harder to plan when a border crossing may take two hours one week and two days the next. Uncertainty forces firms to hold more inventory, promise slower delivery, or abandon a market. For a small business with limited cash, one delayed shipment can be the difference between profit and loss.

Infrastructure Is Part of Trade Policy

Trade rules travel in legal documents. Goods travel on roads, railways, ships, and aircraft. The difference is obvious, yet infrastructure is often discussed as though it were separate from trade policy.

The United Nations Economic Commission for Africa (UNECA) modeled the transport demand that AfCFTA implementation could generate by 2030. Its estimates suggested that road freight could rise from 201 million to 403 million tonnes and intra-African maritime freight from 58 million to 131.5 million tonnes. It also estimated that planned projects could add almost 26,500 kilometers to the continent's rail network (UNECA, 2022).

These figures are projections, not a count of freight already moving or railway already built. Their value lies in the warning they provide. If trade grows while transport capacity remains fixed, congestion and delay may replace tariffs as the binding constraint.

Africa's geography makes the problem uneven. Landlocked countries depend on corridors through neighboring states to reach ports. Island states depend heavily on shipping and aviation. Large countries may face long internal journeys before a product reaches any border. Mountainous terrain, deserts, seasonal flooding, and insecurity affect routes differently. There is no single continental transport solution.

Corridors are useful because they connect systems rather than isolated assets. A functioning corridor may include a port, road and rail links, border posts, storage facilities, digital tracking, customs cooperation, and access for communities along the route. The African Development Bank reported that, by 2022, it had financed 25 transport corridors, more than 18,000 kilometers of roads, 27 border posts, and 16 bridges, representing about $13.5 billion in investment (African Development Bank Group, 2025).

Those numbers describe financing and construction, not the quality of every journey. A new road can reduce travel time, but maintenance, safety, checkpoints, border procedures, and the condition of connecting roads still matter. Infrastructure becomes economically valuable when it links production to a usable market and continues to function after the opening ceremony.

Railways present a similar challenge. Networks in many countries were built to carry particular commodities from the interior to a port.

Gauges differ, missing links remain, and neighboring systems are not always interoperable. Completing a line is only one step. Freight operators also need rolling stock, reliable schedules, terminals, maintenance, and agreements that allow cargo to continue across borders.

Maritime transport should not be treated only as Africa's connection with Europe, Asia, or the Americas. Coastal shipping can link African ports and reduce pressure on roads, especially for bulky cargo. Yet routes, vessel availability, port charges, dwell times, and transshipment patterns determine whether sea transport is practical for an intra-African shipment.

The same principle applies across every mode: a route is not integrated because it appears on a map. It is integrated when a shipment can complete the journey at a cost and level of reliability that make trade possible.

A Border Can Protect and Facilitate

The purpose of trade facilitation is not to remove legitimate border controls. Governments still have to collect lawful revenue, enforce immigration rules, prevent smuggling, protect public health, and inspect animal and plant products. The problem begins when agencies perform these functions in ways that are repetitive, opaque, or unpredictable.

A better border process can include electronic documentation, information submitted before arrival, coordinated inspections, risk-based controls, and one-stop border posts where agencies from neighboring countries work in a shared or closely linked process. Low-risk shipments can move quickly while officials concentrate attention on higher-risk cases.

Standards require the same balance. Product standards protect consumers and make markets more trustworthy. A medicine, electrical cable, or packaged food should not escape necessary scrutiny in the name of speed. But businesses face needless expense when countries require different tests for the same characteristic or refuse to recognize a credible result from a neighboring jurisdiction.

Harmonization does not always mean one identical rule for every country. It may mean agreement on common minimums, mutual recognition of equivalent systems, shared laboratories, or compatible digital records. The goal is to preserve protection while removing duplication that serves no clear public purpose.

The Guided Trade Initiative has helped countries and businesses test AfCFTA procedures while wider implementation continues. It began with seven countries, and the AfCFTA Secretary-General reported in September 2024 that participation had expanded to 39 (Pan-African Parliament, 2024). That is meaningful operational progress. It is still a guided pathway, not proof that ordinary trade across all participating markets has become seamless.

Payments Are Trade Infrastructure

A sale is not complete when the goods arrive. The seller must be paid.

Cross-border payments within Africa often involve different currencies, banking rules, settlement systems, and levels of financial access. In some transactions, money has historically been converted through a major international currency and routed through correspondent banks outside the continent. Each step can add cost, delay, and foreign-exchange risk.

The Pan-African Payment and Settlement System, or PAPSS, was developed by the African Export-Import Bank in collaboration with the

African Union Commission and the AfCFTA Secretariat. It was commercially launched in Accra on 13 January 2022. PAPSS does not create a single African currency. It provides infrastructure intended to help participating financial institutions make eligible cross-border payments more directly while payers and recipients use their local currencies (PAPSS, 2022).

The network has expanded, but it is not yet universal. After the Bank of Central African States joined in July 2026, PAPSS reported connections across 28 African countries, more than 190 commercial banks and fintechs, and 16 switches. It also said participants could reach more than 250 additional financial institutions through extended network partners (PAPSS, 2026).

These are network-coverage figures, not measures of how frequently every business uses the system, what each transaction costs, or whether service is equally available in every connected country. Those questions require transaction and user evidence. Still, the expansion shows that payment integration is moving from concept toward operating infrastructure.

For a business, the practical test is simple. Can a customer pay in a familiar currency? Can the seller receive funds promptly and understand the exchange rate and fees? Can the transaction be reconciled, refunded, and trusted? Continental trade will remain difficult if the movement of money lags behind the movement of goods and services.

Regional Communities Are the Starting Structure

African integration did not begin with AfCFTA. Regional organizations had already developed trade arrangements, movement rules, infrastructure programs, and institutions. The African Union recognizes eight Regional Economic Communities as building blocks of the African Economic Community: the Arab Maghreb Union, COMESA, CEN-SAD, the East African Community, ECCAS, ECOWAS, IGAD, and SADC (African Union, n.d.-b).

This inherited structure offers experience and working institutions. A customs process that already functions within a region does not need to be discarded merely because a continental agreement exists. Regional power pools, corridor authorities, courts, standards bodies, and trade systems can provide a base for wider integration.

The same structure also creates complexity. Several countries belong to more than one regional community, and regional rules do not always match. Tariff schedules, rules of origin, movement rights, and administrative practices may overlap. A continental market must therefore connect existing arrangements without making the rulebook impossible for traders to understand.

The best result would not be a choice between regional and continental integration. Regions can move faster where cooperation is already deep, while continental rules can make those regional markets more compatible with one another. The principle developed earlier in this book remains useful: build nationally, connect regionally, compete globally.

Trade in Goods Does Not Equal Free Movement of People

AfCFTA is sometimes discussed as though it gives every African the right to live and work anywhere on the continent. It does not.

The African Union adopted a separate Protocol on Free Movement of Persons, Right of Residence and Right of Establishment on 29 January 2018. The AU status list dated 8 August 2023 recorded 32 signatures and only four deposited ratifications (African Union, 2023). The age of that status list should be stated openly, but it demonstrates a clear legal difference: progress on continent-wide mobility has been much slower than progress on the trade agreement.

Movement of people raises questions that a tariff schedule cannot answer. Governments consider labor-market effects, professional licensing, residence rights, social protection, security, documentation, and public services. Regional arrangements already permit different degrees of mobility, but those rights do not automatically apply across the entire continent.

This separation can create an economic contradiction. A country may want more trade in services while making it difficult for the engineer, installer, consultant, driver, artist, or technician providing that service to travel. Firms may be allowed to bid for work across a border but unable to deploy staff efficiently. Integration of goods, services, and people cannot be identical, yet the systems must be coherent enough to support real commerce.

Aviation is part of that coherence. The Single African Air Transport Market seeks to liberalize air services among participating states. Malawi became the thirty-eighth country to sign the solemn commitment in February 2025, a sign of broad but still incomplete participation (African Union, 2025). Better air links matter for tourism, but also for business travel, high-value cargo, professional services, family connections, and the movement of knowledge.

Electricity and Digital Services Cross Borders Too

Continental integration is larger than merchandise trade.

Electricity illustrates the point. Africa has regional power pools, and the African Union launched the African Single Electricity Market in 2021 as a framework for deeper continental power trade (African Union, 2021). One country may have hydropower available during a particular season, another may have geothermal generation, and another may develop solar or gas capacity. Cross-border trade can allow those different systems to support one another.

But electricity does not respond to a declaration. It requires transmission lines, synchronized or technically compatible grids, financially credible utilities, agreed prices, reliable settlement, and operators who coordinate in real time. The regional market is therefore both physical and institutional.

Digital trade removes some physical distance but creates its own borders. Software, design, professional advice, education, entertainment, and financial services can be delivered electronically. A small firm can reach customers in another country without a shipping container. It may still face uncertainty over consumer protection, electronic signatures, taxation, data governance, cybersecurity, licensing, and payment.

The AU adopted the AfCFTA Protocol on Digital Trade on 18 February 2024. Its objectives include more predictable rules, interoperability, secure digital commerce, and a common legal framework among State Parties (African Union, 2024). Adoption is the beginning of implementation. The commercial value will depend on domestic rules, affordable internet access, digital identity, payment links, trust, and the ability of regulators to cooperate.

These systems reinforce one another. Reliable electricity supports digital services. Digital customs can shorten a physical border process. Payment platforms can make both online and merchandise trade easier. Air transport can move people who deliver services that cannot be completed entirely online. Integration succeeds when the links work together.

The Market Must Work for Smaller Firms

Large companies can hire customs specialists, lawyers, logistics providers, and foreign-exchange experts. They can maintain stock while a shipment is delayed and spread compliance costs across many sales. Smaller firms usually cannot.

This creates a serious test for AfCFTA. If the system remains complicated, large firms may benefit first while micro, small, and medium-sized enterprises remain confined to local markets. The agreement may be continental, yet access to its opportunities could still be unequal.

The answer is not to exempt every small trader from necessary rules. It is to design procedures that a legitimate smaller business can understand and afford. Clear online information, simplified documentation for suitable consignments, transparent fees, accessible standards guidance, efficient dispute channels, and workable payment options all matter. So do roads from farms and workshops to the main corridor. A modern border post is of limited use to a producer who cannot reach it.

Informal cross-border trade must also be understood rather than treated as invisible. In many border communities, traders move food, clothing, household goods, and other products in small quantities. Women are prominent in many of these activities, although patterns differ by route and country. Official merchandise statistics may not record all of this exchange (United Nations Economic Commission for Africa, 2023).

Formalization can bring access to finance, legal protection, larger customers, and more reliable trade channels. It can also impose taxes, paperwork, and costs that a very small trader cannot bear. People will not enter a formal system simply because officials tell them to. The system must offer a benefit that justifies the cost.

Integration should therefore be judged from the bottom as well as the top. Can a small food processor find the tariff and origin rule for its product? Can a trader obtain the required document without paying an unofficial fee? Can a woman crossing a border report harassment safely? Can a new exporter receive payment and resolve a dispute? These questions reveal whether a continental market is becoming usable rather than merely impressive.

Opportunity Is Not a Guarantee

Trade liberalization creates opportunities and adjustments. It does not guarantee that every country, sector, company, or worker will gain at the same time.

Firms that are already productive may enter new markets quickly. Others may face stronger competition before they are ready. Governments that depend heavily on customs revenue may need time and administrative reform. Some workers may find opportunities in expanding industries while others face disruption in sectors that lose protection. Consumers may benefit from greater choice and lower prices, but those gains can be reduced when transport, market concentration, or currency weakness keeps costs high.

The distribution of gains is not a reason to reject integration. It is a reason to prepare for it. Countries need competition policy, adjustment support, social protection, skills development, and credible domestic institutions. Chapter 11 examined these capabilities in detail. AfCFTA can enlarge the field on which businesses compete; it cannot supply electricity to every factory, train every worker, finance every firm, or ensure that every court enforces a contract fairly.

Economic models help show what may be possible under stated assumptions. A 2022 World Bank report estimated that a trade and trade-facilitation scenario could raise Africa's real income by about 7 percent by 2035 and help 40 million people leave extreme poverty relative to the modeled baseline. A deeper-integration scenario that also included investment, competition, e-commerce, and intellectual-property policies estimated income gains of about 9 percent, or $571 billion, nearly 18 million additional jobs, and as many as 50 million fewer people in extreme poverty (World Bank, 2022).

These are scenarios, not promises. They depend on assumptions about implementation, investment, behavior, and the future economy. The reference point is a modeled baseline, not today's income or poverty count. Their most important message is not the precision of a number in 2035. It is that reducing tariffs alone produces less benefit than combining trade reform with lower non-tariff barriers, better facilitation, and deeper institutional cooperation.

From Selling Products to Building Supply Chains

Continental integration matters most when it changes what African economies produce together.

Trade can consist largely of finished goods moving from one producer to one consumer. It can also connect firms through intermediate goods, the materials and components used to make something else. Yarn becomes fabric. Fabric becomes clothing. Refined chemicals become medicines or fertilizer. Steel becomes machinery. Packaging, software, transport, finance, and professional services support the physical product.

No country has to produce every input. A firm can specialize in one stage while buying from suppliers elsewhere. That is how regional value chains can give smaller economies a place in production that would be difficult to build entirely within their own borders.

The possibility should not be romanticized. A supply chain chooses locations according to cost, quality, reliability, skills, energy, logistics, policy, and risk. A regional label will not keep an uncompetitive supplier in business. Nor should every raw material be processed in the country where it is extracted. Energy use, water, technology, scale, environmental damage, and transport all affect what is economically and socially sensible.

Larger regional markets can nevertheless change the calculation. A processing plant that cannot survive on one national market may become viable if it can serve several. Common standards can reduce the cost of producing for those markets. Rules of origin can reward regional inputs. Reliable transport and payments can turn potential demand into actual sales.

This is the connection between Chapter 10's discussion of value addition and the present chapter. Value addition is not only a national project. It can be distributed across countries, with each location contributing a capability. The more difficult task is to make those contributions fit together.

What a Functioning Market Would Feel Like

A functioning continental market would not be measured first by the number of declarations signed. It would be visible in ordinary transactions.

A producer would be able to identify the tariff, origin rule, and required documents before accepting an order. Customs agencies would receive information electronically and apply rules consistently. Necessary inspections would protect the public without being repeated simply because a border had been crossed. Transporters would know the route, charges, and expected crossing time. Payment would arrive through a trusted channel at a disclosed cost. A dispute would have a credible path toward resolution.

Infrastructure would connect production areas to regional corridors. Ports and rail terminals would work with roads rather than as isolated investments. Electricity could be traded where grids and agreements permit. Airlines would connect more African cities directly. Digital services would operate under rules that protect consumers while allowing legitimate cross-border business.

Most important, the system would not be usable only by large corporations. Smaller firms and traders would be able to find information, comply without hiring a team of specialists, and seek help when an official or private operator acted unfairly.

Not every border would become invisible. States would retain immigration laws, security responsibilities, public-health controls, and legitimate national interests. Integration would change how borders function. A border could become a place where lawful trade is recorded, assessed, and allowed to continue, rather than a point where uncertainty consumes time and money.

Africa's market will be built in summit halls, but it will be proven elsewhere: at customs windows, warehouses, testing laboratories, truck terminals, banks, airports, power-control rooms, mobile phones, and factory gates. That is where a continental vision meets the discipline of daily work.

The legal foundations are stronger than they were before AfCFTA. Preferential trade has begun, the Guided Trade Initiative has widened, payment infrastructure is expanding, and complementary frameworks for aviation, electricity, and digital trade are taking shape. At the same time, intra-African trade remains limited, physical and administrative connections are incomplete, and implementation differs widely among countries.

The evidence supports neither dismissal nor celebration without qualification. Africa has not yet created a fully functioning single market. It has created a serious framework and begun testing the machinery required to make it real.

The next stage depends on people as much as rules. Customs officers must understand the procedures. Engineers must build and maintain the connections. Entrepreneurs must identify opportunities. Regulators must cooperate. Workers must have the skills to produce goods and services that can compete. Chapter 14 turns to that human foundation, because no market can become more capable than the people who make it work.

Evidence Note

AfCFTA implementation changes over time and does not advance through one measure. This chapter distinguishes signature, domestic approval, deposited ratification, tariff readiness, and actual preferential trade. The AU depositary list dated 22 May 2026 is used for the formal count of deposited ratifications. The free-movement count comes from an AU status list dated 8 August 2023 and is identified as such. PAPSS coverage is dated July 2026. UNECA and World Bank figures are model estimates, not observed outcomes or guarantees. The intra-African trade share refers to recorded trade under UN Trade and Development's reported measure; other sources or periods may use exports as the denominator, and informal exchange may be undercounted.

CHAPTER 14

Africa's Greatest Resource Is Its People

Education, Health, Skills, Science, and the Capacity to Create

Chapter 13 ended at the point where a continental vision becomes daily work. Trade agreements need customs officers who understand the rules. Railways need engineers and technicians who can keep them running. Factories need skilled workers, reliable managers, and researchers who can improve what they produce. These capabilities do not appear because a government signs an agreement or discovers a deposit of copper, iron ore, oil, or natural gas.

Natural resources do not transform themselves. Land does not improve its own soil. A mineral deposit cannot decide whether it will leave the continent as raw ore or become an input for African manufacturing. Electricity does not maintain the grid that carries it. In every case, people supply the judgment, skill, labor, care, and imagination that turn an asset into something useful.

Calling people Africa's greatest resource is therefore a way of making an argument, not a statistical claim. It should not reduce human beings to units of production. People have worth that is not measured by wages, output, or national income. The deeper point is that development happens through human capability. A society becomes more able to shape its future when its people can learn, remain healthy, master difficult skills, ask questions, conduct research, create businesses, and participate in public life.

Africa's population passed 1.5 billion in 2024, according to the United Nations Economic Commission for Africa. Its future size will be significant, but size alone tells us very little about what that future will feel like. The more important questions are practical. Will a child learn to read well enough to keep learning? Will a young person find a path from school into useful work? Will a nurse have a functioning clinic in which to practice? Will a scientist have a laboratory, a research community, and the freedom to investigate? Will a woman with a good idea be able to obtain training, finance, and access to a market? Will digital technology allow Africans to create, or mainly invite them to consume what others have created?

The answers will differ from country to country and community to community. Yet one principle holds across the continent: population becomes possibility only when people have the means and the opportunity to develop what they can do.

A Young Continent, a Conditional Opportunity

Africa has the world's youngest population structure. That familiar statement can sound like a promise, but it is better understood as a responsibility. A large generation of children and young adults creates urgent demand for schools, teachers, health services, housing, transport, and eventually work. If these systems expand in quality as well as size, the continent can gain from a larger, healthier, and more capable working-age population. If they do not, demographic growth can intensify pressure on households, public services, and labor markets.

The idea of a *demographic dividend* is often used too casually. It does not mean that a young population automatically produces faster economic growth. It describes a possibility that may emerge when the share of working-age people rises relative to dependent age groups and when supportive conditions allow those people to be productive. Those conditions include health, education, employment, savings, investment, competent institutions, and meaningful participation by women. Age structure opens a window. Policy, economic change, and human choices determine what happens through it (United Nations Economic Commission for Africa, 2024).

This distinction matters because ***demographic confidence can easily become demographic complacency.*** It is not enough to say that Africa will supply the world's future workforce. A workforce has to be educated, healthy, skilled, connected, and able to find work that uses its capabilities. A population forecast cannot build those foundations.

The pressure is already visible in the scale of educational demand. The World Bank reported in 2024 that roughly 270 million children and adolescents were enrolled in primary and secondary education across sub-Saharan Africa. It also projected that, if countries were to reach universal education by 2030, systems would need to accommodate about 170 million additional learners, build millions of classrooms, and recruit millions of teachers. These are projections based on a policy goal, not a count of facilities already funded or under construction. Even so, they reveal the magnitude of the task (World Bank, 2024).

Numbers of this size can make the problem feel abstract. In practice, expansion is experienced one classroom at a time. It is a teacher facing sixty pupils, a family deciding whether it can afford transport, a rural student walking farther when the nearest school ends at the primary level, or a ministry trying to recruit teachers faster than trained candidates become available. Access matters, but the quality of what happens after a child enters the classroom matters just as much.

Schooling Must Become Learning

Africa has made important gains in school enrollment over several decades. More children are entering school, and more are progressing through it. Those gains should not be dismissed. For a family whose parents or grandparents were denied an education, a child entering a classroom can represent a profound change.

But attendance is not the same as learning. A student can spend years in school and still struggle to read a short passage, use basic mathematics, or explain an idea in writing. When that happens, every later stage of education becomes harder. Science textbooks assume literacy. Technical training assumes numeracy. Digital instruction assumes both. Foundational learning is not a narrow concern for primary schools. It is the platform on which the rest of an education system stands.

The World Bank defines *learning poverty* as being unable to read and understand a simple, age-appropriate text by about age ten. The measure combines the share of children who are out of school with evidence about reading among children who attend. A joint 2022 update by the World Bank and partner organizations estimated that learning poverty in sub-Saharan Africa may have reached about 89 percent after the disruption caused by COVID-19, compared with an already severe pre-pandemic estimate of 86 percent. These figures were modeled from data collected in different countries and years. They were not the result of one examination taken by every ten-year-old in the region. Even with that caution, the evidence points to a foundational learning crisis (World Bank et al., 2022).

The causes are not identical everywhere. Some schools lack books, electricity, safe buildings, or water. Some classrooms are overcrowded. Teachers may have limited training, delayed pay, or little support. Conflict displaces families and closes schools. Hunger makes concentration difficult. Children may be taught in a language they are still learning, while suitable materials in the language they know best are scarce. Disability can become exclusion when schools are inaccessible or teachers lack appropriate support. Poverty can pull children into work or keep girls at home when families cannot meet the direct and indirect costs of schooling.

That variety matters because a single reform will not solve every problem. Distributing textbooks can help where books are missing, but it will not reopen a school closed by conflict. Recruiting teachers can reduce crowding, but recruitment alone will not improve instruction if training and supervision remain weak. Testing can reveal what students know, but testing without support may only document failure more precisely.

A serious response begins with the classroom rather than the slogan. Teachers need clear curricula, useful materials, practical training, and time to help students who fall behind. Schools need leaders who can support instruction, not merely complete paperwork. Governments need assessment systems that reveal problems early and use the results to improve teaching. Families need confidence that the time and sacrifice invested in school will lead to real learning.

This is not an argument for reducing education to reading scores. Children should encounter history, science, art, civic life, physical education, and the ideas that help them understand themselves and the world. But if foundational literacy and numeracy are weak, access to that wider education becomes unequal. The child who cannot read fluently is present in the classroom but separated from much of what the classroom can offer.

The Foundations Begin Before Primary School

The learning challenge begins before a child enters Grade One. Early nutrition, health, language, play, safety, and responsive care shape readiness to learn. Children do not arrive at school with identical experiences, and a good education system cannot pretend that they do.

In 2024, the World Bank reported that seven in ten children in sub-Saharan Africa lacked access to pre-primary education. This regional figure does not describe every country, and access alone says nothing about the quality of a particular program. It does show how many children may begin primary school without the benefit of organized early learning (World Bank, 2024).

Pre-primary education should not become an academic race imposed on very young children. Its value lies in age-appropriate learning through language, movement, curiosity, social interaction, and play. It can also help identify hearing, vision, developmental, or nutritional problems before they silently undermine a child's progress.

The home remains important, but responsibility cannot be placed entirely on parents, especially where adults are working long hours, have limited literacy, or lack access to books and safe childcare. Community programs, health services, schools, and local-language materials can help families create a stronger beginning. An education system that waits until primary school to notice inequality has already waited too long.

Language deserves particular care. A child may think, joke, and understand complex relationships in one language while encountering formal schooling in another. Learning a national or international language can expand opportunity, but abrupt language transitions can also make a capable child appear incapable. Countries must make choices suited to their own linguistic realities. The guiding question should be whether language policy helps children understand what they are learning while gradually gaining access to wider communication.

More Than One Path to Expertise

Education is sometimes discussed as though its natural destination were a university degree. Universities are essential. They educate physicians, teachers, engineers, lawyers, economists, researchers, and many other professionals. They preserve knowledge, test ideas, and create new ones. A continent that wants scientific and technological capability needs strong universities.

Yet a modern economy also depends on expertise that is developed through technical and vocational education, apprenticeships, professional certification, and learning at work. The electrician who wires a clinic safely, the machinist who produces a precise component, the refrigeration technician who protects a food supply, and the mechanic who keeps a bus fleet moving all hold knowledge on which other people rely.

The World Bank reported in 2024 that fewer than 1.5 percent of people aged 15 to 24 in sub-Saharan Africa were enrolled in formal vocational education, compared with about 10 percent in high-income countries. The comparison does not capture every apprenticeship or informal path through which skills are learned. It does suggest that formal technical training remains limited relative to the scale of need (World Bank, 2024).

Expanding technical education should not mean treating it as a second-class destination for students who are assumed to have failed academically. That attitude damages both learners and economies. High-quality technical work requires judgment, mathematics, discipline, problem-solving, and continuous learning. Modern equipment changes. Safety standards improve. Digital systems enter occupations that once appeared entirely manual. The boundary between intellectual and practical work is far less rigid than educational hierarchies often suggest.

Training also has to be connected to real conditions. A college can advertise a program in solar installation, but students need equipment on which to practice, instructors who understand current systems, and employers or customers who value the qualification. A nursing program needs supervised clinical experience. Agricultural training has to respond to the crops, soils, water conditions, markets, and risks of the region it serves. Curricula cannot remain fixed while the economy changes around them.

Employers should participate without being allowed to narrow education to their immediate staffing needs. Businesses can help identify changing standards, offer placements, lend equipment, and explain where graduates struggle. Educators must also prepare students for a working life longer than any one job. A good program teaches a current skill and develops the ability to learn the next one.

There is no single curriculum for fifty-five African countries. A coastal economy developing port logistics will need a different mix of expertise from a landlocked agricultural economy, a mining center, or a city building a technology-services sector. National and local priorities must guide the balance. The common requirement is respect for competence, wherever it is developed.

Skills Need a Place to Work

Education policy cannot be separated from the structure of the economy. A country can train engineers, but engineers need firms, utilities, laboratories, construction projects, and public agencies where engineering is actually practiced. It can graduate scientists, but research careers will remain fragile without laboratories, funding, mentors, journals, equipment, and institutions willing to use evidence. It can train nurses, yet still leave communities underserved if public budgets cannot hire them or if jobs are concentrated far from where the need is greatest.

This is why the common question, "What should young Africans study?" has no simple answer. Students should not be promised that one fashionable degree guarantees employment. Nor should unemployment among graduates be used as proof that education has no value. The problem may lie in poor training, a weak labor market, a mismatch between fields of study and available work, discriminatory hiring, economic stagnation, or a combination of these.

Education has value beyond earnings. It can widen a person's choices, strengthen health decisions, improve participation in public life, and enrich the way people understand their society. At the same time, students and families are reasonable to expect that years of study will improve the chance of a dignified livelihood. When that connection repeatedly fails, frustration is not a moral weakness. It is evidence that educational expansion and economic transformation have moved out of step.

The informal economy must be part of this discussion. Many Africans create livelihoods outside formal wage employment. A tailor, mechanic, trader, builder, farmer, or repair technician may acquire considerable skill without a recognized certificate. Policy can support these workers through better apprenticeships, short upgrading courses, recognition of prior learning, safer workplaces, finance, and pathways into formal contracts. Treating informal work as if it contained no knowledge wastes experience that already exists.

Entrepreneurship is also important, but it should not become a polite way of telling every unemployed graduate to solve a structural employment problem alone. Starting a viable enterprise requires customers, capital, reliable power, transport, payment systems, enforceable contracts, and the ability to survive failure. Education can help people recognize and build opportunities. It cannot replace the wider environment in which a business must operate.

A capable economy creates a productive conversation between schools and work. Employers communicate emerging needs. Educators protect depth and quality. Governments invest in sectors with credible potential. Workers return for further training as technology changes. None of these actors can carry the whole burden alone.

Health Protects Human Capability

A child who is frequently ill misses' lessons. A parent living with untreated disease may lose income while also carrying the cost of care. A pregnancy without safe maternal services can become a family tragedy. Malnutrition can limit development before a child has a fair opportunity to learn. Health is therefore not a benefit that arrives after economic progress. It is one of the conditions that makes participation in education, work, and community life possible.

The long-term direction in the WHO African Region has been encouraging. According to the World Health Organization's regional data platform, life expectancy at birth rose from 53.0 years in 2000 to 63.6 years in 2021. Healthy life expectancy rose from 46.0 to 55.2 years over the same period. These are regional averages, and they do not describe every country or the effect of every disease outbreak. They nevertheless represent substantial progress in survival and years lived in better health (World Health Organization Regional Office for Africa, n.d.).

Progress came through many routes: vaccination, treatment of infectious diseases, improved maternal and child health, stronger surveillance, cleaner water in some communities, better knowledge, and wider access to services. It was not uniform, and it was not irreversible. Conflict can destroy facilities. An epidemic can exhaust workers and budgets. Climate-related shocks can alter disease patterns and food security. Weak supply systems can leave a clinic standing without essential medicines.

Health systems are often judged by visible buildings, but a building is only the shell. A functioning system needs trained people, laboratories, medicines, information, referral networks, ambulances, maintenance, electricity, water, financing, and public trust. A woman who reaches a clinic and finds no midwife has not received access in any meaningful sense. A laboratory machine that cannot be repaired is not capacity merely because it appears on an inventory.

Public health also extends beyond hospitals. Safe roads prevent injury. Clean air and water reduce illness. Nutrition, housing, sanitation, occupational safety, and reliable information shape health every day. The people who design cities, regulate food, teach children, inspect workplaces, and manage water systems all influence human capability, whether or not they wear a medical uniform.

The Health-Worker Paradox

Africa needs more health workers, but the problem is not solved by counting graduates.

The World Health Organization's *State of the Health Workforce in Africa 2026* estimated that the WHO African Region had 5.72 million health workers across twenty-seven occupational groups in 2024, including about 1.15 million community health workers. The report also estimated that the available workforce represented only 46 percent of the region's needs under its needs-based model. At the same time, it modeled a large pool of trained people who might be unemployed or not absorbed into appropriate work. The apparent contradiction is real: severe shortage can coexist with unemployment (World Health Organization Regional Office for Africa, 2026).

Several failures can produce this result. A ministry may need nurses but lack the budget to hire them. Workers may be concentrated in major cities while rural facilities remain understaffed. A trained professional may accept unrelated work because salaries are delayed or conditions are unsafe. Facilities may lack equipment, housing, transport, or career paths. Data systems may not show clearly where workers are, what they are trained to do, or which vacancies remain open.

Community health workers deserve particular attention. They often connect households with formal services, support prevention, provide health information, and help people continue treatment. Their local knowledge can make them trusted guides through systems that otherwise feel distant. Yet praise for their importance is not a substitute for proper training, supervision, supplies, protection, and fair compensation.

Migration adds another layer. When a physician, nurse, scientist, engineer, or lecturer leaves, the country that financed part of that person's education may lose scarce expertise. But migration should not be described only as betrayal or loss. People move for safety, family, professional growth, better equipment, reliable pay, and the chance to do work for which they trained. Diaspora professionals may also send money, mentor younger colleagues, invest, conduct joint research, teach, or eventually return.

The better question is not how to prevent every skilled African from moving. It is how to build institutions in which skilled people can do serious work, live with dignity, and remain connected to Africa wherever they reside. Retention begins with opportunity and trust, not guilt.

Science Is Working Infrastructure

Science can appear distant from daily development, especially where governments face immediate needs. A laboratory may seem less urgent than a road, a classroom, or a clinic. Yet all three depend on accumulated knowledge. Engineers test materials before a bridge carries traffic. Agronomists study soils, seeds, pests, and water. Public health laboratories identify pathogens. Meteorologists improve warnings. Food scientists help products remain safe from farm to market. Research is one of the systems that allows visible infrastructure to work.

African countries already contain strong universities, research institutes, public-health centers, technology firms, and communities of expertise. The point is not that the continent lacks science. It is that scientific capacity is uneven, often underfunded, and sometimes disconnected from the institutions that could use it.

The African Union's *Science, Technology and Innovation Strategy for Africa 2034* places stronger human capabilities, research systems, innovation, and the application of knowledge at the center of the continent's development agenda. It is a continental policy strategy, not evidence that its goals have already been achieved. Its significance lies in the direction it sets: science is not an optional prestige project reserved for a few universities. It belongs in agriculture, health, manufacturing, environmental management, public administration, and business (African Union, 2025).

Funding matters, but so does continuity. Research cannot mature when grants arrive unpredictably, equipment sits in customs for months, or promising teams dissolve as soon as one project ends. Institutions need technicians who maintain equipment, librarians who provide access to knowledge, administrators who manage grants honestly, and career paths that allow researchers to remain productive. A scientist cannot build a field alone.

Governments and firms also need the capacity to use research. Evidence has little public value when it is produced, filed, and ignored. Researchers must communicate clearly, and decision-makers must be willing to ask questions whose answers may complicate a preferred policy. The relationship works best when neither side treats the other as decoration.

Africa Must Generate and Adapt Knowledge

International knowledge is indispensable. African researchers should collaborate globally, learn from discoveries made elsewhere, and contribute to shared scientific work. Intellectual isolation would weaken the continent, not protect it.

But knowledge travels with assumptions. A seed developed for one climate may fail in another. A medical protocol may need adjustment where electricity, transport, staffing, or disease patterns differ. A public-transport model designed for a highly formal city may misunderstand the routes and livelihoods of an African city in which informal transport carries most passengers. Technology created for dominant global languages may perform poorly when users speak languages that are scarcely represented in its training data.

Local research helps reveal these differences. It does not mean that every country must invent every tool independently. That would waste resources and ignore the collaborative nature of science. The more realistic goal is sufficient capability to evaluate a technology, understand its risks, adapt it to local conditions, regulate it competently, repair it, and improve it where necessary.

This distinction separates technological access from technological dependence. Buying equipment can expand capacity quickly, but a system remains vulnerable if no one can diagnose a fault, negotiate a license, secure the data, or judge whether the product is appropriate. Importing knowledge is useful. Building the ability to question and adapt it is essential.

Language is part of that capacity. UNESCO reported in 2025 that more than 7,000 languages are spoken worldwide, while only about 1,000 have a meaningful presence online. This is a global measure, not an African count, but the imbalance has obvious consequences for a continent of extraordinary linguistic diversity. When digital content, search, translation, and voice systems do not work well in the languages people use, the barrier is not merely cultural. It can limit access to education, services, markets, and public information (UNESCO, 2025).

African knowledge also includes experience that may never have entered a formal journal. Farmers, craftspeople, healers, builders, and communities understand environments through generations of observation. Such knowledge should not be romanticized or accepted without testing. Nor should it be dismissed because it developed outside a university. Respectful research can examine what works, what does not, and why.

Digital Access Is More Than a Signal

Digital technology has shortened some distances that physical infrastructure leaves in place. A small business can advertise beyond its neighborhood. A student can reach a course unavailable nearby. A health worker can consult a specialist. A family can send money without spending a day traveling to a bank. Governments can provide information and services more efficiently.

These possibilities are real, but access remains profoundly unequal. The International Telecommunication Union estimated that 36 percent of people in its Africa region used the Internet in 2025, compared with 74 percent globally. It also estimated mobile-phone ownership at 66 percent among people aged ten and older in the region. The thirty-point difference is a useful warning: owning a phone is not the same as using the Internet (International Telecommunication Union, 2025a, 2025b).

Even Internet use is an incomplete measure of meaningful access. A person may connect briefly through an inexpensive bundle but be unable to watch an instructional video, download a large document, or run a business online. A family may share one device. Coverage may disappear when electricity fails. A farmer may have a signal but find that relevant services are unavailable in a familiar language. A student may technically be connected while studying on a small screen in a crowded room.

Affordability, devices, electricity, digital skills, language, safety, and useful content all determine what connectivity can accomplish. So does geography. ITU's 2025 estimates indicated that the urban Internet-use rate in its Africa region was about 2.6 times the rural rate. That gap affects far more than entertainment. It can shape access to market prices, banking, education, health information, agricultural advice, public services, and customers (International Telecommunication Union, 2025c).

The phrase *digital divide* can make the problem sound like a clean line between those online and those offline. Reality is more layered. Some people have high-speed fixed connections and several devices. Others depend on unstable mobile access. Some connect only at work or school. Others have never used the Internet. Policy has to see these different levels of access if it is to close the right gaps.

Digital literacy is equally important. People need more than the ability to open an application. They need to judge whether information is trustworthy, protect personal data, recognize fraud, communicate professionally, and use digital tools to solve problems. These capabilities should be developed across subjects and occupations rather than confined to one computer class.

Artificial Intelligence Raises the Cost of Exclusion

Artificial intelligence has intensified the stakes. The technology may support medical analysis, crop monitoring, translation, education, financial services, logistics, scientific research, and public administration. It can also reproduce discrimination, spread convincing falsehoods, threaten privacy, displace some tasks, and concentrate power in companies or countries that control computing infrastructure, data, and advanced expertise.

The African Union's Continental Artificial Intelligence Strategy, endorsed in 2024, calls for investment in infrastructure, skills, research, data, innovation, governance, and safeguards. Like the science strategy, it is a policy framework, not a record of completed implementation. It correctly identifies that participation in AI requires an ecosystem, not a collection of imported applications (African Union, 2024).

African countries do not all need to build the same capabilities, and no country needs to reproduce the entire global AI industry. Regional cooperation may make more sense for costly computing resources, specialized research, safety testing, and shared standards. Universities, businesses, and public institutions can focus on problems where local knowledge matters and where a useful application can be sustained.

The immediate danger is not simply that machines will replace every worker. It is that existing inequalities in electricity, connectivity, language representation, education, and research will shape who can benefit from the technology and who remains subject to systems they do not understand. A farmer whose language is absent from a service, a patient whose data are poorly protected, or a public agency that cannot audit an automated decision is not fully included because an AI product has reached the market.

Education must therefore prepare people both to use and to question technology. Programmers and data scientists are necessary, but so are teachers, lawyers, ethicists, linguists, domain experts, regulators, and citizens who can ask what a system does, whose data trained it, where it fails, and who is accountable. Technical capability without public judgment can make a society efficient at doing the wrong thing.

Women Must Be Able to Participate Fully

No account of human capability is credible if it treats women and girls as a special topic at the edge of the economy. Women are farmers, traders, professionals, workers, researchers, caregivers, entrepreneurs, and public leaders. Barriers that limit their education, health, safety, mobility, property rights, finance, technology, or employment reduce individual freedom and constrain the capabilities available to society as a whole.

The barriers are not the same everywhere. A girl may leave school because the nearest secondary school is too far away. A market trader may lack collateral because property is registered in someone else's name. A professional woman may have a degree but carry a disproportionate share of unpaid care. An entrepreneur may have customers but lack access to a formal account or a safe means of traveling to a regional market. National averages can hide each of these experiences.

Inclusion requires more than opening a classroom or passing a law. Rules have to be understood, enforced, and supported by practical services. Safe transport, childcare, maternal health, protection from harassment, reliable identification, financial access, and fair hiring can determine whether a formal right becomes an actual opportunity.

Care work deserves particular recognition. Children, older people, and family members living with illness or disability need care. Much of that work is unpaid and performed by women. It sustains households and economies, yet it can also limit time for education, paid work, rest, and public participation. Better care services and a fairer sharing of responsibilities expand human capability on both sides of the relationship.

The objective is not to describe women only in terms of how much economic output they can add. It is to ensure that gender does not determine whose intelligence is developed, whose health is protected, whose work is rewarded, or whose ideas reach the public world.

Migration, Return, and the Wider African Community

Africa's human-capability story does not end at the continent's coastline. Africans living abroad include health professionals, scientists, engineers, artists, academics, business owners, technicians, and workers in nearly every field. Their relationship with countries of origin is often discussed through remittances, but money is only one part of it.

Diaspora communities can connect institutions, introduce firms to new markets, mentor students, support research, invest, share professional standards, and return with experience. These possibilities should not be exaggerated. Not every person abroad has wealth, time, or a desire to serve as a development program. Many face insecure status, discrimination, difficult work, and obligations to relatives in more than one place.

Governments get better results when they build relationships rather than issue moral demands. A researcher is more likely to collaborate when institutions answer messages, agreements are honored, equipment clears customs, and colleagues can continue the work after a short visit. A business owner is more likely to invest when rules are predictable and contracts mean something. A professional is more likely to return when family members can live safely and a career can grow.

Movement within Africa matters too. A teacher, engineer, nurse, artist, or entrepreneur may find opportunity in another African country, yet face difficulty with visas, recognition of qualifications, residence rights, or professional licensing. Chapter 13 showed that a market for services cannot deepen if the people providing those services cannot move under clear and lawful rules. Human capability is strengthened when knowledge can circulate, but circulation depends on trust between institutions.

Capability Is Uneven, and That Matters

Continental averages can help establish scale. They can also hide the story that policy needs most.

School completion, literacy, life expectancy, Internet use, research capacity, and employment differ greatly among African countries. They also differ within countries, between cities and rural areas, wealthy and poor households, peaceful and conflict-affected regions, men and women, and people with and without disabilities. A national average can improve while a remote community sees little change. A fast-growing technology sector can coexist with schools that lack electricity. A country can have excellent surgeons and districts without a physician.

This unevenness is not a reason to abandon continental analysis. Shared problems can justify shared research, pooled infrastructure, regional universities, mutual recognition of qualifications, and the exchange of successful practice. It is a reason to resist a single story. The appropriate intervention depends on what is missing in a particular place.

There is also much to learn from progress already achieved. Some African health systems have built effective community networks. Some universities conduct internationally respected research. Some vocational programs work closely with employers. Some technology firms design products for conditions that global companies overlooked. Serious analysis should ask not only where Africa is behind, but where African institutions have solved difficult problems and what made those solutions possible.

The goal is not a contest in which one country proves itself more advanced than another. It is to understand capacity honestly enough to strengthen it. Pride that cannot tolerate evidence is fragile. Criticism that cannot recognize achievement is equally unhelpful.

The Resource That Multiplies Other Resources

Oil can be depleted. A mineral deposit can be exhausted. Soil can lose fertility when it is badly managed. Commodity prices can rise or collapse for reasons far beyond the control of the country that produces them. Human knowledge behaves differently. It can be shared without leaving the first person empty.

A teacher may educate thousands of students over a career. One engineer can help train a team that later designs projects of its own. A nurse can teach families practices that prevent illness beyond the walls of a clinic. A researcher can produce knowledge that allows other researchers to ask better questions. An experienced craftsperson can pass judgment, technique, and pride in workmanship to an apprentice.

This multiplication is not automatic. Skills can become outdated. Poor institutions can silence expertise. Professionals can be unemployed, underpaid, or driven away. Education can reward memorization while discouraging curiosity. Technology can widen inequality when only a few can use it. Human capability needs a surrounding system that protects, employs, and renews it.

Still, the effect on every other resource is profound. Farmland has different possibilities when farmers can reach agronomists, finance, machinery, weather information, storage, and markets. A mineral deposit has different possibilities when geologists, engineers, chemists, environmental scientists, financiers, and manufacturers can work together. Digital infrastructure has different possibilities when people can create software, secure networks, develop local-language tools, and build businesses on top of it.

The question is therefore not only how many Africans there will be. It is what knowledge, health, freedom, and opportunity they will have, and what they will be able to build.

If schools produce learning, if health systems protect life and ability, if technical training is respected, if universities conduct serious research, if women and men can participate fully, and if technology becomes a field of African creation as well as consumption, demographic scale can support a more capable continent. But the word *if* cannot be removed. Population is not destiny.

Nor is capability the final answer. Skilled people still need institutions they can trust. Businesses need rules that are applied fairly. Researchers need freedom and continuity. Citizens need peace. A society can educate people and then waste their knowledge through corruption, violence, exclusion, or arbitrary government. Chapter 15 turns to these conditions, because institutions, peace, and the rule of law determine whether human capability can remain, cooperate, and build.

Evidence Note

The phrase "greatest resource" is an interpretive framing, not a statistical ranking, and this chapter treats human dignity as broader than economic productivity. The numerical evidence comes from several geographic groupings that must not be combined silently. Population figures refer to the African continent. Education figures cited from the World Bank refer to sub-Saharan Africa. Health figures refer to the WHO African Region. Digital estimates refer to the ITU Africa region. These groupings do not contain exactly the same countries.

The post-pandemic learning-poverty figure is a modeled regional estimate based on data from different countries and years, not the result of one simultaneous examination. World Bank classroom and teacher requirements are projections tied to the goal of universal education by 2030. WHO health-workforce totals depend partly on the availability and quality of country reporting, and the estimate of unmet need is model-based. African Union science and artificial-intelligence documents are strategies that state priorities; they are not evidence that the proposed programs have already been implemented. All dates and scopes are retained so that progress, estimates, and policy ambitions are not mistaken for one another.

CHAPTER 15

Institutions, Peace, and the Rule of Law

Why Resources and Markets Are Not Enough

Chapter 14 examined Africa's greatest resource: its people. Yet education, health, skill, and imagination do not operate in open space. A nurse may be well trained, but she/he cannot keep a clinic running if medicines disappear between the warehouse and the patient. An engineer may design a sound bridge, but the bridge will not last if procurement rewards the wrong contractor or maintenance money is never released. A farmer may improve the soil for years, but hesitate to invest further if a legitimate claim to the land can be overturned without a fair hearing.

These are institutional questions. They concern the rules a society adopts, the organizations created to apply them, and the habits that determine whether those rules mean the same thing in practice as they do on paper. Institutions include courts, parliaments, ministries, local governments, regulators, auditors, police services, tax authorities, electoral bodies, statistical offices, and regional organizations. They also include less visible arrangements: how officials are appointed, how records are kept, how a citizen challenges a decision, and whether wrongdoing has consequences.

A country can possess minerals and remain poor. It can build roads and fail to maintain them. It can collect taxes without turning them into reliable services. It can pass impressive laws that few people can enforce. It can hold elections and still struggle to administer schools, courts, borders, or public finances. None of this means that governance alone explains development. History, geography, war, global markets, technology, and the structure of an economy all matter. But institutions influence what happens after a resource is discovered, a budget is approved, a law is passed, or a promise is made.

That is the concern of this chapter: how capable, accountable institutions and a durable peace give people room to build.

Institutions Are What Happens After the Announcement

Governments announce policies. Institutions decide whether those policies reach ordinary life.

Imagine a new program intended to provide textbooks to rural schools. The announcement may be sincere, the budget may be approved, and the books may even be printed. Success still depends on a chain of less dramatic tasks. Officials must know how many pupils attend each school. Contracts must be awarded fairly. Deliveries must be tracked. Roads must remain passable. Head teachers must confirm what arrived. Auditors must be able to investigate missing supplies.

When any link breaks, the difference is felt by a child sitting at a desk without a book.

The same chain exists across public life. A vaccination program depends on procurement, refrigeration, transport, staffing, local trust, and accurate records. A power plant depends on fuel arrangements, competent regulation, maintenance, billing, and financial discipline. A court judgment depends on clerks, files, enforcement, and respect for judicial authority. The public usually encounters the state not as a theory but as a queue, a classroom, a police station, a permit, a tax form, a land record, or a hospital visit.

This is why government effectiveness is not mainly about the elegance of a policy document. It is about implementation. It asks whether a civil service can carry out decisions, whether agencies can coordinate, and whether public systems can keep working when a minister changes. A capable state does not have to own every factory, farm, bank, or airline. It does need to perform the functions it has accepted with enough competence and continuity to make public authority credible.

Nor is institutional capacity the same as the size of government. A large bureaucracy can be ineffective, and a smaller administration can perform selected duties well. The central issue is whether responsibilities, staff, money, information, and authority are aligned. An agency cannot reasonably be judged for failing to perform a task it was never funded or empowered to carry out. Equally, a generous budget does not excuse weak management. Capacity has to be understood in practical terms: who must do what, with which skills, under whose supervision, and with what evidence that the work was completed.

Governance Cannot Be Reduced to One Score

Governance is a broad and sometimes carelessly used word. The World Bank's Worldwide Governance Indicators organize it into six dimensions: voice and accountability, political stability, government effectiveness, regulatory quality, rule of law, and control of corruption. The 2025 revision draws on perception data from 35 cross-country sources, including household and business surveys and expert assessments. It covers more than 200 economies, with a revised historical series extending from 1996 through 2024 (World Bank, 2025).

The framework is useful because it prevents several different questions from being collapsed into one. Can citizens participate and hold power to account? Is political authority threatened by violence or unconstitutional change? Do public agencies deliver? Are regulations workable? Can rights and contracts be enforced? Is public power used for private gain? These questions interact, but they are not identical.

A country may be relatively stable yet have slow or unreliable public services. Another may administer some services effectively while restricting political voice. Competitive elections do not automatically produce competent procurement, professional regulation, or independent courts. Strong technical agencies do not by themselves guarantee accountability. The World Bank therefore reports the six dimensions separately rather than combining them into one overall governance index (World Bank, 2025).

The indicators also have limits. They measure perceptions, not governance in the same physical sense that a surveyor measures a road. Perceptions matter because people and firms act on what they expect institutions to do. A business deciding whether to invest cares whether it believes a contract will be enforced. A citizen deciding whether to report a crime cares whether the police are expected to respond fairly.

Yet perceptions can also be influenced by ideology, recent events, publicity, and different expectations. The World Bank advises treating the indicators as a broad comparative lens and combining them with country-specific evidence such as audits, administrative records, case-processing data, and service-delivery results (World Bank, 2025).

This caution is especially important in a book about Africa. There is no single African governance condition. Countries differ in political systems, administrative traditions, judicial performance, civil liberties, tax capacity, local government, corruption risks, and security. Performance also varies within countries and across institutions. A well-run central bank may coexist with a weak land office. One municipality may manage permits efficiently while another does not. A country that improves on one dimension may stagnate or decline on another.

The statement "Africa has bad governance" is therefore not an analysis. It is a generalization that hides more than it reveals. Agenda 2063 itself treats good governance, human rights, justice, rule of law, capable institutions, peace, and security as connected but distinct aspirations (African Union, n.d.-a). Serious discussion begins by asking which institution, in which country, performing which function, during which period.

Capacity and Accountability Must Grow Together

Debates about governance sometimes create a false choice. One side emphasizes state capacity, the ability to decide and act. The other emphasizes accountability, the need to restrain power and expose abuse. Durable institutions require both.

Authority without capacity produces promises that cannot be fulfilled. Capacity without accountability can make misuse of power more efficient. A tax authority needs enough information and legal power to collect what is owed, but taxpayers also need clear rules, appeal procedures, and protection from arbitrary treatment. A police service needs the ability to investigate crime, but it also needs lawful limits, professional discipline, and independent oversight. A procurement agency needs staff who understand complex contracts, but it must also disclose decisions and permit review.

Accountability takes different forms in different constitutional systems. It may involve parliaments, courts, auditors, electoral bodies, journalists, professional associations, civil-society organizations, access-to-information laws, and internal controls within government. No mechanism guarantees honest or competent government. Auditors can be ignored. Courts can be delayed. Elections can be poorly administered. Journalists can make mistakes. But institutions that allow decisions to be questioned, evidence to be examined, and authority to be corrected make abuse harder to hide and failure easier to diagnose.

Continuity matters as well. A capable public service should not have to start from the beginning after every election or cabinet reshuffle. Political leaders are elected or appointed to set direction, but functioning administrations also need professional memory. Engineers must preserve maintenance records. Health officials must retain surveillance systems. Budget officers must know the history of long-term commitments. When each change in leadership sweeps away skilled staff and records, the public pays repeatedly for lost knowledge.

The aim is not an institution without politics. Public institutions exist within political societies, and many of their goals are properly decided through political debate. The aim is to prevent every routine function from becoming a personal favor, a partisan reward, or a fresh experiment. Citizens should not have to know the right person to receive a birth certificate, register a business, report a crime, or obtain medicine already paid for from public funds.

The Rule of Law Is Economic Infrastructure

Infrastructure usually brings to mind roads, ports, railways, electricity, water, and communications. Economic life also depends on legal infrastructure.

Every day, people make commitments to one another. A shopkeeper orders goods on credit. A worker expects to be paid. A bank lends money. A farmer leases land. A transport company agrees to deliver a shipment. An investor contributes capital to a business managed by someone else. These relationships cannot function entirely on trust between friends. They need rules that are understandable and institutions able to resolve disputes with reasonable fairness and speed.

The rule of law does not mean that every disagreement ends in court. Most contracts are honored without a lawsuit. Courts matter partly because the possibility of enforcement shapes behavior before a dispute occurs. When both parties believe that a serious breach can be reviewed by an impartial institution, each has a stronger reason to keep the agreement. A court's influence therefore reaches far beyond the cases that judges actually decide.

The same principle applies elsewhere. A credible auditor can influence conduct before an audit begins. A regulator known to apply rules consistently can improve compliance without punishing every violation. An independent electoral body can reduce conflict by making procedures more predictable. Institutions guide behavior partly through what people reasonably expect them to do.

This is why delays matter. A legal right that takes ten years to enforce may be useless to a small business that will close in six months. A land dispute unresolved for a generation can prevent investment and deepen community tension. A commercial court that publishes reasoned decisions and manages cases predictably can support trust even when one party loses. The purpose is not to guarantee victory. It is to provide a process in which evidence, law, and procedure matter more than wealth, connection, or threat.

Rule of law also requires that public authority be bound by law. Businesses cannot plan if a license granted today can be cancelled tomorrow without reasons or appeal. Citizens cannot feel secure if rules are applied selectively. Consistency need not mean rigidity. Laws can change, and sometimes they should. But legitimate change should follow known procedures, be communicated clearly, and allow people a reasonable chance to adjust.

Property, Land, and the Confidence to Invest

Property arrangements across Africa include statutory ownership, customary tenure, communal rights, leasehold systems, and combinations of these. The diversity reflects different histories, legal traditions, livelihoods, and relationships to land. It would be careless to declare one identical model appropriate for every society.

The more useful principle is predictability. A family that has farmed land for decades needs confidence that a legitimate claim will be recognized. A pastoral community needs rules that account for movement and shared access, not only fixed plots. Women need the practical ability to exercise rights recognized by law, including inheritance and ownership. Communities affected by mining, dams, or urban expansion need transparent procedures for consultation, compensation, and appeal. Lenders and buyers need records that can be checked, but formal registration should not erase valid customary interests simply because they were not previously written into a central database.

Poorly designed reform can create new insecurity while claiming to solve an old problem. Digitizing land records may reduce lost files and make searches easier, but technology cannot decide whose claim was legitimate in the first place. If disputed or incomplete records are entered into a computer, the uncertainty becomes digital. Reform therefore requires legal care, local knowledge, accessible dispute resolution, and protection for people with less money or political influence.

The connection to development is straightforward. Long-term investment requires some confidence in the future. A farmer is more likely to plant trees, improve irrigation, or protect soil when lawful use of the land is reasonably secure. A business is more likely to build a workshop when the lease is enforceable. A city is better able to plan roads and services when land records are credible. Secure rights do not solve every economic problem, but uncertainty about rights can discourage people from improving what they have.

Public Money Must Become Public Results

A national budget records choices. It does not, by itself, prove that those choices reached the public.

Two countries can spend similar amounts on education and produce different results. Two road projects can have the same design while differing greatly in cost, quality, and completion time. Medicines can be purchased but fail to arrive at clinics. A water system can be inaugurated and then stop working because maintenance was never funded. The distance between money approved and service delivered is where institutional quality becomes visible.

Corruption is one reason that distance can grow, but it is not the only one. Bribery, embezzlement, procurement manipulation, favoritism, and the use of public power for private benefit can raise costs and weaken public trust. Because such acts are concealed, corruption cannot be measured simply by counting what is reported. This is one reason perception surveys are used, alongside audits, prosecutions, procurement data, and unexplained patterns in public spending.

It is equally important not to label an entire continent, country, or public service as corrupt. Such language treats millions of people and many different institutions as though they behave alike. It also discourages careful diagnosis. A delayed project may reflect theft, but it may also reflect inflation, a shortage of materials, a design error, difficult terrain, conflict, or a contractor's bankruptcy. Accountability requires evidence, not suspicion presented as fact.

The practical question is whether public systems make wrongdoing harder and detection more likely. Are tenders genuinely competitive? Are beneficial owners known? Are contract changes recorded? Can auditors follow money from the treasury to the final delivery point? Are findings acted upon? Can citizens see what was promised to their school, district, or clinic? Transparency is valuable when it makes responsibility traceable. Publishing thousands of unreadable pages after decisions are finished may satisfy a formal rule without enabling meaningful scrutiny.

Good financial management is not only about stopping theft. It is also about planning, value, and maintenance. A procurement system that buys the cheapest equipment without considering spare parts may waste money honestly. A ministry that starts many projects but finishes few may spread resources so thinly that no community receives the promised benefit. Public money becomes public value when institutions select priorities, purchase competently, monitor delivery, correct failure, and maintain what has been built.

Reliable Information Is Public Infrastructure

Development requires a society to know itself.

Where are children being born? Which districts are growing? How many teachers are present, not merely on a payroll? Which crops are failing? Where are disease cases rising? Which firms are hiring? How long do court cases take? How much money reached a local health center? Without reliable answers, policy becomes guesswork and accountability becomes argument.

National statistical offices, civil registries, health-surveillance systems, land records, customs databases, budget systems, and court files may not look like roads or power plants. Yet they perform an infrastructure-like function. They carry information on which decisions depend.

Data quality is not a technical concern reserved for statisticians. A population estimate affects where schools and hospitals are built. An incomplete death-registration system can hide a health crisis. Weak employment data can lead governments to announce job programs without knowing whether unemployment is changing. Poor trade records make it harder to identify delays or understand who benefits from regional integration. If citizens cannot compare a budget with actual spending, public debate is deprived of evidence.

Digital systems can improve speed, access, and traceability, but they also create risks. Personal information can be misused. Rural communities may be excluded when services become digital before connectivity and identification are widely available. Separate agencies may build systems that cannot communicate. A broken paper process does not become fair merely because it moves online. Technology is useful when it is built around clear responsibilities, good records, privacy, security, and a realistic understanding of how people will use it.

Trust is essential. People are more willing to provide information when they understand why it is collected and believe it will not be used against them. Officials are more likely to act on evidence when data producers are professionally independent and transparent about uncertainty. Reliable statistics do not eliminate political disagreement. They give disagreement a more honest foundation.

Regulation Should Protect Without Paralyzing

Regulation is sometimes described only as a burden on business. That view is incomplete. Medicines need safety standards. Banks require prudential oversight. Buildings must be safe. Workers need legal protection. Food should not be contaminated. Electricity networks require technical rules. Environmental harm does not remain within a company's accounts.

The real choice is rarely between regulation and no regulation. It is between rules that manage legitimate risks and rules that are unclear, duplicative, selective, or impossible to administer.

Predictability matters as much as the number of rules. A business can often plan for a known license fee or safety requirement. It struggles when the required documents change from one office to another, when approval time has no limit, or when an unofficial payment appears to be the only way forward. Rules that are formally identical can produce unequal effects when enforcement depends on personal connection.

Small firms often feel these weaknesses first. A large company may employ lawyers, accountants, customs specialists, and compliance teams. A small manufacturer or trader may have none of them. If a permit takes six unpredictable months, a large corporation may be able to wait. A new firm with one rented room and limited cash may close before approval arrives. Unclear administration can therefore protect established interests even when the written rule appears neutral.

Reform should not be judged only by how many procedures are removed. Eliminating an unnecessary signature may help. Removing a safety inspection without improving any other control may create harm. Better regulation asks what risk the rule addresses, whether the requirement is proportionate, whether agencies duplicate one another, how long a decision should take, and how an applicant can appeal. It protects the public while reducing opportunities for delay, discretion, and extraction.

Regional Integration Is an Institutional Project

Chapter 13 examined the infrastructure, production, and commercial systems required to make a continental market work. The AfCFTA also depends on institutions that can translate agreements into daily practice.

A paved road may connect two countries, but goods will still move slowly if customs systems cannot exchange information, officials interpret rules differently, or border agencies open at incompatible hours. A tariff commitment matters only if it is reflected in procedures used by customs officers and understood by traders. Rules of origin must be administered. Product standards must be recognized or reconciled. Trade disputes need credible mechanisms. Payment systems, transport insurance, and banking rules must operate across jurisdictions.

The challenge is not simply to sign more agreements. It is to build habits of implementation. Ministries must coordinate with one another at home before countries can coordinate across borders. Businesses need clear guidance. Border staff need training and equipment. Data must reveal where delays occur. Smaller traders, including many women who depend on cross-border commerce, need procedures they can use without hiring specialists or relying on informal payments.

Regional institutions also require trust among states. Governments must believe that partners will honor commitments, share relevant information, and address legitimate concerns. Disagreements are inevitable. The test is whether institutions can manage them without allowing every dispute to paralyze the wider project.

Continental integration is therefore physical, commercial, legal, and administrative at the same time. Infrastructure creates a route. Institutions determine whether that route becomes a dependable economic connection.

Peace Is an Economic Asset

Peace does not appear in a table of mineral reserves. It cannot be exported in a container, and it has no daily commodity price. Yet it gives value to nearly everything discussed in this book.

Peace allows a child to remain in school long enough to learn. It allows a farmer to plant with some hope of harvesting. It lets a truck travel after dark, a clinic retain its staff, and a business invest in equipment expected to last for years. It allows records to remain in public offices, electrical lines to stay standing, markets to open, and taxes to be collected for public use.

Conflict can destroy these gains quickly. Roads and hospitals can be damaged. Schools can close. Crops can be abandoned. Trade routes can shift. Businesses can lose workers, stock, credit, and customers. Governments may redirect scarce resources from development to emergency security. Skilled professionals may leave. Some losses are less visible but equally serious: institutional memory, community trust, professional networks, interrupted education, and the belief that long-term plans are worth making.

Peace alone does not guarantee development. A peaceful society can still be poor, unequal, badly governed, or economically stagnant. But sustained violence makes almost every development goal harder. This is why security cannot be treated as a separate chapter that begins after economics ends. It is one of the conditions under which economic and social life can continue.

The overlap between conflict and poverty is increasingly important. The World Bank's strategy for engagement in settings affected by fragility, conflict, and violence for 2026 to 2030 states that more than half of the world's people living in extreme poverty are in countries affected by those conditions (World Bank, 2026). This is a global statement based on the Bank's classifications and poverty measures, not a claim about Africa alone. It nevertheless matters for the continent because several African countries face acute or prolonged fragility.

Sudan and the Human Scale of Institutional Breakdown

The war that began in Sudan in April 2023 shows how quickly institutional breakdown and organized violence can enter everyday life. By the end of 2025, UNHCR reported about 9.1 million people displaced inside Sudan, the largest internal displacement crisis in the world at that reporting date. Nearly 3.8 million Sudanese refugees and asylum-seekers were outside the country. More than 2.8 million internally displaced people had returned during 2025, mainly toward Khartoum and Al Jazirah, but many returned amid damaged homes, missing services, and explosive hazards (UNHCR, 2026).

Those figures describe different categories and should not be added casually. They are also dated because displacement changes as people flee, return, or are displaced again. Behind every category is a household making decisions under pressure: whether a road is safe, whether food will be available, whether children can travel, whether an elderly relative can survive the journey, and whether a home still exists.

The economic consequences extend beyond Sudan's borders. Refugees and asylum-seekers have been received in neighboring and nearby African countries, including Chad, Egypt, South Sudan, Libya, Ethiopia, the Central African Republic, and Uganda (UNHCR, 2026). Host communities may share schools, clinics, water, housing, transport, and employment with new arrivals while donor funding and local budgets remain limited. Trade corridors can be disrupted. Border regions can become more insecure. Families and communities divided by colonial borders may experience the conflict on both sides.

It would be equally wrong to let Sudan, the Sahel, eastern Democratic Republic of the Congo, Somalia, or any other conflict-affected area become an image of the whole continent. Africa is not one continuous war zone. Conflict is concentrated in particular places, though its effects can spread. Responsible writing must hold both truths at once: African conflicts demand serious attention, and conflict does not define Africa or the daily life of every African society.

Forced displacement is humanitarian and economic at the same time. People forced from their homes need safety first. They also need the ability to work, learn, receive healthcare, and rebuild ordinary life. Host communities need support that strengthens shared services rather than creating resentment around scarce resources. Return is not automatically a durable solution if people go back because conditions elsewhere are intolerable or arrive where schools, clinics, homes, and livelihoods no longer function.

Sudan also warns against measuring peace only by the movement of front lines. A city may become calmer while fear, hunger, unexploded weapons, destroyed records, and broken services remain. The end of active fighting is indispensable. It is the beginning of institutional recovery, not its completion.

Peace Requires More Than a Ceasefire

A ceasefire can save lives immediately. Durable peace asks what happens next.

Communities emerging from conflict may need security arrangements, political settlements, justice, reconstruction, the restoration of schools and health services, and pathways for displaced people to return or settle elsewhere safely. Property records may have been destroyed. Former neighbors may distrust one another. Armed groups may still control income, territory, or movement. Young people who lost years of schooling may have few lawful opportunities. Skilled public servants may have fled.

No single institution can repair all of this. National and local governments, community leaders, women's organizations, youth groups, religious institutions, courts, security services, businesses, humanitarian agencies, and regional organizations may each hold part of the work. Their roles will differ by conflict. What matters is that reconstruction is treated as more than rebuilding walls.

Justice is among the hardest questions. A society may need accountability for grave abuses, but legal institutions may be damaged or distrusted. Demands for punishment, reconciliation, truth, compensation, and immediate stability can pull in different directions. There is no universal sequence that guarantees success. Ignoring injustice can preserve grievances, while pursuing justice without security or credible institutions can expose victims and witnesses to further danger. Decisions must be grounded in law, local conditions, and the voices of those most affected.

Economic recovery is also part of peacebuilding. A former combatant without a livelihood, a displaced family without land, and a graduate without work face different circumstances, but all need a realistic place in a lawful economy. Jobs cannot replace political settlement or justice. They can, however, restore routine, dignity, and a reason to invest in stability. This is one reason the World Bank's current fragility strategy places strong emphasis on employment while acknowledging that peace, security, and political settlements involve actors beyond a development bank's mandate (World Bank, 2026).

The deepest work may be the rebuilding of trust. Trust cannot be legislated into existence. It grows when people see that agreements are kept, services are shared fairly, complaints are heard, and violence no longer decides every dispute. Institutions earn trust through repeated conduct. That process is slow, but there is no shortcut around it.

Africa Has Built Institutions for Collective Security

African states have not treated peace and security only as national or external concerns. The African Union's Peace and Security Council is its standing decision-making body for the prevention, management, and resolution of conflicts. The protocol establishing it was adopted in Durban on 9 July 2002 and entered into force in December 2003. The Council became fully operational in early 2004 and is the principal pillar of the African Peace and Security Architecture (African Union, n.d.-b).

The wider architecture includes the Panel of the Wise, the Continental Early Warning System, the African Standby Force, and the Peace Fund. It is designed to work with regional economic communities and regional mechanisms, as well as with the United Nations and civil society (African Union, n.d.-b). These regional bodies include the Economic Community of West African States (ECOWAS), the Intergovernmental Authority on Development (IGAD), the Southern African Development Community (SADC), the East African Community (EAC), and the Economic Community of Central African States (ECCAS). They have participated in diplomacy, mediation, security cooperation, or conflict management in different circumstances.

The existence of an institution is not proof of its effectiveness. A protocol cannot prevent conflict merely by being adopted, just as a national law cannot enforce itself. Political divisions, financing, competing interests, delayed decisions, and weak implementation can limit regional action. The right standard is performance: Were risks identified early? Was mediation timely? Were civilians protected? Were decisions implemented? Did institutions learn from failure?

Still, their existence establishes an important fact. African states have created continental and regional mechanisms to address collective threats. Agenda 2063 places capable institutions, accountable governance, rule of law, and a peaceful and secure Africa within the same vision (African Union, n.d.-a). That connection is not accidental. Institutions can provide peaceful ways to manage disagreement before it becomes violence, while peace gives institutions time to develop.

International cooperation remains necessary. The United Nations, humanitarian agencies, development banks, foreign governments, and international organizations all play roles in diplomacy, relief, peace operations, and reconstruction. Cooperation is not the opposite of African agency. Problems that cross borders often require action at local, national, regional, continental, and international levels. The real question is whether those levels reinforce one another and remain accountable to the people living with the consequences.

Institutions Cannot Simply Be Imported

International partners can finance equipment, provide technical advice, train officials, share research, or support oversight. They cannot permanently perform the daily work of domestic government.

A court must decide cases in the language and legal system of the society it serves. A tax authority must understand local businesses and sources of income. A municipality must know where people live and which services fail. A regulator must earn authority from law and consistent practice. Citizens, businesses, professional bodies, universities, journalists, and civil-society organizations all shape whether institutions are trusted and corrected.

Imported models often look attractive because they arrive as complete organizational charts, laws, software systems, or performance frameworks. Yet a design that worked elsewhere may depend on staffing, revenue, technology, political agreements, or legal traditions that do not exist in the receiving country. Copying the visible form without the supporting conditions can produce an institution that performs well during a donor-funded pilot and weakens when external support ends.

This does not mean countries should reject international experience. Learning across borders is sensible. The distinction is between learning and imitation. Reformers must ask which problem a model solved, what resources sustained it, who gained or lost power, how it was adapted, and whether domestic institutions can maintain it.

African countries can also learn from one another. Differences across the continent create a large field of practical comparison. Why does one tax office make compliance simpler? How did a city reduce delays in issuing permits? Why does one public-health system identify outbreaks faster? What allowed a particular court or audit office to preserve professional independence? Which peace arrangements survived a political transition, and which did not?

Answers must be studied, not romanticized. A reform praised from a distance may have costs that local people understand better. A successful policy in a small, relatively well-resourced country may not transfer easily to a large state with remote communities. The objective is to identify principles and adapt them to context.

Institutional quality is not a cultural destiny. Courts improve and deteriorate. Tax systems are reformed. Civil services professionalize or lose experienced staff. Corruption controls strengthen and weaken. Peace can be built and broken. No population is born with permanently good or bad governance. Institutions are human creations, shaped by history but also by choices, incentives, organization, and persistence.

Capable States and Productive Markets Need Each Other

Public debate often treats government and private enterprise as rivals. In practice, each depends on the other.

Markets rely on public institutions for currency, security, commercial law, contract enforcement, infrastructure, competition rules, education, public health, and regulation. Businesses cannot flourish for long if roads are unsafe, electricity unreliable, contracts meaningless, or skilled workers unable to reach jobs. Even the most independent entrepreneur operates inside systems built and maintained with others.

Governments, in turn, depend on productive private activity. Firms and workers create goods, services, employment, innovation, and much of the tax base. A state that treats every business as a source of extraction weakens the economy that funds public life. A market in which politically connected firms can buy rules weakens the fairness and legitimacy of the state.

The goal is not maximum government or minimum government. It is a workable relationship in which public institutions set fair rules and provide essential goods, while enterprise has room to experiment, compete, invest, and create value. The proper balance will differ by sector and country. Electricity transmission, primary healthcare, mobile payments, mineral extraction, and neighborhood retail do not present the same risks or require the same institutional arrangement.

Capable states and productive markets can strengthen each other. Better services improve the environment for business. A broader, more formal economy increases public revenue. Higher revenue can support stronger institutions, which can make investment safer and public services more reliable. The reverse cycle is also possible: weak services constrain firms, a narrow tax base limits the state, and poor administration further discourages production. Institutional reform is partly the work of turning a damaging cycle into a productive one.

Institutions as a Multiplier

Institutional weakness does not remain confined to a ministry labeled governance. It travels through the whole economy.

Weak procurement raises the cost of infrastructure. Poor customs administration reduces the value of trade agreements. Delayed courts make credit and contracts riskier. Unclear land rights discourage long-term investment. Weak statistics obscure whether policies work. Political violence damages human capital. Corruption diverts resources. Unpredictable regulation favors those who can purchase access or survive delay.

The reverse is also true. A reliable procurement unit can make the same infrastructure budget build more. A transparent land process can protect communities while reducing uncertainty. A professional statistical office can expose failures early. A court that manages cases well can make business relationships more dependable. A trusted election or mediation process can keep political conflict from becoming armed conflict.

Institutions therefore act as a multiplier. They can increase or diminish the value of investments made elsewhere. That does not mean a single reform transforms a country. Institutions are systems, and systems improve through many connected changes: better recruitment, clearer procedures, usable information, credible oversight, adequate funding, professional leadership, and consequences for failure.

Nor does development wait until institutions are perfect. No country possesses perfect institutions. Progress often occurs while systems remain incomplete and contested. The useful question is whether institutions are becoming more capable of serving the public, more predictable in the exercise of power, more open to correction, and less vulnerable to collapse when leaders change.

Can public money become functioning schools, clinics, roads, and power systems? Can citizens and businesses understand the rules that affect them? Can a person without wealth or connection receive a fair hearing? Can political disagreement occur without violence? Can institutions acknowledge failure and learn? These are not abstract tests. They reveal whether development reaches people's lives.

Africa's future will not be determined only by what lies beneath its soil, how large its market becomes, or how much infrastructure it constructs. It will also depend on the institutions that connect those assets to the public, protect them across generations, and correct them when they fail.

Chapter 16 turns from systems to responsibility. Institutions do not build themselves. They are shaped by public officials, citizens, educators, businesspeople, professionals, community leaders, regional bodies, and the diaspora. The final question is therefore not only what Africa needs, but who must do the work, and what each actor owes to the future being described.

Evidence Note

Governance is harder to measure than physical infrastructure. The Worldwide Governance Indicators used in this chapter are perception-based composite measures. Their 2025 revision covers more than 200 economies and provides a revised series through 2024, but the World Bank presents the six dimensions separately and advises using them as a broad comparative lens rather than a precise diagnosis of particular reforms. They should be read with country-level administrative, legal, financial, and service-delivery evidence. The Sudan displacement figures refer specifically to the end of 2025 and distinguish people displaced inside Sudan from refugees and asylum-seekers outside the country. Such totals change as people flee, return, or are displaced again. The World Bank statement about extreme poverty in settings affected by fragility, conflict, and violence is global and depends on the Bank's classifications and poverty measures. African Union documents establish agreed aspirations and formal institutions; their existence should not be treated as evidence that implementation has succeeded in every case.

CHAPTER 16

From Potential to Practice

Who Must Build the Africa We Have Described?

This book began with knowledge. It asked what Africans should know about the continent's history, people, resources, economies, institutions, and place in the world. Across those subjects, two truths kept appearing together. Africa has extraordinary possibilities, and it also faces serious constraints. There is no contradiction in saying both.

Potential tells us what could be done. It does not tell us what has already been achieved. A mineral deposit is not an industry. A young population is not automatically a skilled workforce. A signed trade agreement is not yet a working market. A new school building is not the same as learning, and a power plant on paper does not light a home or keep a factory running.

Chapter 15 examined the institutions, peace, and rule of law that make durable progress possible. This final chapter turns from systems to responsibility. Institutions do not build themselves. They are shaped by public officials, citizens, educators, businesspeople, professionals, community leaders, regional bodies, and the diaspora. International partners also influence what becomes possible, though they cannot replace African institutions or make African choices.

The practical question is therefore not simply, what does Africa need? It is, who is responsible for what?

That question matters because Africa is not one government, one economy, or one community. The African Union has 55 member states, each with its own political system, laws, resources, geography, institutions, and priorities (African Union, n.d.). Responsibilities also exist below and above the nation. A municipal government manages problems that a continental body cannot. A regional organization can address cross-border systems that a town or province cannot. A business can produce and invest in ways a ministry should not try to imitate. A citizen has duties, but cannot personally repair a national power grid.

The task is not to make everyone responsible for everything. It is to match responsibility with authority, resources, and ability, then make performance visible.

Responsibility Must Match Power

Discussions about African development have often begun with the question, Who will help Africa? Help may be valuable, especially during emergencies or when a country needs financing, technology, or specialized knowledge. But the question is incomplete. It places the continent in the position of waiting and treats development as something delivered from elsewhere.

A better question is, Who has the power to change this condition, and what should that person or institution be expected to do?

National governments possess powers that private companies do not. They make laws, collect taxes, set public budgets, regulate markets, administer justice, negotiate treaties, and provide or finance public services. Businesses make investments, organize production, hire workers, and respond to customers. Universities educate, conduct research, and preserve knowledge. Banks and investors direct capital. Local governments manage services close to daily life. Regional institutions coordinate across borders. Civil society and the media help the public examine decisions. Citizens work, vote where elections are provided, pay taxes, obey laws, organize communities, and hold authority to account.

These roles overlap, but they are not interchangeable. A private company may build a power plant, yet government still has to establish credible regulation and protect the public interest. A university may develop a useful agricultural technique, yet farmers, businesses, extension services, and financiers are needed to carry it into production. A community may maintain a local water point, but it should not be asked to finance a national water system from household contributions.

Shared responsibility must never become a way for powerful institutions to shift blame onto people with little power. When a hospital has no medicine because procurement failed, the patient is not responsible. When customs procedures are slow and contradictory, a small trader cannot solve the system alone. Responsibility should be proportionate. Those who control public money, rules, and institutions should carry the greatest burden of explanation.

This principle is consistent with the African Union's Agenda 2063. Its current implementation period, the Second Ten-Year Implementation Plan for 2024 to 2033, calls for participation by governments, regional economic communities, civil society, the private sector, academia, the media, and the diaspora. It also emphasizes coordination, monitoring, evaluation, accountability, and transparency (African Union, 2024). The list is broad because transformation is a system. The responsibilities within that system still have to be clear.

Governments Must Build the Foundations

Governments cannot and should not operate every farm, shop, factory, bank, or transport company. They remain responsible for the foundations on which productive life depends.

Those foundations include public safety, a functioning legal system, predictable administration, basic education, public health, reliable statistics, sound infrastructure policy, and a macroeconomic environment in which households and businesses can plan. They include the quiet work of keeping records, maintaining roads, paying public employees on time, publishing rules, managing public debt, and making it possible to challenge an official decision.

The distinction is not between a government that acts and one that stays out of the way. Every market is shaped by laws, infrastructure, standards, taxes, public institutions, and the quality of administration. The real question is whether government performs necessary public functions competently and creates room for productive activity.

Consider electricity. In 2025, the International Energy Agency estimated that roughly 600 million people in Africa still lacked access to electricity. Under its ACCESS scenario, achieving universal access in sub-Saharan Africa by 2035 would require nearly US$150 billion in cumulative investment, or about US$15 billion a year (International Energy Agency, 2025). The figure is a modeled pathway, not a forecast, but it conveys the scale of the task.

No ministry can meet that need by announcement. Governments have to set credible policy, plan generation and transmission, regulate public and private providers, protect consumers, and direct scarce public or concessional money toward projects that would otherwise remain unserved. Utilities must improve maintenance, billing, and financial discipline. Private developers and local enterprises can build grids, mini-grids, and stand-alone systems where each is appropriate. Banks and development institutions must structure finance. Technical colleges must train electricians and engineers. Communities need a voice in decisions that affect land, service, and cost.

Electricity also shows why priorities matter. A dependable supply does more than illuminate a room. It supports clinics, schools, water systems, cold storage, digital services, workshops, and factories. Governments with limited resources should ask not only what a project costs, but what other productive activity it will enable.

The same reasoning applies to transport corridors, water systems, ports, digital infrastructure, and education. A project deserves attention not because it is impressive at an opening ceremony, but because it solves a defined problem, connects people to opportunity, and can be maintained after the cameras leave.

Local government belongs in this discussion. In many countries, the quality of daily life depends heavily on municipalities, districts, provinces, counties, or other subnational authorities. They plan streets and markets, manage waste, regulate building, maintain local roads, and deliver services close to households. Rapid urban growth will place even more pressure on these institutions. National policy can establish direction and finance, but local administration often determines whether a neighborhood is safe, connected, and livable.

Build Institutions That Outlast Officeholders

Infrastructure takes years to plan and build. A strong school system takes longer. Research institutions and industrial supply chains may require decades. Development cannot restart each time a minister, mayor, president, or governing party changes.

This does not mean that policies should be protected from criticism. Bad policies should be changed. Wasteful projects should be stopped. Officials should remain accountable to constitutions, laws, elections, courts, and the public arrangements of their countries. Continuity is not an argument for keeping leaders in office. It is an argument for keeping institutions capable of doing their work when leaders leave.

A professional civil service preserves records and knowledge. A statistical agency uses methods that do not change to suit a speech. A regulator explains its decisions. A court follows procedures even when a powerful party dislikes the result. An infrastructure authority keeps maintenance schedules across budget cycles. A university protects serious inquiry. These habits allow a country to learn instead of repeatedly beginning from zero.

Chapter 15 argued that capable institutions and accountability must grow together. Chapter 16 adds a practical test: can the institution continue to perform its legitimate function beyond the individual who currently leads it? A system that works only when an exceptional person is present is not yet strong.

Africa needs ethical and competent leaders. It also needs systems in which good leadership can produce results and abuse is harder to conceal. The future of a country should not depend on finding one remarkable individual in every generation.

Regional Institutions Must Solve Regional Problems

Some problems are mainly national or local. Others cross borders by their nature. Rivers, disease outbreaks, electricity grids, transport corridors, digital networks, migration, financial transactions, and trade do not stop neatly at a customs post.

Regional economic communities, the African Union, the AfCFTA Secretariat, development institutions, and specialized regional bodies are most valuable when national action alone is insufficient. Their purpose is not to administer every African town or replace national governments. It is to create cooperation where separate national systems have to connect.

The African Continental Free Trade Area illustrates both the promise and the difficulty. The agreement was adopted in 2018 and entered into force in 2019 (African Union, 2018). Its economic meaning, however, depends on what happens after ratification. A treaty does not manufacture a product, move a truck, finance an order, or find a customer. Businesses do those things.

For the agreement to matter in daily commerce, a company must be able to understand the rules, prove where its product originated, meet relevant standards, complete customs procedures, make and receive payments, transport goods at a reasonable cost, and resolve disputes. Border agencies need compatible systems. Officials need training. Regulations must be published and applied with enough consistency that a business can plan.

The opportunity remains substantial because regional trade is still shallow. UN Trade and Development reported in its *Economic Development in Africa Report 2024* that intra-African trade accounted for about 16 percent of Africa's total trade (UN Trade and Development, 2025). The precise share varies with the year, dataset, and definition, so the number should not be treated as permanent. Its significance is that African producers still have considerable room to build commercial relationships and production networks within the continent.

Payments provide a concrete example of implementation. A business in one African country that buys from a supplier in another must settle the transaction. The Pan-African Payment and Settlement System is financial infrastructure designed to support cross-border payments through participating banks and payment providers, including payments initiated and received in local currencies. PAPSS describes its core processes as instant payment, pre-funding, and net settlement (PAPSS, n.d.). It is not a single African currency, and it does not remove exchange-rate risk. It addresses a narrower problem: the friction involved in moving money across African borders.

That is the proper standard for regional institutions. Identify a shared obstacle. Decide which level of authority can address it. Build a system that people can actually use. Measure whether cost, delay, risk, or uncertainty falls.

No country must wait for the whole continent before acting. One government can improve a border post. Two neighboring countries can coordinate operating hours. Several countries can build an electricity interconnector. A regional bloc can harmonize a specific standard. Continental progress can grow from practical improvements that begin at different levels and eventually connect.

Businesses Must Turn Markets Into Production

Governments create conditions, but productive firms create goods and services. They invest, hire, train, organize supply chains, adopt technology, and take commercial risks. If Africa's larger markets are to support better jobs and higher incomes, the continent needs more firms able to grow beyond subsistence or very small scale.

This is not an argument against microenterprises. Small businesses support families, serve communities, and often provide the first path into economic activity. The problem arises when capable firms remain small because electricity is unreliable, finance is unavailable, transport is expensive, regulations are unpredictable, or customers beyond the local market are difficult to reach.

Productive capacity means more than registering new companies or celebrating the language of entrepreneurship. It means helping viable firms improve quality, raise worker productivity, obtain equipment, manage accounts, meet standards, and reach larger markets. It also requires honest competition. A protected company that survives only through political connection may employ people, but it can weaken the broader economy by keeping prices high and blocking more capable producers.

African businesses should be able to think beyond national markets. A food processor may begin with domestic customers. If transport improves, standards become compatible, customs becomes more efficient, and payments become easier, neighboring countries can become additional markets. A wider customer base may justify a larger facility, better packaging, quality certification, and more specialized jobs. Regional scale can then help a firm compete internationally.

None of this is automatic. A large market on paper does not guarantee customers, efficiency, or profit. Firms still have to understand demand and offer reliable value. Regional integration should not become permanent shelter from global competition. Its deeper purpose is to help African producers develop the scale and capability to meet it.

African Capital Must Help Finance African Development

International finance will remain important. Many African countries need more long-term capital than domestic markets can presently supply, especially for large infrastructure. Concessional finance can be essential for projects with high social value and limited immediate commercial return. Foreign direct investment can bring technology, management experience, and access to markets.

It would still be a mistake to imagine that every productive investment must begin elsewhere. African economies already contain household savings, banks, pension funds, insurance companies, public financial institutions, businesses, cooperatives, and individual investors. The central challenge is to mobilize capital, domestic and international, toward productive use while managing risk and protecting savers.

Governments contribute by maintaining credible public finances, strengthening financial regulation, improving project preparation, and avoiding sudden rules that destroy trust. Banks have to move beyond lending mainly against familiar collateral when viable firms need working capital or equipment finance. Capital markets can provide longer-term funding where institutions and scale permit. Development banks can absorb selected risks without becoming channels for political favoritism. Pension and insurance funds need prudent regulation because the money they manage belongs to workers and policyholders, not to politicians seeking an easy source of finance.

The question is not whether capital is African or foreign in a symbolic sense. The important questions are practical. What will be built? Who carries the risk? Are the terms transparent? Is the debt sustainable? Does the investment create useful capacity? Can the asset earn enough, directly or through public value, to justify its cost?

Money does not become development simply because it is spent. It becomes development when it finances something sound, useful, and durable.

Education and Research Must Meet Real Problems

Chapter 14 examined the importance of education, health, and human capability. The responsibility of schools, universities, technical colleges, and research institutions is not merely to issue certificates. It is to help people understand the world, perform useful work, solve problems, and create knowledge suited to their societies.

Universities should remain places of broad learning, not narrow training centers for the latest labor-market demand. Yet they cannot be indifferent to the conditions around them. Engineering faculties can work on local construction materials, water systems, energy, and manufacturing processes. Agricultural researchers can study soils, crops, storage, livestock, and climate conditions that farmers actually face. Medical schools can strengthen clinical practice and public-health research. Economists and social scientists can test whether programs achieve what governments claim.

Technical and vocational institutions deserve equal seriousness. An economy cannot maintain electrical systems, medical equipment, water networks, factories, vehicles, or digital infrastructure without skilled technicians. Training should be designed with employers and professional bodies, supported by functioning equipment, and judged by what graduates can do. A classroom course labeled practical is not enough if no student touches the tools used in the occupation.

Employers share responsibility. A company cannot demand experienced workers forever while refusing to train anyone. Apprenticeships, internships, supervised practice, and partnerships with colleges can make the transition from education to work more realistic. Governments can establish standards and incentives, but firms know which skills production requires.

Research also needs patience. Serious institutions are built through stable funding, ethical standards, laboratories, data, libraries, collaboration, and career paths that allow talented people to remain. Not every country can maintain every expensive facility. Regional research networks can share equipment and expertise, especially in fields where the questions and benefits cross borders.

Citizens Should Demand Outcomes, Not Announcements

Citizens are not spectators. They work in public institutions and businesses, teach children, serve communities, pay or evade taxes, follow or break laws, and shape what conduct is socially accepted. Where political systems provide meaningful elections, citizens also choose among leaders and programs.

This role must be described honestly. Citizenship does not erase unequal power. A citizen cannot personally end a war, fix a customs administration, or finance a regional railway. Telling ordinary people to change their mindset can become an easy substitute for fixing structures that constrain them. It is unreasonable to demand patience and sacrifice from citizens while public officials avoid accountability.

What citizens can reasonably demand is evidence of performance. A new hospital building is not the same as functioning health care. A budget allocation is not the same as medicines on a shelf. A school enrollment figure is not proof that children are learning. A trade agreement is not increased trade. A road announcement is not a maintained road.

The questions should become more concrete. Did electricity access improve? Did transport time fall? Are teachers present, and are pupils learning? Can a small business complete a permit without an unofficial payment? Did a water system continue working five years after construction? Did maternal deaths decline? Are courts resolving cases more fairly and promptly? Did the promised funds reach the district?

Civil-society organizations, researchers, journalists, professional associations, and community groups can help people ask these questions. They can translate budgets and policies into language the public can understand, examine procurement, document local experience, and make neglected voices harder to ignore. Independent information is part of accountability.

Critics should be held to the same evidence standard as governments. A false claim does not become useful because it opposes power. Africa needs optimism grounded in evidence and criticism grounded in evidence. Both are forms of respect for the public.

Women, Young People, and the Diaspora Are Not Side Programs

Policy documents often list women, young people, and the diaspora near the end, as though they were special constituencies outside the main economy. They are already part of it.

Women farm, trade, teach, manage households, lead institutions, practice medicine, conduct research, run companies, and serve in government. The question is not how to add women to development after the main plan is complete. It is whether laws, finance, education, safety, property systems, health services, and workplaces allow women to participate fully and receive a fair return for their work.

The same is true of young people. Youth is not a permanent economic category or a substitute for a job. A young population becomes an advantage when children are healthy, schools teach well, training leads to useful skill, and economies create room for productive work. Young Africans should be able to influence decisions that will shape their lives, but they should not be told that enthusiasm alone can overcome weak institutions and scarce opportunity.

The diaspora contributes through family remittances, investment, professional networks, research, business formation, and the transfer of knowledge. These connections can be valuable, but they should not be romanticized. Living abroad does not automatically give someone better judgment about a community at home. Productive engagement begins with listening, understanding local conditions, and building relationships that continue after an initial visit or investment.

Governments can make diaspora participation easier through transparent investment rules, credible institutions, portable professional recognition where appropriate, reliable information, and channels that connect expertise to real needs. Diaspora communities, in turn, should evaluate projects carefully rather than relying on sentiment or personal connection. Trust grows when expectations, ownership, and risk are clear.

International Partners Should Build Capability, Not Dependency

African self-determination is compatible with international cooperation. Every major modern economy participates in global trade, finance, science, investment, and technology exchange. Africa will continue to work with Europe, the United States, China, India, the Middle East, Latin America, Asia, multilateral institutions, foundations, companies, and universities.

The useful distinction is not foreign equals good or foreign equals bad. It is between partnerships that strengthen African capability and arrangements that leave little behind.

Each proposal should be examined on its terms. What problem is it meant to solve? Who selected the priority? Who benefits? What debt, guarantees, resource commitments, or other liabilities are created? Are contracts transparent to the extent legitimate commercial confidentiality allows? What skills and technology will be transferred? Can local institutions operate and maintain what is built? What happens when the outside partner leaves?

Emergency assistance may properly focus on immediate survival. Long-term development cooperation should be judged more broadly. A laboratory that cannot obtain supplies after a grant ends is not a durable research system. Equipment that no local technician can repair may become an expensive monument. A consultant's report that remains on a shelf has not created institutional memory.

Partnership is strongest when African institutions have enough knowledge and bargaining capacity to define their needs, compare options, negotiate carefully, supervise performance, and refuse terms that do not serve the public interest. International partners should respect those responsibilities rather than expecting privileged access in return for assistance.

Coordination Is Where Plans Become Real

Development is often discussed by sector: energy, agriculture, education, health, trade, or transport. Real economies do not respect those administrative divisions.

Imagine an agricultural region trying to sell more processed food. Farmers first need appropriate seed, knowledge, water, and access to inputs. Producer organizations may aggregate crops in quantities a processor can buy. The processing company needs electricity, equipment, workers, quality control, and working capital. A technical college trains operators and maintenance staff. A road connects farms to the plant and the plant to a regional corridor. A packaging company supplies containers. Laboratories certify safety. Customs authorities apply trade rules. A bank or payment system settles cross-border sales. A university helps improve storage or processing. Logistics companies deliver the final product.

No single participant created the result. Farmers produced. Firms invested. Workers applied skill. Banks financed. Government provided rules and infrastructure. Educators and researchers supplied knowledge. Regional institutions connected markets.

This is not a claim that the precise arrangement exists everywhere. It is a way of seeing why isolated projects disappoint. A factory without reliable electricity, raw materials, skills, finance, or customers may remain idle. A road that connects no productive centers may carry less traffic than promised. Agricultural output can rise while farmers lose money because storage and markets were ignored.

Coordination does not require one central authority to control every decision. It requires participants to understand their dependencies, share reliable information, and resolve problems at the appropriate level. Sometimes that work is unglamorous: compatible standards, synchronized schedules, clear contracts, maintenance budgets, and meetings focused on an actual bottleneck rather than a broad declaration.

Sequence, Measurement, and Learning Matter

No country can solve every problem at the same time with equal intensity. Starting points differ. A country at war must give urgent attention to peace, security, humanitarian need, and reconstruction. One with a severe electricity deficit may prioritize energy. A commodity-dependent economy may focus on diversification. A landlocked country may place transport corridors and relations with its neighbors near the center of strategy. Another may have sound basic infrastructure but weak research capability.

There are common foundations, but there is no single sequence for all African countries. Priorities should follow evidence about the country's own constraints, opportunities, finances, and institutional capacity.

Measurement begins before action. What problem is being solved? Who experiences it? What does existing evidence show? What alternatives were considered? What will the project cost to build and maintain? Who is responsible for each stage? What result should be visible, and by when?

Measurement continues after implementation. Did the project reach the intended people? Were costs reasonable? What unintended effects appeared? Is the service still functioning? What should be changed? A project that fails should not be defended merely because an important leader announced it. A project that succeeds should be studied closely enough to understand why.

The discipline is simple: measure, act, measure again, learn, and improve.

Data cannot answer every political or moral question. Communities may value outcomes that are difficult to place in a spreadsheet. Numbers can be selected or presented dishonestly. Yet refusing to measure leaves the public with promises, impressions, and arguments that cannot be tested. Evidence should inform judgment, not replace it.

Copy Principles, Not Countries

This book has drawn lessons from many African countries. Readers may be tempted to ask which country others should copy. That is usually the wrong question.

Morocco, Kenya, Botswana, Mauritius, Rwanda, Ethiopia, Ghana, South Africa, and every other country began with different populations, geographies, histories, institutions, neighbors, and political choices. A policy that works in a small island economy may not transfer neatly to a large landlocked state. A system designed for a relatively strong civil service may fail where administrative capacity is thin. What looks successful nationally may also conceal costs or exclusions that a simple headline misses.

The better questions are narrower. Which principle appeared to work? Was it reliable infrastructure, patient investment, export access, effective regulation, institutional continuity, technical education, industrial clustering, or coordination between public and private actors? What evidence supports that conclusion? Under what conditions did it work? Would those conditions exist elsewhere, or could they be created?

Learning is not imitation. It requires humility from both the country studying an example and the country being praised. No nation is a complete model. A country may perform well in one sector and poorly in another. It may improve during one period and decline during the next. African countries should learn from one another without turning any of them into a myth.

There Is No Single Leader or Miracle Industry

The search for one great leader and the search for one miracle industry arise from the same desire: a complicated problem should have a simple answer.

Leadership matters. A competent, ethical, and determined leader can improve priorities, appointments, public trust, and implementation. But countries that depend entirely on exceptional individuals remain vulnerable when those individuals leave. Durable progress requires courts, public services, local governments, universities, businesses, financial institutions, and rules that can survive a leadership transition.

Nor will one sector transform every African economy. Not oil, mining, tourism, agriculture, technology, artificial intelligence, or manufacturing by itself. Countries have different comparative advantages, and productive sectors depend on one another. Agriculture needs transport, energy, science, finance, and processing. Digital services need electricity, skill, regulation, and paying customers. Mining can generate revenue and industrial inputs, but it does not automatically create broad prosperity. Tourism can support jobs and foreign exchange, yet it can also be vulnerable to shocks.

Resilience usually requires diversification. The mix will differ by country and may include agriculture, manufacturing, services, logistics, finance, energy, tourism, creative industries, technology, and responsible natural-resource production. The goal is not to assemble every sector for the sake of variety. It is to avoid placing a country's future on one narrow source of income and to build connections through which capability in one field strengthens another.

Build Nationally, Connect Regionally, Compete Globally

The practical economic argument of this book can be carried forward in three movements.

Build nationally. Every country has to strengthen its institutions, educate its people, improve health, expand reliable energy, maintain infrastructure, support productive agriculture and business, develop science and technology, and preserve peace. Regional integration cannot substitute for weak domestic foundations.

Connect regionally. Roads, railways, electricity grids, payment systems, digital networks, research partnerships, supply chains, and markets should cross borders where connection creates value. Countries can reduce avoidable barriers, coordinate infrastructure, and treat neighboring economies as potential suppliers, customers, and partners.

Compete globally. African firms need quality, productivity, reliability, technology, skill, strong brands, and competitive costs. Governments and regional institutions can improve the environment, but they cannot guarantee a market for a poor product. The aim is not withdrawal from the world. It is participation from a stronger productive base and with greater bargaining capacity.

These movements depend on one another. National capability without regional connection may leave firms trapped in small markets. Regional agreements without capable national institutions may remain underused. Regional protection without global competitiveness can preserve inefficiency. The sequence is not rigid, but the relationship is important.

Build nationally. Connect regionally. Compete globally.

What Success Should Look Like

Africa's progress should not be measured mainly by speeches about greatness or by rankings celebrated for a week. It should be visible in ordinary life.

A child learns to read well. A mother receives reliable care. A farmer reaches a profitable market. A nurse finds medicine in the clinic. An electrician earns a living from skill. A scientist can conduct serious research. A small firm receives a decision on a permit within a known period. A factory operates without planning every day around a power failure. A truck crosses a border without an unnecessary week of delay. A graduate finds productive work. A court hears a case fairly. A road remains usable years after its opening.

Success also appears in relationships between countries. A neighboring African economy becomes a more familiar customer, supplier, investor, research partner, and source of ideas. Governments cooperate where interests overlap even when they disagree elsewhere. Technical standards, infrastructure, and payment systems make distance and borders less costly without erasing national identity.

Cooperation does not require sameness. Africans will continue to speak different languages, practice different faiths, hold different political opinions, and maintain strong local and national identities. Unity cannot mean universal agreement. It can mean the ability to work together where shared interests are clear.

Development becomes real through millions of outcomes like these. No single statistic captures them all, but future evidence will reveal whether access widened, capability deepened, and institutions became more dependable.

The Africa We Choose to Build

No generation begins with a blank continent. Today's Africans inherited countries and borders, languages and institutions, achievements and conflicts, infrastructure and debt, natural wealth and environmental pressures, memory and unfinished work. The next generation will inherit what this one strengthens, neglects, builds, damages, or leaves unresolved.

That inheritance will be measurable. Will fewer people live without electricity? Will more children learn, not merely enroll? Will African research capacity deepen? Will more goods be processed before export? Will firms trade more easily across African borders? Will public institutions become more capable and accountable? Will fewer families be displaced by conflict? Will roads, clinics, schools, and water systems still function after the projects that created them are no longer new?

The answers will not come from speeches. Future data, institutions, and lived experience will provide them.

Africa's development cannot be outsourced. Others can finance, invest, teach, research, trade, and partner. Those relationships can make a real difference. But Africans will live most directly with the results. African governments will decide whether public institutions earn trust. African businesses will decide whether a market becomes productive capacity. African educators and researchers will decide whether knowledge meets real problems. African citizens will decide what conduct they accept and what performance they demand. Regional institutions will decide whether continental commitments become usable systems.

This is not a call for isolation or a denial of the forces that have shaped the continent from outside. It is a recognition that self-determination carries responsibility. A continent cannot control every global shock, commodity price, climate event, or foreign decision. It can strengthen its ability to respond, negotiate, adapt, and act together.

The evidence in this book gives no reason to pretend that the road ahead will be easy. Large gaps remain in electricity, education, health, infrastructure, research, productive employment, trade, peace, and institutional capacity. Those facts should not be hidden. Neither should they be turned into a permanent story of incapacity.

Africa has people with knowledge, skill, ambition, and experience. It has farms, minerals, energy resources, cities, businesses, universities, communities, and institutions. It has examples of progress as well as warnings from failure. The central challenge is to organize these assets, strengthen capability, connect what remains divided, and insist on performance.

That work belongs to governments, but not only to governments. It belongs to businesses, but markets alone will not complete it. It belongs to schools and universities, farmers and workers, scientists and professionals, communities and citizens, regional bodies and the diaspora. It also calls for international partners willing to support African capability rather than substitute for it.

Each responsibility is different. Each should be judged by what it has the power to change.

My hope is not that every reader will agree with every conclusion in these pages. Thoughtful disagreement is part of serious learning. My hope is that this book encourages curiosity, honest conversation, deeper knowledge of Africa, and a greater willingness to ask not only what the continent possesses, but what can be built with it.

Africa does not need a mythology of effortless greatness. It does not need exaggerated claims about its resources or silence about its failures. Nor does it need to accept a permanent narrative of weakness.

It needs knowledge of what is true, memory of what has been endured and achieved, discipline to learn from evidence, and the courage to correct what fails. It needs people willing to protect what works, build what is missing, and cooperate where cooperation makes them stronger.

Potential is what exists. Capacity is what can be used. Performance is what produces results.

The future is not guaranteed by potential. It is built by what people do with it.

Evidence Note

This concluding chapter combines verified evidence with interpretation and recommendations. Figures retain the geography, reference period, and definitions used by their sources. The International Energy Agency's financing estimate is a modeled pathway rather than a forecast. The intra-African trade share varies with the year and method of calculation. "Build nationally, connect regionally, compete globally" is the book's synthesis of the evidence, not a statistical claim.

References

Acemoglu, D., Johnson, S., & Robinson, J. A. (2003). An African success story: Botswana. In D. Rodrik (Ed.), *In search of prosperity: Analytic narratives on economic growth* (pp. 80–119). Princeton University Press. https://doi.org/10.1515/9781400845897-006

Africa Centres for Disease Control and Prevention. (n.d.). *About us.* https://africacdc.org/about-us/

African Development Bank Group. (2024, August 1). *African Development Bank invests $20 million in infrastructure fund to catalyze continental development.* https://www.afdb.org/en/news-and-events/press-releases/african-development-bank-invests-20-million-infrastructure-fund-catalyze-continental-development-73143

African Development Bank Group. (2025, March 19). *2025 Annual Meetings: Regional corridors as drivers of continental integration.* https://www.afdb.org/en/news-and-events/2025-annual-meetings-regional-corridors-drivers-continental-integration-81924

African Union, UNESCO, & UNICEF. (2025). *Transforming learning and skills development in Africa: Second continental report.* UNESCO. https://unesdoc.unesco.org/ark:/48223/pf0000393250

African Union. (2000). *Constitutive Act of the African Union.* https://achpr.au.int/en/node/884

African Union. (2018). *Agreement establishing the African Continental Free Trade Area*. https://au.int/en/treaties/agreement-establishing-african-continental-free-trade-area

African Union. (2019). *Progress report on the Pan African University.* https://au.int/sites/default/files/newsevents/workingdocuments/37841-wd-pau_progress_report_en.pdf

African Union. (2021, June 4). *African Union launches world's largest single electricity market (AfSEM).* https://au.int/en/pressreleases/20210604/african-union-launches-worlds-largest-single-electricity-market-afsem

African Union. (2022). *AfCFTA rules of origin manual.* https://au.int/sites/default/files/treaties/36437-ax-AfCFTA_RULES_OF_ORIGIN_MANUAL.pdf

African Union. (2023, August 8). *Status list: Protocol relating to free movement of persons, right of residence and right of establishment.* https://au.int/sites/default/files/treaties/36403-sl-PROTOCOL_TO_THE_TREATY_ESTABLISHING_THE_AFRICAN_ECONOMIC_COMMUNITY_RELATING_TO_FREE_MOVEMENT_OF_PERSONS-1.pdf

African Union. (2024, August 9). *Continental artificial intelligence strategy.* https://au.int/en/documents/20240809/continental-artificial-intelligence-strategy

African Union. (2024, February 17). *Agenda 2063: Launch of the second decade of acceleration.* https://au.int/en/newsevents/20240217/agenda-2063-launch-2nd-decade-acceleration

African Union. (2024, February 18). *Protocol to the Agreement Establishing the African Continental Free Trade Area on Digital Trade.* https://au.int/en/treaties/protocol-agreement-establishing-african-continental-free-trade-area-digital-trade-0

African Union. (2025). *Continental Education Strategy for Africa 2026-2035.* https://au.int/en/documents/20250616/continental-education-strategy-africa-2026-2035

African Union. (2025, February 20). *Malawi becomes 38th African country to join Africa's Single Air Transport Market.* https://au.int/en/pressreleases/20250220/malawi-becomes-38th-african-country-join-africas-single-air-transport-market

African Union. (2025, July 18). *Science, technology and innovation strategy for Africa 2034.* https://au.int/en/documents/20250718/science-technology-and-innovation-strategy-africa-stisa-2034

African Union. (2026, May 22). *Status list: Agreement establishing the African Continental Free Trade Area.* https://au.int/sites/default/files/treaties/36437-sl-AGREEMENT_ESTABLISHING_THE_AFRICAN_CONTINENTAL_FREE_TRADE_AREA_1.pdf

African Union. (n.d.). *About the African Union.* https://au.int/en/overview

African Union. (n.d.). *Member states.* https://au.int/en/member_states/countryprofiles2

African Union. (n.d.-a). *Our aspirations for the Africa we want.* https://au.int/en/agenda2063/aspirations

African Union. (n.d.-a). *The African Continental Free Trade Area.* https://au.int/en/african-continental-free-trade-area

African Union. (n.d.-b). *Regional Economic Communities.* https://au.int/en/recs

African Union. (n.d.-b). *The Peace and Security Council.* https://au.int/en/psc

Birmingham, D. (1995). *The decolonization of Africa.* UCL Press.

Bjerk, P. (2015). *Building a peaceful nation: Julius Nyerere and the establishment of sovereignty in Tanzania, 1960–1964.* University of Rochester Press.

Boahen, A. A. (Ed.). (1985). *General history of Africa, VII: Africa under colonial domination, 1880–1935.* UNESCO. https://unesdoc.unesco.org/ark:/48223/pf0000184296

British Museum. (n.d.). *Asante gold regalia*. https://www.britishmuseum.org/about-us/british-museum-story/contested-objects-collection/asante-gold-regalia

Clapham, C. (1988). *Transformation and continuity in revolutionary Ethiopia*. Cambridge University Press.

Cooper, F. (2002). *Africa since 1940: The past of the present*. Cambridge University Press.

Decalo, S. (1990). *Coups and army rule in Africa: Motivations and constraints* (2nd ed.). Yale University Press.

Economic Commission for Africa. (2025). *Assessment of progress on regional integration in Africa* (E/ECA/COE/44/5). United Nations. https://papersmart.uneca.org/download/5565

European Commission. (2026). *Single market*. https://commission.europa.eu/topics/single-market_en

Eurostat. (2025). *International trade in goods: An overview*. https://ec.europa.eu/eurostat/statistics-explained/index.php?title=International_trade_in_goods_-_an_overview

Ezra, K. (1992). *Royal art of Benin: The Perls Collection in the Metropolitan Museum of Art*. Metropolitan Museum of Art. https://www.metmuseum.org/met-publications/royal-art-of-benin-the-perls-collection

Falola, T., & Heaton, M. M. (2008). *A history of Nigeria*. Cambridge University Press.

Federal Foreign Office. (1885). *General Act of the Berlin West Africa Conference, 26 February 1885*. Political Archive of the Federal Foreign Office. https://archiv.diplo.de/arc-en/the-political-archive/general-act-2684414

Federal Foreign Office. (2021, May 28). *Foreign Minister Maas on the conclusion of negotiations with Namibia*. https://www.auswaertiges-amt.de/en/newsroom/news/2463598-2463598

Food and Agriculture Organization of the United Nations. (2025). *Glossary*. In *The state of the world's land and water resources for food and agriculture 2025*. https://www.fao.org/3/cd7488en/online/state-of-the-worlds-land-and-water-resources-for-food-and-agriculture-2025-2025/glossary.html

Food and Agriculture Organization of the United Nations. (2026, July 17). *Land statistics 2001–2024: Global, regional and country trends*. https://www.fao.org/statistics/highlights-archive/highlights-detail/land-statistics-2001-2024.-global--regional-and-country-trends/en

Foreign and Commonwealth Office. (2013, June 6). *Statement to Parliament on settlement of Mau Mau claims*. Government of the United Kingdom. https://www.gov.uk/government/news/statement-to-parliament-on-settlement-of-mau-mau-claims

Ghana Cocoa Board. (2025). *Government will prioritise local processing of cocoa to safeguard prices*. https://cocobod.gh/news/government-will-prioritise-local-processing-of-cocoa-to-safeguard-prices

Herbst, J. (2000). *States and power in Africa: Comparative lessons in authority and control*. Princeton University Press.

Hublin, J.-J., Ben-Ncer, A., Bailey, S. E., Freidline, S. E., Neubauer, S., Skinner, M. M., Bergmann, I., Le Cabec, A., Benazzi, S., Harvati, K., & Gunz, P. (2017). New fossils from Jebel Irhoud, Morocco and the pan-African origin of *Homo sapiens*. *Nature, 546*, 289–292. https://doi.org/10.1038/nature22336

Intergovernmental Panel on Climate Change. (2022). Africa. In *Climate change 2022: Impacts, adaptation and vulnerability* (pp. 1285–1456). Cambridge University Press. https://doi.org/10.1017/9781009325844.011

International Energy Agency. (2022). *Africa Energy Outlook 2022: Key findings*. https://www.iea.org/reports/africa-energy-outlook-2022/key-findings

International Energy Agency. (2024). *Kenya 2024: Executive summary*. https://www.iea.org/reports/kenya-2024/executive-summary

International Energy Agency. (2025). *Financing electricity access in Africa*. https://www.iea.org/reports/financing-electricity-access-in-africa

International Energy Agency. (2025). *Stepping up the value chain in Africa: Minerals, materials and manufacturing*. https://www.iea.org/reports/stepping-up-the-value-chain-in-africa

International Telecommunication Union. (2025a). *Facts and Figures 2025: Internet use*. https://www.itu.int/itu-d/reports/statistics/2025/10/15/ff25-internet-use/

International Telecommunication Union. (2025a). *Facts and Figures 2025: Mobile phone ownership*. https://www.itu.int/itu-d/reports/statistics/2025/10/15/ff25-mobile-phone-ownership/

International Telecommunication Union. (2025b). *Facts and Figures 2025: Internet use in urban and rural areas*. https://www.itu.int/itu-d/reports/statistics/2025/10/15/ff25-internet-use-in-urban-and-rural-areas/

Lal, P. (2015). *African socialism in postcolonial Tanzania: Between the village and the world*. Cambridge University Press.

Library of Congress. (n.d.-a). *The Great Depression: Italy invades Ethiopia*. https://www.loc.gov/exhibits/naacp/the-great-depression.html

Library of Congress. (n.d.-b). *History of Liberia: A time line*. https://www.loc.gov/collections/maps-of-liberia-1830-to-1870/articles-and-essays/history-of-liberia/

Mas, I., & Radcliffe, D. (2010). *Mobile payments go viral: M-PESA in Kenya*. World Bank. https://documents.worldbank.org/en/publication/documents-reports/documentdetail/638851468048259219

Metropolitan Museum of Art. (2000a). *Foundations of Aksumite civilization and its Christian legacy (1st-7th century).* https://www.metmuseum.org/essays/foundations-of-aksumite-civilization-and-its-christian-legacy-1st-7th-century

Metropolitan Museum of Art. (2000b). *The trans-Saharan gold trade (7th-14th century).* https://www.metmuseum.org/essays/the-trans-saharan-gold-trade-7th-14th-century

Mkandawire, T., & Soludo, C. C. (1999). *Our continent, our future: African perspectives on structural adjustment*. Africa World Press.

National Army Museum. (n.d.). *The Battle of Isandlwana, 22 January 1879.* https://www.nam.ac.uk/explore/battle-isandlwana-22-january-1879

Ndlovu, X. A., & Vandome, C. (2024). *Mineral resource governance in Botswana*. International IDEA. https://doi.org/10.31752/idea.2024.117

Nyerere, J. K. (1968). *Ujamaa: Essays on socialism*. Oxford University Press.

Office des Changes. (2025). *Annual report on Morocco's foreign trade for the year 2024*. https://www.oc.gov.ma/en/actualites/publication-du-rapport-annuel-du-commerce-exterieur-du-maroc-au-titre-de-l-annee-2024

Ofoego, O. (2015). *Taytu Betul: The rise of an Itege*. UNESCO. https://unesdoc.unesco.org/ark:/48223/pf0000233138

Organization of African Unity. (1963). *Charter of the Organization of African Unity.* https://au.int/sites/default/files/treaties/7759-file-oau_charter_1963.pdf

Organization of African Unity. (1964). *AHG/Res. 16(I): Border disputes among African states*. African Union Archives. https://archives.au.int/bitstream/handle/123456789/157/FIRST%20ORDINARY_E.pdf

Pan-African Parliament. (2024, September 19). *Significant progress on AfCFTA implementation highlighted at conference*. https://pap.au.int/en/news/press-releases/2024-09-19/significant-progress-afcfta-implementation-highlighted-conference-s

Pan-African Payment and Settlement System. (2022, January 13). *Commercial launch event*. https://papss.com/events/commercial-launch-event/

Pan-African Payment and Settlement System. (2026, July 9). *BEAC joins PAPSS, connecting payments between CEMAC and the rest of Africa*. https://papss.com/media/beac-joins-papss-connecting-payments-between-cemac-and-the-rest-of-africa/

Pan-African Payment and Settlement System. (n.d.). *About us*. https://papss.com/about-us/

Pan-African Payment and Settlement System. (n.d.). *How it works*. Retrieved September 2, 2026, from https://papss.com/how-it-works/

Ragsdale, A. P., Weaver, T. D., Atkinson, E. G., Hoal, E. G., Möller, M., Henn, B. M., & Gravel, S. (2023). A weakly structured stem for human origins in Africa. *Nature, 617*, 755–763. https://doi.org/10.1038/s41586-023-06055-y

Reuters. (2025, September 9). *Ethiopia launches Africa's largest hydroelectric dam.* https://www.reuters.com/sustainability/boards-policy-regulation/ethiopia-launches-africas-largest-hydroelectric-dam-2025-09-09/

Royal Museum for Central Africa. (n.d.). *The viewpoints of the museum.* https://www.africamuseum.be/en/about_us/viewpoints

Smithsonian Institution. (2023, May 17). *No single site for modern human origins.* Human Origins Program. https://humanorigins.si.edu/research/whats-hot-human-origins/no-single-site-modern-human-origins

Smithsonian Institution. (2024a, July 9). *Introduction to human evolution.* Human Origins Program. https://humanorigins.si.edu/education/introduction-human-evolution

Smithsonian Institution. (2024b, January 3). *Homo sapiens.* Human Origins Program. https://humanorigins.si.edu/evidence/human-fossils/species/homo-sapiens

Statistics South Africa. (2026, August 11). *Quarterly Labour Force Survey, Q2: 2026.* https://www.statssa.gov.za/?p=19804

U.S. Department of State, Office of the Historian. (n.d.-a). *Ghana.* https://history.state.gov/countries/ghana

U.S. Department of State, Office of the Historian. (n.d.-a). *Nigerian Civil War.* In *Foreign relations of the United States, 1969–1976, volume E-5, part 1: Documents on sub-Saharan Africa, 1969–1972.* https://history.state.gov/historicaldocuments/frus1969-76ve05p1/ch2

U.S. Department of State, Office of the Historian. (n.d.-b). *Guinea.* https://history.state.gov/countries/guinea

U.S. Department of State, Office of the Historian. (n.d.-c). *The Congo, decolonization, and the Cold War, 1960–1965.* https://history.state.gov/milestones/1961-1968/congo-decolonization

U.S. Department of State, Office of the Historian. (n.d.-d). *Algeria.* https://history.state.gov/countries/algeria

U.S. Department of State, Office of the Historian. (n.d.-e). *Tanzania.* https://history.state.gov/countries/tanzania

U.S. Department of State, Office of the Historian. (n.d.-f). *Mozambique.* https://history.state.gov/countries/mozambique

U.S. Department of State, Office of the Historian. (n.d.-g). *Angola.* https://history.state.gov/countries/angola

U.S. Department of State, Office of the Historian. (n.d.-h). *The Angola crisis, 1974–75.* https://history.state.gov/milestones/1969-1976/angola

U.S. Department of State, Office of the Historian. (n.d.-i). *Zambia*. https://history.state.gov/countries/zambia

U.S. Department of State. (2013). *Foreign relations of the United States, 1964–1968, volume XXIII: Congo, 1960–1968* (Document 1, "Covert action in the Congo"). Office of the Historian. https://history.state.gov/historicaldocuments/frus1964-68v23/d1

U.S. Department of State. (2016). *Foreign relations of the United States, 1977–1980, volume XVII, part 1: Horn of Africa*. Office of the Historian. https://history.state.gov/historicaldocuments/frus1977-80v17p1

U.S. Embassy and Consulate in Nigeria. (2022, October 17). *30 Benin bronzes returned to Nigeria*. https://ng.usembassy.gov/30-benin-bronzes-returned-to-nigeria/

UN Trade and Development. (2022). *Economic Development in Africa Report 2022: Rethinking the foundations of export diversification in Africa: The catalytic role of business and financial services*. https://unctad.org/publication/economic-development-africa-report-2022

UN Trade and Development. (2023). *Commodities and Development Report 2023: Inclusive diversification and energy transition*. https://unctad.org/publication/commodities-and-development-report-2023

UN Trade and Development. (2025). *Economic Development in Africa Report 2024: Unlocking Africa's trade potential: Boosting regional markets and reducing risks*. https://unctad.org/publication/economic-development-africa-report-2024

UNESCO Intangible Cultural Heritage. (2016). *Gada system, an indigenous democratic socio-political system of the Oromo*. https://ich.unesco.org/en/RL/gada-system-an-indigenous-democratic-socio-political-system-of-the-oromo-01164

UNESCO World Heritage Centre. (n.d.-a). *Aksum*. https://whc.unesco.org/en/list/15/

UNESCO World Heritage Centre. (n.d.-b). *Ancient Thebes with its necropolis*. https://whc.unesco.org/en/list/87/

UNESCO World Heritage Centre. (n.d.-c). *Great Zimbabwe National Monument*. https://whc.unesco.org/en/list/364/

UNESCO World Heritage Centre. (n.d.-d). *Archaeological Sites of the Island of Meroe*. https://whc.unesco.org/en/list/1336/

UNESCO World Heritage Centre. (n.d.-e). *Ruins of Kilwa Kisiwani and Ruins of Songo Mnara*. https://whc.unesco.org/en/list/144/

UNESCO World Heritage Centre. (n.d.-f). *Timbuktu*. https://whc.unesco.org/en/list/119/

UNESCO World Heritage Centre. (n.d.-g). *Tomb of Askia*. https://whc.unesco.org/en/list/1139/

UNESCO. (1961). *Final report: Conference of African States on the Development of Education in Africa, Addis Ababa, 15–25 May 1961.* https://unesdoc.unesco.org/ark:/48223/pf0000213338

UNESCO. (2025, November 10). *UNESCO launches global roadmap for multilingualism in the digital era.* https://www.unesco.org/en/articles/unesco-launches-global-roadmap-multilingualism-digital-era

UNESCO. (2025a). *Languages matter: Global guidance on multilingual education.* https://www.unesco.org/en/articles/languages-matter-global-guidance-multilingual-education

UNESCO. (2025b, September 8). *Transforming knowledge for Africa's future.* https://www.unesco.org/en/articles/transforming-knowledge-africas-future-2

UNESCO. (n.d.). *General History of Africa.* https://www.unesco.org/en/general-history-africa

United Nations Economic Commission for Africa. (2022, February 9). *Africa's transport sector to strongly benefit from African Continental Free Trade Area.* https://www.uneca.org/stories/africa%E2%80%99s-transport-sector-to-strongly-benefit-from-african-continental-free-trade-area-

United Nations Economic Commission for Africa. (2023, June 5). *Measuring informal cross-border trade is key to monitoring intra-African trade.* https://www.uneca.org/stories/measuring-informal-cross-border-trade-is-key-to-monitoring-intra-african-trade

United Nations Economic Commission for Africa. (2024, July 12). *(Blog) As Africa's population crosses 1.5 billion, the demographic window is opening: Getting the dividend requires more than numbers.* https://www.uneca.org/stories/%28blog%29-as-africa%E2%80%99s-population-crosses-1.5-billion%2C-the-demographic-window-is-opening-getting

United Nations General Assembly. (1960, December 14). *Declaration on the granting of independence to colonial countries and peoples* (Resolution 1514 [XV]). United Nations Office of Legal Affairs. https://legal.un.org/avl/ha/dicc/dicc.html

United Nations High Commissioner for Refugees. (2026). *Global trends 2025.* https://www.unhcr.org/global-trends

United Nations Statistics Division. (2025a). *UNData profile: Africa.* https://data.un.org/en/reg/g2.html

United Nations Statistics Division. (2025b). *UNData profile: Sub-Saharan Africa.* https://data.un.org/en/reg/g202.html

United Nations. (n.d.-a). *1960: New African states join the UN.* UN Audiovisual Library. https://media.un.org/avlibrary/en/asset/d351/d3517467

United Nations. (n.d.-b). *United Nations Operation in Mozambique: Background.* United Nations Peacekeeping. https://peacekeeping.un.org/sites/default/files/past/onumozS.htm

United Nations. (n.d.-c). *United Nations Transition Assistance Group: Background.* United Nations Peacekeeping. https://peacekeeping.un.org/sites/default/files/past/untagFT.htm

United Nations. (n.d.-d). *Building on the legacy of Nelson Mandela.* https://www.un.org/en/exhibits/page/building-legacy-nelson-mandela

Vidal, C. M., Lane, C. S., Asfawrossen, A., Barfod, D. N., Mark, D. F., Tomlinson, E. L., Tadesse, A. Z., Yirgu, G., Deino, A., Hutchison, W., & Mounier, A. (2022). Age of the oldest known *Homo sapiens* from eastern Africa. *Nature, 601*, 579–583. https://doi.org/10.1038/s41586-021-04275-8

Webuild. (n.d.). *Grand Ethiopian Renaissance Dam Project (GERD).* https://www.webuildgroup.com/en/projects/dams-hydroelectric-plants/grand-ethiopian-renaissance-dam-project/

World Bank, UNESCO, UNICEF, Foreign, Commonwealth & Development Office, U.S. Agency for International Development, & Bill & Melinda Gates Foundation. (2022). *The state of global learning poverty: 2022 update.* https://www.worldbank.org/en/topic/education/publication/state-of-global-learning-poverty

World Bank. (1994). *Adjustment in Africa: Reforms, results, and the road ahead.* Oxford University Press. https://documents.worldbank.org/en/publication/documents-reports/documentdetail/219981468192845881

World Bank. (2018, June 11). *Additional financing for Morocco to develop a second solar power complex.* https://www.worldbank.org/en/news/press-release/2018/06/11/additional-financing-for-morocco-to-develop-a-second-solar-power-complex

World Bank. (2021, April 28). *What is learning poverty?* https://www.worldbank.org/en/brief/2021/04/28/what-is-learning-poverty

World Bank. (2022). *Making the most of the African Continental Free Trade Area: Leveraging trade and foreign direct investment to boost growth and reduce poverty.* https://openknowledge.worldbank.org/entities/publication/09f9bbdd-3bf0-5196-879b-b1a9f328b825

World Bank. (2022, June 30). *Free trade pact could help lift up to 50 million Africans from extreme poverty.* https://www.worldbank.org/en/news/press-release/2022/06/30/free-trade-pact-could-help-lift-up-to-50-million-africans-from-extreme-poverty

World Bank. (2023). *Botswana systematic country diagnostic update: At a crossroads, reigniting efficient and inclusive growth.*

https://documents.worldbank.org/en/publication/documents-reports/documentdetail/099112023112034378

World Bank. (2023, December 8). *Regional integration removes barriers to development in Africa.* https://www.worldbank.org/en/results/2023/12/08/regional-integration-removes-barriers-to-development-in-africa

World Bank. (2024, October 14). *Urgent education reform key to unlocking faster, more inclusive growth in Africa.* https://www.worldbank.org/en/news/press-release/2024/10/14/urgent-education-reform-key-to-unlocking-faster-more-inclusive-growth-in-africa

World Bank. (2025). *The Worldwide Governance Indicators: Revised methodology for measuring governance using perception data.* https://www.worldbank.org/content/dam/sites/govindicators/doc/The%20Worldwide%20Governance%20Indicators%202025%20Methodology%20Revision.pdf

World Bank. (2025, January 24). *Enhancing regional power trade and energy access in West Africa.* https://www.worldbank.org/en/news/press-release/2025/01/24/enhancing-regional-power-trade-and-energy-access-in-west-africa

World Bank. (2025a, October 29). *Africa's Eastern Electricity Highway.* https://www.worldbank.org/en/news/video/2025/10/29/africa-s-eastern-electricity-highway

World Bank. (2025b). *21st-century Africa: Governance and growth.* https://openknowledge.worldbank.org/entities/publication/03bdf5e3-daba-404a-a638-25c5511c2376

World Bank. (2025b, February 28). *New World Bank report highlights four pathways to spur job creation and inclusive growth in South Africa.* https://www.worldbank.org/en/news/press-release/2025/02/28/new-world-bank-report-highlights-four-pathways-to-spur-job-afe-growth-in-south-africa

World Bank. (2026). *A World Bank Group strategy for engaging in fragility, conflict and violence settings, 2026–2030.* https://www.worldbank.org/en/topic/fragilityconflictviolence/publication/a-wbg-strategy-for-engaging-in-fcv-settings-2026-2030

World Bank. (2026, June 24). *655 million people still without electricity underscore urgent need to deliver universal energy access.* https://www.worldbank.org/en/news/press-release/2026/06/16/accelerating-universal-energy-access

World Bank. (2026a, February 18). *Mauritius country climate and development report.*

https://www.worldbank.org/en/country/mauritius/publication/mauritius-country-climate-and-development-report-ccdr

World Bank. (2026b, May 11). *Connecting West Africa through regional power integration and expanded electricity access.* https://www.worldbank.org/en/results/2026/05/11/connecting-west-africa-through-regional-power-integration-and-expanded-electricity-access

World Health Organization Regional Office for Africa. (2026). *The state of the health workforce in Africa 2026: Plan, train and retain.* https://www.afro.who.int/publications/state-health-workforce-africa-2026-plan-train-and-retain

World Health Organization Regional Office for Africa. (n.d.). *African Health Observatory: Regional health data hub.* Retrieved September 2, 2026, from https://data.afro.who.int/

Young, C. (1994). *The African colonial state in comparative perspective.* Yale University Press.

Zewde, B. (2001). *A history of modern Ethiopia, 1855–1991* (2nd ed.). James Currey.

www.ingramcontent.com/pod-product-compliance
Lightning Source LLC
LaVergne TN
LVHW100137061126
851857LV00010B/128
* 9 7 9 8 9 9 7 8 3 4 0 0 5 *